W9-BKR-164

of hierarchy does not apply well to wild baboons, who are normally widely spaced, and there is rarely any confrontation or conflict over food. In a relatively simple group with three adult males, one clearly dominated the others, and the leader behaved in the following way: As females entered their periods of maximum fertility, he mated exclusively with some of them. He drove away the males who were second and third in the hierarchy and who wished to mate with these highly fertile females. The subordinate males 'presented' to the dominant one in a submissive way far more frequently to this male than to the others. (Presenting is a gesture usually involving an exposure of the hindquarters to a dominant animal; occasionally a dominant will present to a subdominant. The gesture is important for many primates in 'ritualizing' social bonds, particularly hierarchical ones.) The leader appeared to be involved in many more aggressive episodes than any other male. When a disturbance happened – for example, when an eland cow charged the group – the dominant male stood his ground, while the rest of the group retreated. Finally, mothers with newborn infants tended to cluster near him and walk near him, and the dominant's retaliation was prompt against any attack on the mothers (p. 56).

In another group DeVore and Hall find a pattern of bonding which may have implications for the analysis of baboon hierarchies;

> It became clear that certain of the adult males constantly associated with each other and tended to support each other in aggressive interaction with other males. Some of these males associated so closely that they were scarcely ever observed acting independently in such episodes, and on this basis three of them came to be designated a 'central hierarchy' (pp. 59–60).

These three males would not seriously compete for food, and combined against other males in the group. They stayed in the centre of the group, acted in concert, decided group movement, and access to goals, etc. 'Thus a male's dominance status was a combination of his individual fighting ability ("linear dominance" . . .) and his ability to enlist the support of other males . . . [in] the central hierarchy' (pp. 61–2). Among four groups intensively studied, dominance relationships varied significantly. Frequently, 'redirection of aggression' occurs; this involves a threat by the dominant to the subdominant, who chases or threatens a third, and so on. This is thought to function as a possible reinforcement of the group's dominance pattern.

Dominance among females was more difficult to establish clearly. Female dominance appears to be more variable and more subtly marked than dominance among males. For one thing, it is sharply affected by estrous condition. For another, it seems to be based on individual interactions rather than coalitions, which partly determine the relative stability of male hierarchies. Female dominance seems to be expressed in virtually continuous minor bickering and harassment and there is little outright biting and attack (pp. 66–7). DeVore and Hall decide that:

> The most significant general finding . . . was the extent to which female aggressiveness against other females was correlated with the frequency of mating by the A (dominant) male with the female who was in full estrous. This . . . seemed to indicate that the social pattern among all the adult females was considerably affected by the close attention of the markedly dominant A male to one of their number . . . (p. 69).

Two or more females commonly 'gang-up' to threaten or attack another female.

Mothers with infants tend to the centre of the group where the dominant males are when the group is on the move, while the less dominant males are to the front, rear, and sides. Consistently, when a crisis occurs the dominant males move from the middle to the front of the group to deal with the situation. The peripheral males act as sentinels both when the group is moving or at rest. The whole group is attentive to the signals and position of the dominant males, and the peripheral 'sentries' govern their movements in reference to these males (p. 71). The overall social pattern of the baboon groups studied by DeVore and Hall suggests that the very complex dominance pattern among males ensures maximum protection for infant-bearing mothers, promotes relative peacefulness in the group, and offers the highest probability that females will be fertilized by the highest ranking males. The genetic significance of this system is apparent.

A detailed account of socialization and maternal behaviour is available (pp. 81–5). By the age of five a sub-adult male is larger than adult females and dominates them. He is daring, truculent, and 'more peripheral in his behaviour to other group members than either sex is at any other stage of the life cycle' (p. 85). Adult males, particularly dominant ones, may hold and touch infants fairly frequently.

What is not yet known from field studies is the association of adolescents and young adults with the adult males. Although some young adult or sub-adult males are somewhat peripheral, or complementary, to a group, others appear to be assimilated into close relationship with dominant males (p. 87).

A provocative related finding by Imanishi is that the offspring of high status Japanese macaque females remain closer to the centre of the group longer than offspring of low status females. Thus they become more familiar with dominant males and appear to derive an effective advantage in gaining high adult status in this way.[1] Imanishi suggests that male offspring of high status females 'identify' with high status males. Perhaps they are more likely to take high status for granted as a result. Low status offspring may lack the vital impetus or encouragement which accompanies 'identification' with high-ranking males. (Incidentally, this is an important indication of the role of socialization among primates. It could be useful in this context to study the applicability of concepts such as role-model and identification among primates.)[2]

A relatively complex communication system, including posture, vocalization, and movements, indicates the states of individual animals as well as those social situations which require action or inattention. Grooming is an important means of affirming social ties. The most common relationship is that females will groom other females. Adult males groom females longer when they are in estrous. Females with infants, and those in estrous, attract particular attention and grooming from other animals. The amount of grooming an individual receives reflects his place in the dominance hierarchy, and the hierarchy itself is expressed in part by grooming patterns. For example, a dominant central male receives more grooming than a peripheral one. But all individuals receive and give some grooming. The process in general both expresses and strengthens social bonds. A subordinate may present his genital region to a dominant, who may mount the subdominant. Such an interaction clearly indicates relative status. Females in estrous will present to a female with a small infant. In

---

1. Kinji Imanishi, 'Social Behaviour in Japanese Monkeys, *Macaca fuscata*', in Charles H. Southwick (ed.), *Primate Social Behaviour*, D. Van Nostrand, Princeton, N.J., 1963, pp. 78–9.
2. Imanishi has provided a good point of departure. See Kinji Imanishi, 'Identification: A Process of Socialization in the Sub-human Society of Macaca Fuscata', K. Imanishi and S. H. Altmann (eds.), *Japanese Monkeys*, Atlanta, Ga., 1965.

groups where tension and unrest exists among the adult males, dominant males may even present to subdominant ones, though mounting is very infrequent; normally a touch of the hindquarters completes the gesture.

Similarities among Kenya and Cape baboons should not obscure the differences between them. However, even if we include the Ethiopian hamadryas, certain underlying similarities in social structure appear. The adaptability of the baboon in coping with considerable diversity in environment is an important function of the pattern of social organization. For example, Crook's studies of the gelada baboons in Ethiopia suggest a new range of possibilities. The gelada lives in a cliff-top ecology, and is often organized into one-male groups. A herd of many of these groups may form when favourable conditions permit. Here the only significant multi-male groups are comprised of sub-adults who form a protective buffer between harems and potential predators. These peripheral males will merge into 'all-male groups' when a herd splits up, and the members of these groups may display considerable loyalty to each other. Membership remains constant over a period of several weeks.[1] Crook proposes that the one-male family structure of the gelada is the most efficient pattern for exploiting the poor and arid terrain of highland Ethiopia. The availability of food is the chief determinant of whether or not multi-male groups will emerge. It appears that psychologically contrasting males receive reproductive advantages in hamadryas and common baboon societies.[2] At this stage, Crook expects the development of interchange between cultural traditions of particular groups and genetic selection. Whether or not this is so, the relationship between gelada prosperity and multi-male grouping is very intriguing. Perhaps here is one analogical clue to the possible significance of bonding in human evolution, and in changes from small-scale to large-scale communities.

2

Now let us look at a primate community in which male bonding plays a very reduced social role. In *Presbytis entellus*, the common langur monkey of north India, male bonding is an inconsiderable feature of social organization. An outline of that organization follows,

1. John Hurrell Crook, 'Evolutionary Change in Primate Societies', *Science Journal* (June 1967), p. 5.
2. ibid., p. 7.

based on the report by Phyllis Jay.[1] Her report describes monkeys in both forest and agricultural conditions. Those in the forest were unfamiliar with man and difficult to observe carefully over long periods; those in the village frequently disappeared over garden and fence walls. The latter village animals were more anxious and aggressive, presumably because of the crowded conditions of the human habitations near where these monkeys have traditionally lived.

Group size varied from five to 120, with averages of eighteen to twenty-five members in the forests and twenty-five to thirty in the dry village regions. The groups were closed; immigration was rare – though the occasional male left to live as a non-group male. No explanation is offered for this phenomenon. Three non-group males living near one group were repelled when they sought to enter it.

Groups move about one to two miles daily, within a group range of about half a square mile to five square miles. There are core areas, which coincide with sleeping trees and, sometimes, water sources. In their movements, groups occasionally meet; but Jay observed no fighting between groups. Larger groups usually take precedence, and smaller ones await the movement away of the larger. Normal patterns of range use and the 'routes' the groups develop separate them very effectively (p. 212). Adult males produce a distinct vocalization when a group is about to move. Predators rarely threaten either forest or village scrub communities.

Social groups are stable and peaceful. The dominance structure is not obvious in the daily routine, and animals relate freely to each other, with apparently little concern about status (p. 216). Group life provides models of adult role performance for maturing langurs. It also provides protection – each individual issues a warning when danger threatens, and this greatly increases an individual's chances of being alerted. When there is danger, 'as part of the social tradition,

1. Phyllis Jay, 'The Common Langur of North India', in I. DeVore (ed.), op. cit., pp. 197–249. All page references in this description are to this article. Since preparing this section I have read Sugiyama's report of his study of another group of langurs. In this group, one-male units are found, as well as cadres of 'dissatisfied' males who are prevented from establishing territories by the population density of the animals. Such differences point up the variety of responses available to animals to solve the problems of survival; male bonding is one such possible response. It accords with ethological theory that a number of patterns are available to solve particular problems, and that some patterns are more likely to emerge than others. The propensity to male-bond, then, would vary from species to species. See Yukimaru Sugiyama, 'Social Organization of Hunuman Langurs', in S. A. Altmann (ed.), *Social Communication in Primates*, op. cit.

all group members are united in a dominance structure that provides a system of predictable behaviour among familiar animals' (p. 217).

Adult males seldom interact with small infants. Adult females appear to be central figures in the groups, while adult males receive less grooming. None the less adult males dominate adult females, though with less intensity than they dominate sub-adult males. The latter also dominate adult females. The birth of a langur infant is very important to the group, and other females congregate around the mother and new infant. The skill of different mothers in caring for their offspring varies considerably. Older experienced mothers are more effective in caring for their young. Dominance appears to be unimportant in the daily lives of langur females – status is infrequently apparent in social relations with other members of the group. Thus it is improbable that a female's status will significantly affect her offspring's development. Rather, the temperament of the mother and not her status seems to influence development (p. 222).

Young males have little or no contact with adult males until about ten months of age. At this time, an infant – squealing loudly – will approach an adult male but veer away just before touching him. With time, the infant musters his confidence and finally touches the male hindquarters. About a week after this, the infant feels able to approach the adult and mount upon the adult's hindquarters. The pattern of infant mounting is similar to male–female mounting or a dominance mounting of two adults, but of course in the infant's case neither sexual nor dominance behaviour is involved. A few weeks later, the infant may face and hug the adult. As many as four infants and juveniles may mount and embrace an adult male in rapid succession. Young males display this sort of behaviour until about the age of four (pp. 226–7).

Sexual differences appear early. Female infants have no contacts with adult males, but are groomed more frequently by and with adult females. More than twice as often as female infants, male infants are threatened and chased by adults. Male play is more active and noisy. The most absorbing and important juvenile activity is play. Early dominance patterns may appear at this stage; dominance is largely a function of size. Female juveniles engage in dominance interaction less frequently than males. Large juveniles almost always play in groups of one sex – large female juveniles rarely play for more than a few minutes with large male juveniles (p. 230). Male juveniles mount adult males about four times as often as they mount male infants, and they may occasionally harass adult males consorting with estrous females.

Sub-adults display frequent submission to adults, and are oriented to them. However, sub-adult males are not subordinate to all adult females and they seek to dominate as many as they are able. Between the ages of about four to six, sub-adult males enjoy fewer social bonds in the group than at any other point in their lives. During this period they are very marginal to group life (p. 231). Dominance interactions among sub-adult males are aggressive and physical; interactions with adult males are tense. Before entering the male dominance hierarchy, the sub-adult male makes his way up through the female structure (p. 232).

Adult females concern themselves primarily with maternal behaviour. Their dominance hierarchy is not well defined. It is relatively unstable – in fact most adult female interactions do not involve dominance. Female dominance encounters are brief – they take about five to thirty seconds – and unlike the males' interactions they are not foreshadowed by an increase of tension (p. 234). Dominant females may take others food. Females tend to accept male dominance except when a male startles an infant or infant-tending female. Estrous females at the height of their receptivity tend to solicit the dominant males in the group, though some males are preferred to others at all times. Consortships last but a few hours.

As in the baboon communities, male langurs lead and co-ordinate group activity, maintain its unity and stability, direct exploitation of the environment, and relate to other langur groups. The basic structure of the group is the stable male hierarchy.

Dominant males appear to be generally less active than sub-dominants, and are given wider ground when irritated. As two individuals pass by each other, just a slight pause indicates sub-dominance.

Another subtle indicator of status is the size of a male's 'personal space', an intangible area surrounding him into which another monkey cannot enter without . . . danger. . . . The more dominant the male, the larger the area of space he can maintain for his exclusive use. When a male is relaxed he does not maintain an area of personal space (p. 243).

Females may also possess a space into which subdominants may not casually intrude.

In grooming, subordinate males present to dominant ones: The subordinate will approach the dominant male, will present, and then is groomed for a few seconds. The high-status male places his hand on the lower-status male. Tension decreases, and both males appear to relax (pp. 245–6).

Because these langurs are primarily arboreal, social grouping is not vital for their survival as it is for the savannah baboon: Macaques and baboons protect themselves by relying for protection on large adult males with well-developed fighting prowess. But langurs protect themselves most securely by slipping up the nearest tree. Perhaps mainly for this reason, sexual dimorphism among north Indian langurs is not pronounced (p. 248). Though they share much the same environment as langurs, ground-living Rhesus monkeys – like baboons – have developed powerful aggressive males in social structures which maintain alertness and can be speedily mobilized against danger. In such communities, the dominant male is obviously the central figure in the group's persistence over time.

In her concluding comments, Jay notes that the major structural differences between langurs and baboons are directly related to the strategies and the means of collective and self-defence. Perhaps marked sexual dimorphism and (this is my extension of the data) male-bonding-based political systems are in part the consequence of savannah as opposed to arboreal life. The relevance of this hypothesis to the discussion of the circumstances and direction of human evolution is clear. As John Napier has noted,[1] the ecological basis of human evolution is central to the development of first behavioural and then physical adaptations during the period when forests were receding and the savannah became the environment within which the hominid life-style and anatomy was selected. Napier's view of the role of sexual dimorphism stresses the importance of the recession of woodlands in influencing primate evolution; *Australopithecus* displayed sexual dimorphism comparatively similar to that of *Homo sapiens*. The implication is drawn that particular social patterns developed to compensate for the reduction of physical sexual dimorphism which followed the branching off of *Homo* from other primates. This division may have taken place as long ago as 20 or 26 million years; the estimates of *Australopithicine* antiquity range from two million to 750,000 years ago. Thus there is the clear possibility that social forms might have evolved to permit this creature to survive.

1. John Napier, personal communication.

Such social forms may in part be the basis of human behavioural infrastructure.

3

Is there any further evidence which can be brought forward in terms of Tinbergen's advice to treat behavioural divergence and convergence as a test of differential evolution of phyletic relations?[1]

One of the original conceptions in this study was that elaborate male bonding was a uniquely human development, that it was a direct consequence of pre-hominid ecological adaptation. The two critical adaptations were the development of patterns of hunting large animals which may have involved tools and, more significantly, a propensity to form co-operative bands which (as I will argue later) would have to be all male. The importance of hunting behaviour in human evolution has been widely recognized. For example, Washburn and Howell comment: 'The tool-using, ground-living, hunting way of life created the large human brain rather than a large-brained man discovering certain new ways of life. The authors believe this conclusion is one which carries far-reaching implications for the interpretation of human behaviour and its origins.'[2] Michael Chance has stressed the importance of cortical and amygdaloid development as a function of dominance behaviour and as a basis for the control of intra-group aggression essential for co-operative hunting behaviour.[3]

After consideration of a variety of ideas and data (to be described in the next chapter), it was proposed that male bonding was a special human adaptation directly connected with co-operative predation and defence.[4]

But the hypothesis has been reformulated as a result of new and more refined primate evidence, in conjunction with Lorenz's conception of the role of aggression in the developing and maintaining social bonds. The hypothesis must now be that a human male bonding propensity may have been a hominid inheritance from the primates.

1. Tinbergen, 'On Aims and Methods of Ethology', in op. cit., p. 428.
2. S. Washburn and F. C. Howell, 'Human Evolution and Culture', in Sol Tax (ed.), *The Evolution of Man*, op. cit., p. 49.
3. M. R. A. Chance, 'The Nature and Special Features of the Instinctive Social Bonds of Primates', in S. L. Washburn (ed.), op. cit., pp. 29–32.
4. L. Tiger, 'A Programme for the Study of the Biological Aspects of Human Male Association Patterns', unpublished paper presented to the meeting of the Association for the Study of Animal Behaviour, Oxford, July 1965.

WAYNESBURG COLLEGE LIBRARY
WAYNESBURG, PA.

Some primates, including man, went on to develop this preadaptation. As a result of the lack of ecological pressure to do so, others did not, or do not show it now in their present circumstances. This appears to follow legitimately from the arguments of Hall,[1] Crook and Gartlan,[2] Reynolds,[3] Butzer,[4] among others. It is basic to primate society that primates generally distinguish between males and females in interactions. This is obvious; but such a distinction must be significant both for the behaviour and social structure of any particular primate community and for the long-run evolution of selected genotypes of maleness and femaleness. After all, the estrous cycle determines intersexual relationships, and there are clear modulations and shifts in the way adult males treat females in different phases of the reproductive cycle. This permits us to ask if, correspondingly, biologically linked mechanisms generally govern male–male interactions in the way male-female encounters depend in part upon such mechanisms. It is known that the biological mechanisms governing sexual behaviour which exist among primates are likely to be closely associated with social learning, particularly at critical periods of growth and development. From the work of Harlow[5] it is clear that both physical *and* social conditions must be met in primate life-cycles for 'normal' sexual behaviour to occur. The effect of higher cortical activity on primates is less than it is in *Homo sapiens*. But in a good discussion of the general field, Michael has noted the underlying community between primate and human sexual behaviour while stressing also the lack of real knowledge about

1. Hall, 'Aggression in Monkey and Ape Societies', in op. cit., p. 63.
2. Crook and Gartlan, op. cit., pp. 1201–3.
3. Vernon Reynolds, 'Kinship and the Family in Primates and Early Man', *Man*, 3, 2 (n.s.) (June 1968). Reynolds describes an outbreeding pattern which involves bands of exploratory adult male chimps and gorillas ranging 'far and wide in small bands finding new sources of food and meeting and mixing with groups elsewhere'. This is an extremely interesting phenomenon in terms of the hypothesis about male bonding and its frequent and provocative association with danger, which will be discussed below.
4. Karl W. Butzer, *Environment and Archaeology: An Introduction to Pleistocene Geography*, Methuen, London, 1965, pp. 353–7. The above authors do not necessarily deal specifically with the phenomenon of male bonding, but it seems reasonable to assume that this is a matter of emphasis rather than the outcome of a decision that such bonds do not exist or have not the significance hypothesized here. Perhaps framing an interpretation of their data and theories in terms of the male-bonding hypothesis will permit these and other workers to accept or reject the hypothesis.
5. H. F. Harlow and M. K. Harlow, 'The Effect of Rearing Conditions on Behaviour', in John Money (ed.), *Sex Research: New Development*, Holt, Rinehart & Winston, New York, 1965, pp. 161–75.

the different forms and quantities of causes and effects involved.[1] It is also of parenthetical interest that human male sexual activity appears to involve more extensive higher cortical control than the corresponding female behaviour. Is this one possible reason for the greatly disproportionate incidence of male pornographic fantasy material? Some general reflections on male–female differences in the use of fantasy materials are to be found in Gillian Freeman's preliminary survey.[2]

Of course, this is not to say that specific identifiable physiological events – like digestion, perhaps – occur internally while a male baboon is engaged in a male bonding. At the same time it is perhaps possible to see this as an aspect of what Count calls an animal's 'biogram' – namely, the general pattern of the actions which are necessary for its survival: 'An animal's organizational morphology must include not only its anatomy and physiology, but its characteristic way of living . . . this life-mode is termed its "biogram".'[3] Thus, just as a male baboon apparently inherits a predisposition to dominate other baboons and achieves 'satisfaction' by exerting dominance, so too a male baboon is predisposed to form male bonds which, equally, provide 'satisfaction' of this particular need in the biogram. Presumably not all individuals will display the same degree of need. Some baboons are more intelligent than others and some more dominant; some will have stronger bonding-valence than others. Possibly it is the individuals with stronger bonding propensities than others who will combine to form the oligarchies to which a number of writers have referred.[4] Presumably individuals with strong bonding abilities began to determine, through their influence on breeding, the evolution of political patterns. Perhaps thus is male bonding linked with dominance.

1. Richard P. Michael, 'Biological Factors in the Organization and Expression of Sexual Behaviour', in Ismond Rosen (ed.), *The Pathology and Treatment of Sexual Deviation*, Oxford University Press, 1964, pp. 24–54.
2. Gillian Freeman, *The Undergrowth of Literature*, Nelson, London, 1967.
3. Earl W. Count, 'The Biological Basis of Human Sociality', *American Anthropologist*, 60, 6 (December 1958), p. 1049. This essay provides a searching analysis of the implications of biological analysis for social anthropology and sociology.
4. I. DeVore and K. R. L. Hall, 'Baboon Ecology', in I. DeVore (ed.), op. cit., pp. 59–60; Charles H. Southwick, Mirza A. Beg, and M. Rafiq Siddiqi, 'Rhesus Monkeys in North India', in ibid., pp. 142–51. See also Paul Simonds, 'The Bonnet Macaque in South India', in ibid., pp. 184–5; Clarence Ray Carpenter, 'The Howlers of Barro Colorado Island', in ibid., pp. 285–6; Vernon Reynolds and Frances Reynolds, 'Chimpanzees of the Budongo Forest', in ibid., p. 397; Jane Goodall, 'Chimpanzees of the Gombe Stream Reserve', in ibid., pp. 454–5.

Natural selection has to do with the leaving of progeny and not necessarily the survival of the fittest or most dominant. In this context the mobile bachelor bands to which Reynolds[1] refers and which may have carried genes within groups, may be another form of selective device favouring individuals whose unisexual gregarious activities apparently could lead to strengthening of this tendency in the population. At the same time, it is clear that under other circumstances this function of gene-carrying, if it is performed at all, may be the result of single-male rather than multi-male movements between groups.[2] The pattern of this gene transfer is not consistent and the evidence about it is very inconclusive. In some primates, maintaining and reinforcing the bonding pattern is partly a function of the internal political structure. But perhaps, also, there was external movement of bonded individuals who would bear a different but special relationship to the genetic pool. Michael Chance has suggested also that bachelor bands may have played an important role in 'cultural' innovation, particularly with respect to occasional hunting and changes in provident behaviour.[3]

This interpretation of data on inter-group exploration by bonded males and its relationship to the genetic pool is somewhat idiosyncratic. But it may be a useful foil for the development of harder explanations. The whole issue of bachelor bands raises some questions about the relevance of territory or range affiliation to reproductive ability. Among Australian magpies, for example, Carrick finds breeding possible among permanent groups only. Males without territory are not fertile. While there is no reason for the same principle to apply to primates, Carrick's analysis suggests a perspective within which the discussion of primate bachelor bands and lonely males can proceed.[4] In general, the known relationship between territory and reproduction would tend to deny the efficacy of bachelor-band inter-group genetic transfer. This is an issue which must be studied *in situ* by researchers aware of the phenomenon to

1. Vernon Reynolds, 'Kinship and the Family in Primates and Early Man', in op. cit., p. vii. For an intriguing science-fictional treatment of this and other Pleistocene social patterns, see Roy Lewis, *The Evolution Man*, Penguin Books, Harmondsworth, 1963.
2. Clarence Ray Carpenter, 'The Howlers of Barro Colorado Island', in I. DeVore, (ed.) op. cit., pp. 269–70: George C. Schaller, 'Some Behavioural Comparisons of Free-Living Apes', in ibid., p. 479.
3. Michael Chance, personal communication.
4. Robert Carrick, 'Ecological Significance of Territory in the Australian Magpie' (unpublished MS., 1965).

which they must attend, if only to be able to assert it does not occur. Of particular interest here is Rowell's finding, in a five-year study period, that baboon males moved extensively from group to group: '. . . among three groups of baboons in Uganda studied over five years, all the males have changed groups at least once. The idea of these as relatively (or even absolutely) "closed" breeding systems is thus disproved.'[1]

It is valid to try to relate biological principles to sociological ones. But it is unnecessary in this discussion to insist upon a direct connection between human and other primate societies – or at least a connection which remains relevant to present-day social patterns. The fossil material recently excavated by Louis Leakey and provisionally dated at about 20 million years suggests that human evolution may have been proceeding independently of that of other primates for such a very long time that any similarities between the two lines is the result primarily of parallel evolution rather than common inheritance. This would imply that the evolution of cooperative carnivorous propensities of human males boasts a more ancient history than ever imagined, and that the comparable social forms found among some primates are the result of separate development by primates. Various physical, maturational, and blood-type similarities have been maintained between humans and some other primates. On the basis that physical structure and behavioural function are related, it may be scientifically economical if not intuitively obvious to consider whether there were initial behavioural similarities on which selective pressures operated, and which have yielded social patterns which remain significantly similar.

This possibility is more interesting among primates which have had to contend with terrain and other circumstances comparable with evolving Homo's. On the other hand, if development has been parallel and related, then it is extremely interesting that the political and defensive male bonding patterns which have been identified should have occurred in both Homo and other primates. To learn why is an important scientific question. Not only important, but perhaps a question which lies at the heart of the most basic questions about the evolution of man. How indeed did man become the political animal?

1. Robin Fox, 'Aspects of Hominid Behavioural Evolution', in op. cit., p. 421. Also see Rowell's excellent discussion 'Variability in the Social Organization of Primates', in Desmond Morris (ed.), Primate Ethology, Weidenfeld and Nicolson, London, 1967.

And has this something to do with the fact that little bands of male primates roam their homelands and that when primate communities increase their number there is a tendency for the males to bond together in worldless but not meaningless oligarchies?

The issue remains very contentious. In the next chapter I try to draw together some of the material which may be pertinent to the preparation of an answer. Those readers who are uninterested in reconstructions of evolution and in the application of palaeo-anthropological data to contemporary social life can swiftly flip the relevant pages and turn to the following chapters, which deal directly with human social behaviour in its present forms and variations. I hope that those who read the chapter but conclude that they cannot accept its suggestions will none the less evaluate on its separate merits what follows in the rest of the book.

Obviously I see human behaviour as evolved and the process of genetic transmission of information about the human life cycle as fundamental to the forms and rhythms of that cycle's expression. Perhaps some will consider it too grand a claim that not only individual component bits of behaviour are constrained by genetic programming, but that structures of society and the *gestalt* of social action are also so constrained. In this chapter on primate systems I have sought to indicate how the complex structures of social action which some animals display is the clear result of interaction between genetic and cultural factors. Bearing in mind the distinctiveness of human culture, we are now free to try to find out how this works in man. Let me turn, therefore, to a discussion of how we got 'this way', and after that to what we do, where, when, for how long, with whom, and maybe even why.

CHAPTER THREE

The Male Bond and Human Evolution

My next task is to sketch out the ways in which male bonding operates, and why it may be regarded as a species-specific pattern. But first, I want to try to suggest how this propensity of behaviour may have become part of the biological infrastructure of man. With a sense of the relative perilousness of any prehistoric analysis by a person untrained in the geological, biological, and medical disciplines which underlie the study of evolution, I must emphasize the necessarily hypothetical quality of what follows. Even for specialists, the difficulty is acute of making judgements about the distant past by inference from bone and fossil remains. But despite this, and because the study of phylogeny may be too important to be left exclusively to 'phylogeneticists', there may be some real point in approaching issues raised by evolutionary analysis from a sociological point of view. As I noted in the Introduction to this book, if there is to be a community of interest and fruitful symbiosis between the natural and social sciences, it is necessary for some practitioners in each to strive to make their work pertinent to the concerns of their counterparts. I have no diplomatic ambitions, but I am interested in the possibility of linking the microhistory of social sciences to the macrohistory of species biology. The ensuing discussion of the way in which male bonding perhaps evolved is an effort in this direction.

It is very difficult, if not impossible, to prove my point about evolution. However, my argument about the significance and incidence of male bonding in contemporary human communities is more amenable to proof or disproof. There will be readers who are dubious about attempts to link history with prehistory under current conditions of knowledge. I hope these readers can restrict their scepticism to this prehistorical enterprise, and consider independently the argument about the role and incidence of male bonding in contemporary society.

In this chapter, I will discuss briefly what is known about pre- and early hominid social patterns and, in particular, try to indicate the role of male bonding for the development of the hunting-gathering way of exploiting the environment. The general genetic consequences of hunting and its relationship to home-based community behaviour will be considered. I also want to elaborate one of my hypotheses – that male–male bonds are of the same biological order for defensive, food-gathering, and social-order-maintenance purposes as the male–female bond is for reproductive purposes. On the assumption that they derive from behavioural as well as physical evolution, male–female somatic (physical) and behavioural differences will be very generally reviewed, and I will make some suggestions about the possible specific mechanisms underlying bonding and the relationship of these mechanisms to cultural differences.

Campbell has commented that:

> Only in the Middle Pleistocene do we find evidence of a major change in early man's adaptation to plains living, and this change involved *cooperative hunting* [Campbell's italics] – a change in food-getting behaviour of central importance to the story of human evolution. It seems clear that man survived the climatic changes of the Middle Pleistocene by a new behavioural adaptation that affected fundamentally and irrevocably his psychosocial character; it was this change in food-finding behaviour that finally made man.[1]

In the discussion of work (Chapter Five), I discuss further the importance of hunting in human evolutionary history. It is unnecessary to document extensively here the result of recent findings about the possible route of human development; a number of fine summaries – of which Campbell's is the most recent – are available to the interested reader. As early as 1921, Karl Pearson suggested that 'the notion of profiting by violence must have come to an ancestor of man', and on the basis of various other sources of evidence Pearson concluded that man was by nature violent.[2] Carveth Read, as we

1. Bernard Campbell, *Human Evolution*, Aldine Books, Chicago, 1967, p. 202.
2. Karl Pearson, *Side Lights on the Evolution of Man*, Eugenics Laboratory Lecture Series, No. XIII, Cambridge University Press, 1921.

know, agreed that man was by nature violent but that he was violent in terms of a co-operative hunting pack. Since the time of Read and Pearson, extensive findings by archaeologists support the contention that strategic violence in association with meat-eating and hunting constituted an important behavioural specialization and advantage of creatures early in human life. We have Pilbeam's estimate that hunting may have begun 14 million years back in human evolution.[1] Considerable speculation on the relative timing of human brain development and other somatic changes has led to wide agreement that the distinctive human brain evolved after, and perhaps partly in consequence of, changes in food-finding which were associated with predatory co-operative hunting.[2] The recent discovery of *Homo habilis* does not appear to invalidate the proposition that dietary change for *Australopithecus* was accompanied by the use of tools,[3] and presumably it is applicable to both *Australopithecus* and *Homo habilis*.[4] The anatomical concomitants of increasing reliance on tools for predation and defence are reflected in changing dentition and body structure – the teeth get smaller, for example. The fauna fossils suggest the existence of huntable animals providing sufficient appropriate nourishment to justify the dietary change.[5]

Obviously we cannot consult written histories of social structure or other such direct insights into the social organization of pre- and early Man. They don't exist. To try to reconstruct social patterns it is necessary to proceed inferentially from discussions of artifacts, geological information, knowledge of food supply, etc. The minimal and initial inference must be that changes in diet and food-gathering methods were accompanied by changes in social organization. The effect on his social behaviour of changes in modern man's economic

1. David R. Pilbeam, 'Man's Earliest Ancestors', *Science Journal*, **3**, 2 (February 1967).
2. For example, see L. B. Leakey, 'Facts Instead of Dogma on Man's Origin', in Paul DeVore (ed.), *The Origin of Man*, op. cit.; Clifford Geertz, 'Summary; Next Steps in Research', in ibid.; S. L. Washburn, 'An Ape's-Eye View of Human Evolution', in ibid.; S. L. Washburn and F. Clark Howell, 'Human Evolution and Culture', in Sol Tax (ed.), *The Evolution of Man*, University of Chicago Press, 1960: Derek Freeman, 'Human Aggression in Anthropological Perspective', in J. D. Carthy and F. J. Ebling (eds.), *The Natural History of Aggression*, op. cit.
3. P. U. Tobias, 'New Discoveries in Tanganyika: Their Bearing on Hominid Evolution', *Current Anthropology*, **6**, 4, pp. 391–411.
4. L. B. Leakey, 'Facts Instead of Dogma on Man's Origin', in op. cit.
5. François Bourlière, 'Observations on the Ecology of Some Large African Mammals', in Howell and Bourlière (eds.), *African Ecology and Human Evolution*, op. cit.

patterns – for example, from hunting–gathering to agriculture to industrialization – is clear. It is an understandable assumption that prehistoric dietary changes of the important order described above were accompanied by changes in social structure. The nature of these social-structural changes will be established only with difficulty – if at all – but it is important to try.[1]

1

My proposition is that specialization for hunting widened the gap between the *behaviour* of males and females. It favoured those 'genetic packages' which arranged matters so that males hunted co-operatively in groups while females engaged in maternal and some gathering activity. Not only were there organic changes in perception, brain size, posture, hand formation, locomotion, etc., but there were also social structural changes. The male–female link for reproductive purposes and the female–offspring link for nutritive and socialization purposes became 'programmed' into the life-cycles of the creatures. It is suggested here that the male–male link for hunting purposes also became 'programmed' to ensure equal non-randomness in the conduct of social relationships in this matter as in reproductive ones.

The change in dietary pattern was reflected in and accompanied by anatomical changes. Concomitantly, because of the nature of the prey involved, hunting increasingly required more sophisticated patterns of co-operation than had presumably existed in communities where all non-infants provided their own food and where a complex division of food-gathering labour was unnecessary.[2] The co-operative groups involved with hunting would have been all-male,[3] and there would be strong selective pressure in favour of all-maleness. Given the reproductive system of the species, the sexual dimorphism which then existed and which was based on child-rearing, child-care, defence, hierarchy, and exploratory activities would be adapted to include the new task of hunting.[4]

Two consequences would follow the fact that females would

1. S. L. Washburn, 'An Ape's-Eye View of Human Evolution', in P. DeVore (ed.), op. cit., p. 143.
2. For an outstandingly thorough and sophisticated discussion of these issues, see John F. Eisenberg, 'The Social Organization of Mammals', *Handbuch der Zoologie*, 10 (7) (May 1964), pp. 1–92.
3. Campbell, op. cit., p. 203.
4. Vernon Reynolds, 'Open Groups in Hominid Evolution', in op. cit.

normally be pregnant or nursing their infants virtually all of the time: (1) Most adult females would be unable to participate without encumbrance in the hunt. (2) Any who did take part would be at least marginally more prone than their sisters to loss of offspring, miscarriage, and early death by accident. The contributions of non-maternal female behaviour to the genetic pool would be less than the contribution to the pool of those females who accepted a clear-cut sexual dimorphism and enhanced the group's survival chances chiefly by full-time maternal and gathering behaviour. An interesting contemporary version of perhaps the same process is the lesser reproductivity of career women. The higher her occupational position, the less likely a North American female is to be married and bear children. Perhaps a widespread use of contraception will reinforce this trend. At the same time it is clear that under modern conditions survival in itself does not confer the same genetic advantage as it does in marginally viable communities. But the dynamism of demographic systems under contemporary conditions is such as to make any prediction about the future composition of the genetic stock quite unrealistic and fanciful. As Campbell has noted,[1] a general shift from economy-based to sexually based family life, and the world-wide trend to conjugal family life rather than wholly kin-based nuclear family patterns, will have wide and unknown effects on the biological composition of human populations.[2]

Conversely, just as females who hunted with males would be at a long-run genetic disadvantage, so would those males who permitted females to join the hunting party. Even unencumbered by pregnancy or infants, a female hunter would be less fleet, generally less strong, possibly more prone to changes in emotional *tonus* as a consequence of the estrous cycle, and less able to adapt to changes in temperature than males. Also, they could interfere with the co-operative nature of the group by stimulating competition for sexual access. Males who accepted females into their hunting groups would be, like those females themselves, less likely to add to the genetic pool than presumably more efficient hunters who maintained male exclusiveness at these times. A variety of extant male–female somatic differences seem to affirm the correctness of this reconstruction of the evolutionary history which produced them. For example, there are differences in

1. Campbell, op. cit., p. 278.
2. See W. J. Goode, *World Revolution and Family Patterns*, Free Press of Glencoe, Glencoe, Ill., 1963, p. 369.

methods of locomotion between males and females,[1] in the ability to throw spears, bolas, rocks, etc.,[2] in adaptability to temperature changes presumably related to hunting;[3] males show greater spatial-geographical ability,[4] they are more aggressive,[5] etc. – these are all differences which relate more clearly (or as clearly) to differences in activities like hunting or defence, than to child-bearing and rearing. Other major male–female differences must be principally rooted in reproductive activity. Differences such as the ones I have noted may be more economically linked to hunting–defence than to reproduction. I take the existence of these differences to be an indication and outcome of the process of human evolution:[6] The inference follows that the differences were of survival value in this process.[7]

If sex differences are perforce related to male bonding, and if male bonding is related to breeding advantage (which my proposition requires), what sociological processes would have led to breeding advantage for those males who entered into effective male bonds and for those females who were receptive to such males and who tended to reject non-bonded males? One of the most striking analogical suggestions arises from the primate data. These data confirm that in all but two species, lemurs and hamadryas, male bonds exist between dominant members of a troop or community of primates, and that it is the members of the dominant bonds who have sexual access to estrous females. Whatever it is that distinguishes bond from non-bond males – and neither size nor strength themselves provide that dis-

1. John Napier, 'The Antiquity of Human Walking', *Scientific American*, 216, 4 (April 1967), p. 57; 'The Evolution of Bipedal Walking in the Hominids', *Extrait des Archives de Théologie*, Liège, 1964. These are differences which are of course related directly to pelvic structure associated with hunting if only because female pelvic structure inhibits females from the sort of locomotion useful and possibly essential for hunting. When it is recalled that contemporary Bushmen hunters stalking an animal may cover more than twenty miles in one day, the utility of specialized locomotor adaptations is very clear.
2. A. Kortlandt and M. Kooij, 'Protohominid Behaviour in Primates', *Symposia of the Zoological Society of London*, No. 10, 1963. Throwing style of chimpanzees and gorillas is evidently similar to human female throwing style; human male throwing is unique among primates.
3. J. S. Weiner, personal communication.
4. Margaret Mead, *Continuities in Cultural Evolution*, Yale University Press, 1964, p. 98.
5. Maccoby (ed.), *Readings in Social Psychology*, op. cit., pp. 323–6.
6. A procedure suggested by M. R. A. Chance, 'Social Behaviour and Primate Evolution', in Ashley Montague (ed.), *Culture and the Evolution of Man*, Oxford University Press, 1962, p. 85.
7. See Niko Tinbergen, 'On the Aims and Methods of Ethology', in op. cit., pp. 417–23.

tinction – bonding among most primates is a clear correlate of productive copulation. If it is so among primates, as I have already argued, a logical basis exists for the possibility that it may also be so among humans, taking forthrightly into account the fact that separation of human from other primate stock began many millions of years ago. Should male bonding have been as widespread a primate characteristic when *Homo sapiens* began his particular evolution as it is now, the development of co-operative hunting could increase the relevance of bonding for group survival by adding another dimension to its utility. Michael Chance[1] proposes another line of argument – discussed and elaborated by Robin Fox[2] – which complements my own. Briefly, the argument is that hierarchy is a crucial feature of social cohesion and organization. To breed at all, non-dominant males must learn to 'equilibrate' their aggressive hostility to members of the dominant cohort. But, as well, they must be *able* to form bonds to maintain their breeding potential, when and if they become senior in the community. Chance's proposition is that the development of patterns of inhibition was crucial to the enlargement of the evolving human brain. Dominant males possessed breeding advantage; to maintain the cohesion of the community it was essential to inhibit aggression directed at the dominant males. That dangerous weapons were available which could lead to deaths within the community as well as without, must be seen as an additional factor of great importance in the development of mechanisms for inhibiting in-group male rivalry. This complex equilibration spurred the enlargement of the brain, which was part of the essential pattern of preadaptation which *Homo sapiens* subsequently exploited.[3] Fox has enlarged on the

1. M. R. A. Chance, 'Social Behaviour and Primate Evolution', in op. cit.
2. Robin Fox, 'In the Beginning: Aspects of Hominid Behavioural Evolution' (Malinowski Memorial Lecture, 1967, given at London School of Economics and Political Science), *Man*, 2, 3 (September 1967). For a more recent review of this material, see also Robin Fox, 'Incest, Inhibition and Hominid Evolution' (paper presented to Wenner-Gren Symposium, Burg Wartenstein, August 1968).
3. In Chance's words '. . . a potent influence causing enlarging of the cortex and related parts of the amygdala which is found in man, could have been the result of competition for dominance. . . . The more intense this competitive behaviour is, the more it is correlated with a breeding premium, which means a very rapid rate of selection for the characteristics that lead to dominance, the most important of which is the ability to control motive expression at high levels of social excitement. This latter faculty, dependent on an enlarged amygdala, would also be a predisposing mechanism for the development of "tameness", the suggested basis upon which co-operative social life can emerge in hunting communities' – M. R. A. Chance, 'The Nature and Special Features of the Instinctive Social Bonds of Primates', in S. L. Washburn (ed.), *The Social Life of Early Man*, op. cit., pp. 29–32.

relationship of this conception to anthropological and psychoanalytic theories of human kinship and incest, stressing the importance of the fact that, for the human brain to have expanded as rapidly as it did, it was likely that very selective breeding took place.[1] Subdominant males able to inhibit indiscriminate aggressive responses and yet later able to assert their dominance if and when they achieved it, would possess markedly greater reproductive advantage over low status males gaining access only to non-estrous females. Only such genetic inequity, it is claimed, could result in the so-rapid growth of brain tissue. Only such a social system could leave its profound effect on the basic processes of the brain and on the behavioural propensities deriving from this organ which controlled and recorded behaviour, and which most dramatically and effectively reflected man's changed ecological condition, his development and adaptation.

The implications of this are curious. Perhaps the most intriguing is the possibility that what we may here call 'the sense of guilt' is one of the primary and distinct experiences of the human being. As Campbell rather boldly but appropriately states: 'The key to man's social nature lies in his evolution of social hunting; like the dog, man was a social carnivore.'[2] In the interaction between the group and the individual and from the awareness that loyalties and actions could be chosen derived the particular form of self-consciousness out of which the sense of guilt arose. To use my analogy, this may be the necessary component to the process of social cohesion implicit in the 'spinal cord' of male bonds which gives location and structure to human communities.

This is not to say that the phenomenon of guilt is restricted to the relations between males; it is often even more involved with sexual and possibly incestuous matters – though this will vary between cultures. But the striking implication of Chance's and Fox's contribution is that the development of male-bond-type guilt preceded sexual or familial guilt. Perhaps guilt was a useful psychological characteristic in modulating and refining community patterns which were centred around hunting and which were structured hierarchically. This accords with my own independent proposition about the social-structural primacy of the male bond. It also provides a clue to what

1. Robin Fox, 'In the Beginning: Aspects of Hominid Evolution', in op. cit.
2. Campbell, op. cit., p. 319. See also A. Kortlandt, 'Comment on the Essential Morphological Basis for Human Culture', *Current Anthropology*, 6 (1965), pp. 320–5. Kortlandt suggests dogs may experience guilt too.

may be the most elusive aspect of the reality with which I am concerned – an identifiable physiological mechanism underlying the social behaviour I call male bonding.

2

Let us explore this question of physiological mechanisms. If dominance behaviour can be regarded as biologically based, and if Chance is correct that this pattern is linked to cortical and amygdaloid expansion, and if dominance behaviour itself directly relates to bonding – an apparent precondition of reproductive success – then we may see how male bonding might have become programmed into the brains of the descendants or inheritors of the process of bonding-cum-dominance I have described. The transition to hunting-based social organization would augment and reinforce the tendency for successful breeding males to be members of close, co-operating, aggressive groups, and it would more sharply mark the division of labour on socio-sexual grounds. One of the clearest suggestions so far by palaeo-anthropologists of the existence of sexual division of labour, here among the Neanderthal Mousterians, is by Lewis R. Binford and Sally R. Binford:[1]

> Could it be that what is being reflected is a primary difference in terms of social division of labour between males and females? The model we have in mind is that of women carrying out restricted tasks close to the site, making use of local flint sources, and making tools by slightly different techniques than did the men. The men . . . are envisioned as engaging in more far-ranging tasks like hunting, and working flint with techniques better suited to the production of points, scrapers, and knives (p. 283).

The Binfords perceive a distinction between base camps and work camps; the work camps were devoted to hunting and butchering, while the base camps were protected and presumably sheltered women, children, and any non-hunting males (p. 269). A much wider range of activities is represented at the base camps than at the work camps (p. 289). The interesting speculation is advanced that changes in composition and type of assembled groups of artifacts is related more to different use of a specific location over time than to

---

1. Lewis R. Binford and Sally R. Binford, 'A Preliminary Analysis of Functional Variability in the Mousterian of Levallois Facies', *American Anthropologist*, **68**. 2 (April 1966). References are to this publication.

changes in social system (p. 284). Incidentally, Binford and Binford make the methodological assumption that *'The minimal social processes and organizational principles exhibited by human groups today were operative in the past'* (their italics), and use contemporary units 'as baselines against which to compare social units of the past' (pp. 291-4). Desmond Clark notes that in Acheulian sites it is possible to observe differentiation of types of site which indicate that spatial dispersion reflected, 'temporary segregation or dispersal of the component elements – adult and juvenile, male and female, for example – which were now able to engage separately in various activities that previously had not been possible except in conjunction with the group co-operating as a whole'. Clark suggests that possibly regular use of fire was chiefly instrumental in permitting this to happen. Comparable classes of tools exist in south-west Asia, Africa, and Europe, and Clark does not regard this as explicable by the diffusion hypothesis. He concludes that 'type and level of exploitation' was probably more or less similar throughout[1] (p. 226).

A conception along these lines of the possible evolution of male bonding mechanisms would accord with Count's important comment about:

> the emergence of a humanized Primate society during the Pleistocene as the *genuine* evolution of the human way of life, and to the subsequent elaborations upon socio-cultural patterns within the genus-species Homo sapiens as a *spurious* evolution. In genuine evolution, the brain itself was evolving to human calibre, and its externalized output evolved ineluctably; both brain and behaviour were variables against time's parameter – the brain an independent variable and behaviour a dependent variable.[2]

What is crucial here is the possible association between the brain's growth and the adoption of the male bonding pattern for not only political but now food-gathering purposes. Again, it must be recalled that, historically, hunting has been the most profound characteristic of Homo sapiens. So if these hypotheses are correct, one would expect contemporary non-hunting societies to reflect the male bonding propensity in different ways from hunters, but none the less identifiably related to the overall process of male bonding as it has

1. J. Desmond Clark, 'Acheulian Occupation Sites in the Middle East and Africa: A Study in Cultural Variability', *American Anthropologist*, 68, 2, Part 2 (April 1966).
2. Earl W. Count, 'Comment on Steps toward a Unified Anthropology', *Current Anthropology*, 8, 1-2 (February–April 1967), p. 80.

been described here. Of course, we do not know now the actual cortical-amygdaloid processes involved in bonding among men, or even the neurological differences among males and females in this respect. However, for my purposes it is suggestive that brain-process differences exist between males and females and that these certainly reflect themselves in sexual and reproductive activity and possibly in politics and economics.

It is at least possible if not scientifically economical to suggest that the neurological difference in sexual/reproductive patterning may extend to the realm of non-sexual, non-reproductive social relationships.[1] If the widespread stereotype that females are more emotionally labile than males is a correct finding of folk-science and not only an expression of the anti-female tradition, it may have to do with differences in that some ability to inhibit emotional responses which Chance has suggested characterized breeding males in the line of human evolution. Given the overwhelming portion of human history in which females' chief functions have been maternal, it was presumably advantageous for females to be closely and uninhibitedly attuned to their young. For males this responsiveness could be a disadvantage beyond the point at which it does not interfere with political and economic activities. Conceivably, the Euro-American contemporary family system, in which there is relatively close contact between father and children, represents one attempt to solve the problems which arise when males selected by one breeding system find themselves many thousands of years later compelled to live in quite a different one. Robin Fox has suggested that the theme of dominance still maintains its importance in our sexual and familial activity.[2] And, for example, in a public lecture in Seattle, Washington, Margaret Mead in 1963 suggested that American men had been so effectively domesticated by their women that they had too little time and energy to engage in the national and communal tasks which needed doing.[3]

1. For a pertinent discussion of the relationship between brain and behaviour, see Benjamin B. Rubenstein, 'The Mind–Body Problem', in Norman S. Greenfield and William C. Lewis (eds.), *Biology and Psychoanalysis*, University of Wisconsin Press, 1967, pp. 35–56. For example: 'Clinical as well as experimental neurological findings accumulated over the years strongly indicate that every phenomenal event is correlated with a neurophysiological event' (p. 37).

2. Robin Fox, 'The Evolution of Human Sexual Behaviour', *New York Times Magazine* (24 March 1968).

3. Reported to me by Dr Gordon Orians. By contrast, an interesting and candid discussion of the difficulties of mothers with interests other than their children is

I have suggested, then, that the relationship between male bonding, political organization, and sexual difference is possibly a function of human brain development which was based upon a particular breeding and ecological system and which culminated in *Homo sapiens*. This system was characterized by the genetic advantage of those males who could dominate, who were willing and able to bond to dominate and hunt, and who could none the less maintain 'affectionate' if undemocratic relationships with females and young. If this is so, we may have partly interpreted the strong emotion which accompanies bonding, political, and hunting and hunting-type behaviour, and explained the marked sexual differences in participation in these activities. This explanation boasts the virtue of parsimony – though some may see it as merely bald rather than a smooth product of Ockham's razor. But if it is an acceptable explanation, it will also help our understanding of the wider range of phenomena with which I have been dealing, as well as being pertinent to a more limited concern with the intimate process of bonding and the specific process of politics. It may also throw light on the adolescent 'crushes' young boys develop for sports, military, and other heroes. Of course girls also have these crushes, but for female 'role models'; this suggests that the process of identification may depend on neurologically based predispositions or propensities of the same order as those possibly basic to male bonding and other socio-sexual differences in social behaviour.

Such an explanation may be pertinent at two levels of analysis. First, there are clearly many overt differences between males and females which can be explained in terms of natural selection and which, using Count's criteria, represent *genuine* rather than spurious *evolution*.[1] Such differences are, for example, those directly involved in reproduction, metabolism, size, maturation rate, distribution of body hair, posture, and movement, etc.

These differences must lead to associated differences in what perhaps we may call 'microbehaviours'. At the second level of analysis are 'macrobehaviours' – which are related but distinguishable social-systemic differences in economic activity, political leadership, child-rearing, participation in the 'attention-structure' (or 'access to

Iris Andreski, 'The Baby as Dictator', *New Society* (15 December 1966). The conflict between the non-maternal tasks mothers wish to pursue, and their responsiveness to the relatively unceasing demands for attention of their young children, is described and briefly discussed.

1. Earl W. Count, 'Comment on Steps toward a Unified Anthropology', in op. cit.

a public forum'), exploration, etc. If only because of the economy of the evolutionary process, it is a fair assumption that physical sexual differences are related to socio-sexual differences, which I have here extended to include differences in social systemic behaviour. Following the injunctions of such theorists as Talcott Parsons, Walter Goldschmidt, and Marion Levy, who anticipate the use of biological data in the analysis of social systems,[1] I take the existence of somatic or physical sexual differences to point the way to possible social and social-systematic differences. It has been in good part the effort of this book to describe these latter differences and to relate them to physical ones.

There are two major and important features of the process linking somatic sexual differences to systemic behavioural differences which I have not treated here in sufficient detail and scope. The first is the genetic variable – the specific manner in which the encoded information of one generation is fertile or sterile in terms of the succeeding generation. Now it is the case that male and female body cells differ, and that the very DNA molecules of males and females look different under the electron microscope. There is also the suggestion that mammalian sex differences may depend upon hormones acting on the brains of the newborn.[2] The knowledge of how these and similar phenomena are reflected in evolution – with particular reference to such a hypothesized pattern as male bonding – must depend on investigation by specialists.

But it seems appropriate here to repeat my argument of Chapter Two; namely, that if male bonding patterns exist among other animals, particularly primates, and if these patterns appear to be broadly 'programmed', then this provides the analytic freedom to assume that any human equivalent of this bonding phenomenon *may* be subject to the same or comparable biological influence and pressure. Secondly, such evidence as I have been able to consult in this context does not seem to deny that human male bonding can exist. I would also be less than honest to fail to record that I am persuaded that the evidence in fact supports the hypothesis – but readers will have ample opportunity to arrive at their own opinions.

The other important matter I have failed to treat with the comprehensiveness it requires is how learning and transmission goes on

1. See above, pp. 12–14.
2. Seymour Levine, 'Sex Differences in the Brain', *Scientific American*, **214**, 4 (April 1966).

of such a species-specific pattern as male bonding. In discussing ethological method, Chance comments,

> A science begins when we first of all restrict our attention and then define the limits of the region within which we seek to elucidate the operation of the constituent part. This process of isolation has two aspects: the practical sphere of operation, within which attention is restricted, and theoretical isolates or concepts which are used to identify the whole or constituent parts of the practical isolate.[1]

I have been mainly interested in defining the region of investigation and in describing one possible 'isolate' for the better study of human behaviour and social structure.

In so doing, I implicitly affirm the significance of related factors – in other words, the obviously cultural features of any particular community co-operative with the isolate. Therefore it becomes important to know how the male bonding pattern factor interacts with communities' economies, traditions, political systems, sexual moralities, family and educational patterns, and so forth. Empirical data about such phenomena as imitation, learning, the interplay of personality differences and bonding behaviour, ways of socializing children, father–son relationships, and religious sexual symbolism become necessary and relevant. Groups of primates of the same species organize themselves differently under varying economic and environmental circumstances, but always within limits set by their evolution. Study of human cultural variation in the forms and style of male bonding – as well as of family, political, or other social processes – will permit some test of hypotheses about evolution. Also, such research should provide information about the *limits* of human variability; this can in turn guide the formation of more refined hypotheses. And necessarily, of course, such an enterprise must point up the variety and role of cultural differences among and within human communities and permit comparative study of pertinence, some rigour, and cumulativeness.

1. M. R. A. Chance, 'Attention Structure as the Basis of Primate Rank Orders', *Man*, 2, 4 (November 1967).

CHAPTER FOUR

The Male Bond in Human Communities: Politics and War

So far I have discussed male bonding among some animal societies, particularly several primate groups, and have offered a sketch of human evolution which stresses the male bonding factor. In the previous two chapters I have been concerned with major biological processes of a general kind and have been required to consider systems of life and explanations of them which involve conceptions of cause and effect of wide scope and elaborate involvement. In a real sense I have been confronting the explanatory universe. Now I want to turn to the empirical world and begin to describe the relations between human males and the significance of these relations for human communities.

My task is quite straightforward: I want to look at some social institutions which usually have been seen as involving relations between people; I will try to see these relations as encounters between males. I will use data about armies, politics, economic power, religious structures, sports organizations, secret societies, family systems, and training patterns. These data should not only help us to understand the substantive groups and processes involved, but should also lead to discussion about human sexual differences and the associative behaviour of males. After this, some general questions about behavioural 'universals' will be raised and some answers proposed. In this chapter I will deal with politics and war, in the next with work. These two chapters can be taken both for what they imply about human society *per se*, and for what they suggest about the biologically based hypotheses I want to examine.

The frame of reference will be mainly macrosociological – in other words, I will look at whole systems, not bits of systems. I will not be concerned as much with the systems of meaning and belief which people have about their social lives as with their actual behaviour and that perceptibly patterned organization of their behaviours we can call 'social institutions'. The symbolic aspects of socio-sexual behaviour will be only briefly discussed. Hopefully, readers will not consider it simple bias if I seem surprised by the extent to which the significance of sexual dimorphism has been overlooked by students of social behaviour (though not, typically, by the common-sense or folk sociology of the people actually doing the behaviour). So let us now look cross-culturally at some major social institutions to see the effect of treating them as male groups as well as human groups.

1

Obviously, being human is more pervasively characteristic of a human male than being male. Sociability and the formation of many kinds of bond are the most eventful and intriguing characteristics of *Homo*: 'Man comes to sociability not by "arrangement", by rational decision, but from the natural primary disposition which he shares with all other higher animals.'[1] That this disposition exists is undoubted; why it exists, in both animals and man, is by no means certain. Perhaps it will be useful to consider one aspect of human relationship before considering the fundaments of the process.[2]

In a review of *Femmes d'Afrique Noire*,[3] Murphy writes:

Certain recurrent ideas in all the contributions give striking verification to the thesis that sex roles and the interaction between the sexes are not at all as malleable and culturally relative as they are sometimes made out to be. Intersexual relations are charged with distance and antithesis, a form of structural opposition that one would expect in any similarly profound form of identification. And this social distance has often been mistaken for basically superordinate–subordinate relationship despite the existence of

1. Adolf Portman, *Animals As Social Beings*, Hutchinson, London, 1961, p. 70.
2. I am grateful for discussion with Desmond Morris of this point, if only for gaining a firmer sense of the lack of knowledge which surrounds the general question: Why do animals bond? One recent study concerned with the process of social aggregation is Stanley Schacter, *The Psychology of Affiliation: Experimental Studies of Sources of Gregariousness*, Tavistock Publications, London, 1961.
3. Robert F. Murphy, review of Denise Paulme (ed.), *Femmes d'Afrique Noire*, in *American Anthropologist*, **64**, 5 (October 1962), p. 1077.

ample documentation that the status of a woman in most societies varies immensely during the life cycle. More importantly, personal power has often been equated with access to a public forum.

I accept Murphy's estimate of the importance of the finding contained in Paulme's edition. It is true that females may have much power in some types of family structure and undoubtedly exert decisive influence over socialization of the young. Females may also participate fully in economic activity (though here again it is significant that lower status typically attaches to female work) and in many communities may play political, religious, intellectual, etc., and certainly 'expressive' roles of consequence. But it may be incorrect to belittle the importance of 'access to a public forum' in symbolizing the actual power relationships between the sexes in a community. When a community deals with its most vital problems, when statements of internal and external importance are made, when – particularly in warfare – decisive actions must be taken, at these times females do not participate. The public forum is a male forum.

(For the purposes of the present argument, I assume that the differences in social behaviour between so-called 'primitive' and so-called 'modern' societies are at the institutional level – so that a very wide variety of formal and informal social arrangements may be composed of a limited number of constituent behavioural patterns and interactional units. Thus, the forms of male dimorphic dominance may vary widely in different societies and within them. But these forms are reducible to relatively simple components, one of which is the access to a public forum.)

It is men who dominate the public and private State Councils of the world; men are the Ambassadors, the Linguists (in west Africa); there are few 'Spokeswomen'. Chance's notions about 'attention structure' are particularly relevant here; females may simply not release 'followership' behaviour. The 'look' of them may be wrong for encounters of high state and gravity.

At this point I am not concerned as much with the structure of communities as with process, and not as much with the forms which dominance by males takes as with dynamics. Structures vary in this respect between 'complex' and 'simple' societies – though to no obvious and general pattern. But the processes of sexual differentiation are identifiably common in a wide range of societies with different kinds of socio-economic systems. Hence it seems useful to deal with the forms as functions or correlates of the process, rather than the other way around. Basically, my proposition is that cultural forms result from the interaction of behavioural propensities – or inborn biological programmes – with existing social patterns and expectations in any community. An analogy is with intelligence. All individuals have some talent for the solution of problems and the accomplishment of tasks. Each community will have a set of appropriate tests and standards in terms of which individual ability can be applied. In one community tracking giraffes may express intelligence; in another tracking missiles. One culture may applaud intelligent war-making, another transcendental meditation. The point is simply that a particular feature of the human endowment is reflected in different ways by different cultures, but what is of interest to us is *how* it is thus reflected, and, more centrally, *what* is being reflected.

So the scheme here is that the behaviour of an individual is not determined by impingement of culture on a *tabula rasa*, but by the co-ordination of a genetically arbitrated life cycle with the more or less appropriate responses evoked by a particular community.[1] For example, females in both the U.S. Federal Civil Service[2] and in

1. This is similar to the distinction made by Simmel between the 'contents' and 'forms' of social life. Simmel did not deal explicitly with the nature of 'drive, interest, purpose, inclination, psychic state, or movement', but he does appear to allow an 'instinctive' factor to underly the development of social patterns. These may then become 'autonomous' – ends in themselves no longer directly related to 'the materials that we wish to wrest from life'. The submission here is that while 'autonomization of contents' may occur, it does so within limits set by a predisposing need to link certain structures to certain features of the 'biogram'. Simmel's work remains a brilliant feat of analysis and exposition. His study of interaction, particularly in small groups, predates the ethological method though his findings and discussion are at least as 'modern' and dispassionate. It is very unfortunate his work appears to be unknown or irrelevant to ethological theorists. His discussion of 'adornment' (pp. 338–44) is a classic elaboration of the concept of 'releaser' and of the interactional nature of an individual's existential stance. The essay is a close kin of the less rich and less successful efforts of ethologists to paint the nature of individual life and social interaction. Because they have had ample evidence of the dangers of anthropomorphism, ethologists may overcompensate, to lose the evident source of possible understanding of other species through an elaborate awareness of their own. No better and no more artful advocacy (by quality not dialectic) of the value of formal sociology in the understanding of social behaviour exists than Simmel's writing. See Kurt H. Wolff (trans. and ed.), *The Sociology of Georg Simmel*, Collier-Macmillan, London, 1964 (Free Press Paperback Edition).

2. Margaret Mead and Frances B. Kaplan (eds.), *American Women: The Report of the President's Commission on the Status of Women*, Charles Scribner's Sons, New York, 1965, pp. 49–53.

the Marri Baluch tribe of West Pakistan[1] lack access to public forum. If this is a regular pattern which occurs regularly across cultures, we may infer that the reason for the pattern lies not only in females' enforced modesty and the cross-cultural diffusion of this pattern, but in the simple but curiously perplexing fact that all the creatures involved are the same in some basic and influential respects.[2]

Does the pattern exist? This is, of course, the heart of our pre-occupation. To find or suggest the answer, a number of procedures could have been followed, separately or simultaneously. I might have drawn a sample of cultures for which good monographs exist, and have analysed the relations between sexes and the distribution of power and influence. I might have consulted secondary sources which, while they may not have dealt directly with our problem, have relevant assessments to offer in this area. I might have projected a series of field studies of various cultures. I might have studied behaviour in my own society.

But this was an exploratory study. It seemed premature to engage in formal study of either my own or other cultures. To have used a sample of cultures from, for example, the Human Relations Area File, would have involved edited data collected and presented in analytic categories developed for quite different purposes.[3] Better would have been an extensive perusal of ethnographic monographs. In the end, I used a *mélange* of several of the above methods, chiefly because I found this more illuminating and efficient at this point.

What follows is a series of discussions of institutional areas of social life, such as politics, religion, economy, based on a variety of kinds of data. The results can be no more than suggestive. Basing generalizations on secondary sources is hazardous for confirming or disconfirming any hypothesis. But in the interests of some theoretical progress, and to benefit from the division of scientific labours, I have used the material of others. The full body of materials used cannot be described and quoted, but I have quoted extensively from some sources to minimize distortion. Whenever full quotation

---

1. Robert N. Pehrson, *The Social Organization of Marri Baluch* (compiled and analysed from his notes by Frederick Barth), Wenner-Gren Foundation, New York: Viking Fund Publications in Anthropology, Vol. 43, 1966, pp. 49–70.
2. See Cohen, *The Transition from Childhood to Independence*, op. cit. 'Biology is always molded by culture and culture always has limits set for it by, among other things, human biology' (p. 17).
3. See ibid., p. 207, for comments on the difficulties in using Human Relations Area File data in some comparable situations.

is impractical, I indicate what I have interpreted and extrapolated rather than summarized.

POLITICS

Let us look at politics first and let us use an organic analogy. Male bonding I see as the spinal column of a community, in this sense: from a hierarchical linkage of significant males, communities derive their intra-dependence, their structure, their social coherence, and in good part their continuity through the past to the future. I share Schapera's broad conception of politics as the result of the occupation of territory coupled with the maintenance of law[1] rather than as the outgrowth and expansion of kinship systems. The territory is the arena within which the law operates. The law represents the cumulative decision-making and tradition of the dominant males. Conceptually, no distinction will be introduced between 'law' as a process and 'politics' as a process. The separation of judiciary and politics is a relatively exotic notion which is in practice very incomplete. This is so not only through error or corruption, but also because legal systems require the protection and sanction of political systems, and because frequently legal functionaries are appointed through or by political process. Even though holders of legal appointments may be formally independent of politicians, they depend none the less on the legislation of politicians for their guidance. Where legislation may be overruled by the law, as in the U.S. Supreme Court decisions on segregation, it can be argued reasonably that the law assumes part of the general responsibility for not only maintaining social order but for deciding what this order is to be.

On the question of territoriality, it may be wisest to accept Lowie's cautious formulation that territoriality and male groups are the basis of political activity.[2] There is much more to be said about the interrelationship between maleness, territoriality, and politics than can be given here. The matter is, of course, tentative. It has been, and will be, difficult to gather data about human territoriality or non-territoriality which satisfies many of the criteria of evidence. None the less it would be very unwise to discount the possibility that a territorial propensity exists and is in part the basis for a variety of human behaviours and institutions. The suggestion has been made

1. I. Schapera, 'Introduction', Government and Politics in Tribal Societies, Watts, London, 1965.
2. Robert Lowie, Primitive Society, Routledge, London, 1949, pp. 380–1.

that it is likely future research will show that territoriality is a more important factor in primate life than present evidence allows;[1] a similar suggestion may well be applicable to humans. A recent general attempt to synthesize the available material on territoriality is by Robert Ardrey.[2] The works of Hall,[3] Carpenter,[4] Calhoun,[5] and Wynne-Edwards,[6] among others, suggest the nature of the 'territorial-type' mechanisms operating among humans and other animals. There is a growing awareness of the effects of crowded conditions upon social organization and personal health. Architects and planners have begun to acknowledge this in their discussions of the possibility that there are inelastic features of man's ability to use space.[7]

2

At an anecdotal level, it is clear there is a close relationship between maleness, politics, and territory. The relationship may be causal, merely circumstantial, or the reflection of a syndrome. My own view is that it is the latter, and that when the syndrome is disrupted there are predictable consequences which we shall have occasion to consider later.

For the time being, let us see to what extent politics is a male enterprise and why this is so. Ardrey defines

. . . the biological nation . . . [as] a social group containing at least two mature males which holds as an exclusive possession a continuous area of space, which isolates itself from others of its kind through outward antagonism, and which through joint defense of its social territory achieves leadership, co-operation, and a

1. S. L. Washburn, The Origin of Man, op. cit., p. 90.
2. Robert Ardrey, The Territorial Imperative: A Personal Inquiry into the Animal Origins of Property and Nations, Atheneum, New York, 1966.
3. E. T. Hall, The Hidden Dimension, Doubleday, New York, 1966.
4. C. R. Carpenter, 'Territoriality: A Review of Concepts and Problems', in A. Roe and G. G. Simpson (eds.), Behaviour and Evolution, Yale University Press, 1958.
5. John B. Calhoun, 'A Behavioural Sink', in Eugene L. Bliss (ed.), Roots of Behaviour, Harper, New York, 1962, Ch. 22.
6. V. C. Wynne-Edwards, Animal Dispersion in Relation to Social Behaviour, Hafner, New York, 1962.
7. For example, see Robin Best, 'Against High Density', New Society (24 November 1966), p. 217; Lionel Tiger, 'Diplomats, Monkeys, and the New Biology', International Journal (Winter 1967); David Stea, 'Territoriality, The Interior Aspect: Space, Territory and Human Movements', Landscape 15, 1 (Autumn 1965); Alvin L. Schorr, Slums and Social Insecurity, U.S. Government Printing Office, Washington, D.C.: Nelson, London, 1965.

capacity for concerned action. It does not matter too much whether such a nation be composed of twenty-five individuals or two hundred and fifty million.[1]

From our point of view, the interesting feature of the definition is the specification that at least two mature males must form the core of the group; this is a similar conception to the spinal cord analogy ventured above. The evidence suggests it is valid to assert that political groups occupying territory are centred and dominated by hierarchies of adult – usually senior – males. (Age limits for office-holders, e.g. U.S. Presidents must be at least thirty-five, reflect general concern with the broad biological characteristics of age and the experience it may represent.) In his Introduction to *The Political Role of Women*, Maurice Duverger notes the hostility which exists in Europe to female political activity and alludes to the

. . . traces of that primitive mentality which regards war as a 'sport for men'; there is a similar tendency to regard politics as a man's affair. The club, the forum, debates, Parliament and political life in general are still considered to be typically masculine activities. . . . The existence of this more or less anti-feminist attitude, which despite an undeniable process of evolution, is still very strong, seems to be a directly observable fact so far as the recent survey is concerned.[2]

Duverger studied four countries intensively – France, the German Federal Republic, Norway, and Yugoslavia. He also gathered less detailed comparative data from fifteen other countries. The familiar but freshly striking general finding of his research is that women play a small role overall in the politics of their communities. Duverger explicitly denies that this is the result of biological differences: 'There is nothing here to suggest an essential peculiarity in woman's nature or a fundamental difference in men's and women's behaviour.'[3] This is a very curious statement, in as much as it is the burden of Duverger's book to show that indeed there are differences in the political behaviour of men and women. Presumably Duverger's implication is that those differences which do exist – and this argument is made at various points in his book – are chiefly the consequences

1. Robert Ardrey, op. cit., p. 191.
2. Maurice Duverger, *The Political Role of Women*, UNESCO, Paris, 1955, p. 10.
3. ibid., p. 122.

of cultural tradition, economic opportunity, and conscious governmental decision.

None the less it is with behavioural differences that we are concerned. These Duverger's evidence affirms. Of particular relevance to our concern with positions of generalized dominance and access to a public forum is that – invariably – there are fewer women in any organization the higher up its hierarchy a count is made:

> This progressive decline in women's influence as the higher levels of leadership are reached is not only noticeable in the structure of the State and political organs, but is also to be found in the government service, the political parties, the trade unions, private business, etc. Nor are there any perceptible signs of improvement in this respect. Although the difference in the proportions of men and women non-voters sometimes tends to lessen in certain countries, nothing similar can be noted at the Parliamentary and governmental levels. The percentage of women members of parliament, for instance, is hardly increasing. On the contrary, it tends to fall after the first elections in which women have had the suffrage, and to become stabilized at a very low level.[1]

For example, after female suffrage was introduced in Japan, thirty-five females were elected in national contests, but this has now dropped to eleven. American experience suggests females are less likely to vote for females than males for males.[2] Canadian material corroborates this.[3] In Australia, though females had the vote earlier than in the U.S. or the U.K. and did not have to struggle for it, the relative unimportance of voting is expressed in the fact that 'over the entire period since women were eligible to sit in the Australian parliament, only a fraction of 1 per cent have been women'.[4]

Duverger notes an important disparity between women's voting behaviour and their political behaviour. There is considerable similarity in male and female *voting* behaviour, but there is an extreme

1. ibid., p. 123.
2. Nona B. Brown, 'Inquiry into the Feminine Mind', *New York Times Magazine* (12 April 1964).
3. Kathy Hassard, 'Spirit of Feminism Political Lack Today', *Vancouver Sun* (2 October 1963). Even in the relatively 'modernizing' government of Pierre Elliot Trudeau, there are only two women out of 264 Members of Parliament.
4. Thelma Hunt, 'Australian Women', *The Australian Quarterly*, 35, 1 (March 1963), p. 80.

dissimilarity in male and female *political* behaviour. Not only is there an extensive quantitative difference in political participation, there is also a qualitative one:

> In party leadership, in senior administrative posts, in parliaments and in governments, the few women included concentrate on specialized matters, such as health, education, motherhood, family welfare, housing, etc. – that is, on all problems which, in the general opinion, are considered to be of special interest to women . . . there are signs . . . of a very definite aggravation of this tendency towards specialization.[1]

While, as Duverger notes, it is not difficult to counter the various arguments which men raise to exclude females from politics, none the less

> the small influence of women in State leadership is in large measure due to women's own inertia. . . . Not only do women show little desire to win a place in political leadership, but the great majority of them accept the system of justification invented by men to rationalize their standing aside from it. Curiously, they sometimes seem to be more uncompromising than men in this regard, and more anti-feminist.[2]

Duverger provides some cross-cultural data on female participation which are worth summarizing in some detail. With the exception of the U.S.S.R., where 17 per cent of the Supreme Soviet (which has very little power) are female, 5 per cent appears to be the maximum of female participation in various parliaments. It is a maximum 'seldom attained': Netherlands, 5 to 6 per cent, French Assembly, 3·6 per cent, Norway, 4 per cent, U.K., 3 per cent, United States Congress, 2 per cent.

> In the local and municipal bodies, the proportion is seldom higher and often lower. . . . At the governmental level, women play an even smaller part.[3]

> . . . in 1949, out of 59 countries where women had the right to vote, women held ministerial office in only 11; none of these countries was a leading power; no country had more than one woman minister; and Rumania was the only country where the ministerial office held by a woman was of any real political im-

1. Duverger, op. cit., p. 124.   2. ibid., p. 126.   3. ibid., p. 145.

portance (foreign affairs). . . . Not only is an extremely small proportion of women admitted to association with the government, but the number does not appear to be increasing. On the contrary, in the countries where women's right to vote was recognized over 30 years ago, there is a decided tendency towards a stabilization of the number of women members of parliament – after an initial surge in the years immediately following the electoral reform.[1]

There is no evidence that these situations vary between societies with more and less liberal views on feminist principles and the political equality of the sexes. For example, the United States is commonly thought to be feminist and in general women are supposed to wield considerable influence. They are relatively well-educated and economically advantaged. Yet the U.S. has one of the smallest proportions of female members in its national government – about 2 per cent.

Of special interest is the fact that, in communities in which female representation has increased, this has been the result of the effort of left-wing parties:

> . . . it is the left-wing parties, particularly the Socialist and Communist parties, which have done most to increase the number of women entering Parliament or holding office in the government – an attitude which may well appear paradoxical, since women electors . . . are, in the majority, conservative. One might almost say that parties which do the most for women are the parties for which women do the least.[2]

For example, the French Communist party has elected the greatest number of females to office. Yet it commands the smallest proportion of women voters of any major party.[3] In view of the traditional theory of democratic politics, which contains the proposition that political parties broadly represent the groups electing them, this is

---

1. ibid., p. 146.   2. ibid., p. 147.
3. For an interesting statement of the French Communist party's general position on the position and rights of women, see Roger Garaudy (Preface), *Femmes du XXe Siècle: Semaine de la Pensée Marxiste*, Presses Universitaires de France, 1965. For current data on female office-holding in France, see his p. 71. One suggested reason for the lack of participation is: '. . . *les femmes refusent le role qu'elles pourraient jouer dans la vie politique, parce qu'elles sont psychologiquement mal preparées* . . .' (p. 74). For detailed data on female status in public and commercial organization, see pp. 47–61.

indeed paradoxical, and of considerable relevance to the notion of representative democracy. There is another distortion of the theory of representative democracy; this reflects the fact that only exceptionally have women's suffragette organizations actually succeeded in securing female suffrage: 'This extension of the suffrage seems attributable to the two world wars rather than to the work of women's associations.'[1] Even before this time, for example in America, female suffrage occurred first in states where there was no strong female agitation for the vote, but where females' votes were desired by men for their own particular political purposes.[2]

The changes in women's rights were effected largely by men. It could not be otherwise because usually – as in Switzerland, for example – men must vote on the very constitutional amendments accepting female suffrage.[3] Significantly, in many countries women received the right to vote as the result of executive decrees by revolutionary provisional governments which later ratified such decrees in the new terms of their drastically won legitimacy.[4]

This suggests the depth and complexity of the connection between political order and male dominance. It will be discussed more fully below. In one description of the constellation of attitudes and actions in this area, Young and Bacdayan demonstate a provocative if bizarre correlation between menstrual taboos, the position of women in communities, and the extent to which communities are politically, religiously, and socially rigid.[5] They sketch the kind of variation which may occur in this area and show how the notion of 'woman' a community holds – of which attitudes to menstruation are an important index – occurs not capriciously but as a function of political system.

Thus where women have been allowed the vote – and it is essential to bear in mind that even voting is, in terms of an individual's participation in the polity, a relatively unimportant action – this has

1. Duverger, op. cit., p. 139.
2. In the nineteenth century, the only states with female suffrage were Wyoming, Utah, Colorado, and Idaho. For an excellent account of these early and subsequent changes in American female political activity, see Alan P. Grimes, *The Puritan Ethic and Woman Suffrage*, Oxford University Press, New York, 1967. See also Andrew Sinclair, *The Emancipation of the American Woman*, Harper and Row, New York, 1966.
3. ' "No" to Vote for Women in Zurich', *Guardian* (21 November 1966).
4. Duverger, op. cit., p. 10.
5. Frank W. Young and Albert A. Bacdayan, 'Menstrual Taboos and Social Rigidity', *Ethnology*, 4, 2 (April 1965).

apparently been largely the result of effort by males on females' behalf. Not infrequently it has been associated with reformist or revolutionary changes in political structure.

A major study should be done of the role of women in political activity of newly independent countries. It is clear that in India, for example, women play a political part with considerable energy and effect. In so far as the U.S.S.R. can be seen as a newly independent state, women have been important in achieving social change and their improved status is an index of this change. On the other hand, this new participation of women in politics may be 'artificial' in the sense that it was created as a result of conscious contentious action (the whole question of consciousness will require more discussion later), and it will be interesting to observe the long-term effects of changes quite precipitously introduced. In Ghana, for example, President Nkrumah by executive *fiat* appointed ten female M.P.s, very generally representing regions and clearly possessing different representative status in the National Assembly from elected male members. Apparently he did this upon suggestion by various persons, one of whom was a Canadian lady who challenged him at a Commonwealth function in London with, 'What are you doing for women?'

Because of the special manner of their elevation to high status in Ghana, at least several of the female M.P.s were surrounded by allegation and innuendo about the role of their sexual activity in maintaining their favour among senior politicians. Their frequent and disproportionate participation in delegations and missions representing Ghana abroad was noticed by persons who attributed to this – whether out of prurience or concern for the 'moral' conduct of state matters – an immoral significance which would only hinder the advancement of the status of women, in aid of which the posts of the female M.P.s had been created. The point here is not that female M.P.s in Ghana behaved or did not behave in any special manner. It is not necessarily of public interest nor is it a new phenomenon that the sharing of beds may accompany the sharing of political spoils. But the *femaleness* of the individuals led to considerable *special* consideration of their political roles. The fact that a number of the persons were physically very attractive is another factor which we shall have occasion to discuss again. The whole matter of the relationship between sexual and political behaviour is not only popularly intriguing – as the Profumo episode indicated – but there may be an underlying process involved which is of considerable scientific interest. For example, there is a report of the difficulties which white female civil rights workers experienced in their attempts to secure social change in the U.S. South because of the historically tense and complex sexual relationship between white women and black men.[1]

Where women have achieved the vote, it is not clear that changes commensurate with doubling the number of voters in fact occurred; Duverger suggests that one of the chief direct effects of enfranchisement of women in America was prohibition, and in France the closing of brothels.[2] While there are undoubtedly many indirect effects of female enfranchisement, such as greater concern with child health, school conditions, and issues of public morality, it may be possible to argue that, relatively speaking, the franchise for women has had less direct political implications than, for example, registration of Negro voters in the U.S. South, the abolition of property qualifications in British national elections, or the 'racialization' of West Indies politics in the 1960s.

Without wishing to disparage either the importance of voting as a political action when taken *en masse* in a community or the value and sophistication of voting studies, it should be said that the significance of voting may be easily overestimated, particularly as a factor in political behaviour. The relationship of voting to female political participation is an excellent case in point. Almost a sacred aura surrounds voting in some circles, especially those concerned with the 'export of democracy' to recently independent societies. The example of the role of voting (in Communist countries most conspicuously, and many others as well) suggests that voting is often part of a 'ritual of intensification' seen to be useful in maintaining the formal legitimacy of the government in power. In fact, with the exception of the few countries in which it is the crucial means of selecting governments, voting as a behaviour is of little account in the actual emergence of a dominance hierarchy in most societies. (While particularly in Euro-American societies it may be thought to be the best way of choosing governments, this is a value judgement which should not distort scientists' choices in studying what is most significant in the political life of communities.)

In no way do I wish to minimize the effect of female voting participation. However, it is important that no direct appeal to the

1. Alvin F. Poussaint, 'The Stresses of White Female Workers in the Civil Rights Movement in the South', *American Journal of Psychiatry*, 123, 4 (October 1966).
2. Duverger, op. cit., p. 150.

female 'block of votes' which is made by political parties is then followed by specific legislation supposedly pertinent to female interests. Females are treated as a minority group, rather like an ethnic one. But policies designed to appeal to them do not have the anticipated electoral effect; those parties most concerned with female issues and rights perversely receive the lesser share of the female vote.

This is surprising on another ground as well. Women generally tend to vote as their husbands do. So when reformist parties with a feminist orientation receive significantly less than a duly proportionate share of the vote, the implication is that women have deliberately chosen the (statistical) innovation of voting differently from their husbands. There is a Western European exception to this. Explicitly 'Christian' parties – namely those having some formal commitment to Christian principle as a feature of political stance – tend both to receive a slightly greater than proportionate female vote and as well to be somewhat more favourably inclined to appoint females to high posts than non-Christian, non-left parties. None the less the Christian parties are less 'progressive' than the left-wing parties which remain unfavoured by female voters. It must also be recalled that European Christian churches are largely male-dominated organizations, and that any decision of female voters to support Christian parties reflects a favourable view the females must have of the importance and influence of these male-dominated religious structures.

3

The data indicate that the attitudes of males and females to female participation in the political arena remain stable. Apparently even major changes in political form and ideology can have little effect on the role of women. For example, during the Nazi era in Germany, the female role was – in the famous phrase – supposed to revolve around 'Kinder, kirche, und küchen'. Goebbels elaborated the position:

> . . . the National Socialist Movement is in its nature a masculine movement. . . . While man must give to life the great lines and forms, it is the task of woman out of her inner fullness and inner eagerness to fill these lines and forms with colour. The realms of directing and shaping . . . politics . . . must without qualification be claimed by man. When we eliminate women from public life, it is not because we want to dispense with them but rather because

we want to give them back their essential honour. . . . The out-standing and highest calling of woman is always that of wife and mother and it would be an unthinkable misfortune if we allowed ourselves to be turned from this point of view.[1]

Until Hitler specifically organized women's groups – defined as such – the female Nazi party membership was less than 3 per cent. German women never undertook military service, even in the Second World War.[2] Now, after the war, an at least superficially quite different political structure exists. But females are still excluded from or do not participate in party political leadership;[3] and it appears that little substantial difference exists between current atti-tudes of the community to female political activity and those in evidence before the trauma of the war.

It has already been noted that females in the U.S. have not so far successfully penetrated higher political circles in numbers in any sense related to the potential political influence which could be based on their 51 per cent voting strength. Tiny numbers occupy high posts in the judicial and administrative hierarchies; 'under the past 3 ad-ministrations women have comprised a constant per cent – 2·4 – of a rising number: 79 of 3,273 in 1951–52; 84 of 3,491 in 1958–59; 93 of 3,807 in 1961–62'.[4] Changes of political administration appear to mark no effective changes in appointments of females to the Federal Administrative Service, though it is thought that conditions are becoming more favourable to the employment of women in high posts. This is because of decreasing resistance by men ('though few political inner circles are free of it') and because females may in future prepare themselves more self-consciously for careers – which may include politics – and may be psychologically and experientially better equipped to compete for high office.[5]

But the significant point remains that the political élites of the U.S. and other societies are male. The backroom boys of legend do exist. They have not yet accepted women either easily or in any numbers. In a study of the American élite,[6] C. Wright Mills makes

1. Goebbels, then Minister of Propaganda, quoted in Clifford Kirkpatrick, *Nazi Germany: Its Women and Family Life*, Bobbs-Merrill, New York, 1938, p. 116.
2. Corinna Adam, 'Gretel's Old Look', *New Statesman* (21 February 1964).
3. Duverger, op. cit., p. 107.
4. Mead and Kaplan (eds.), op. cit., pp. 72 and 74.   5. ibid., p. 74.
6. C. Wright Mills, 'The Structure of Power in American Society', *British Journal of Sociology*, 60, 1 (March 1958). See also Mills's *The Power Élite*, Ocford University Press, 1956.

no reference to females, while in his outstanding analysis of the stratification patterns in Canada, John Porter does not find it necessary to be directly concerned with females.[1] Lipset's influential study offers no contrary evidence.[2]

The exclusion of females is not a phenomenon peculiar to the wealthier Euro-American societies. The error is commonly made that matriarchal societies are societies where females dominate social and political affairs. But the truth is that matriarchy is a principle of hereditary succession, not a political pattern, and should in usage properly be replaced by matrilineality. In his study of 'primitive' society, Lowie flatly states that matrilineal descent patterns do not symptomize female government. There are a very few instances,

> . . . they can be counted on the fingers of one hand, . . . in which women either exercise unusual property rights or play a remarkable part in public life. . . . Even among the Iroquois (where women play a role in the election of chiefs) no woman had a place in the supreme council of the league. . . . A genuine matriarchate is nowhere to be found.[3]

Allen's comprehensive study of Melanesian secret and age-grade societies reveals that the vast majority of these are male societies. There are 'no true examples in Melanesia of bisexual associations – those in which females may have some role confine females to less than full membership'.[4] Without indicating what the reasons for the probability are, Allen states:

> In all probability there are a considerable number of unrecorded women's associations entered by rites of initiation. The only definite examples that I know of are the women's secret societies of the Seniang and Lambumbi districts of Malekula Island in the northern New Hebrides.[5]

Allen's major reason for the statement of probability (personal communication) is that the majority of field-workers are males and would be less likely to discover female groups than male groups, and less likely to be told about them, given the severe intersexual hostility which characterizes many communities of Melanesia. His

1. John Porter, *The Vertical Mosaic*, University of Toronto Press, 1965.
2. Lipset, *Political Man*, op. cit.   3. Lowie, op. cit., pp. 180–2.
4. Allen, *Rites de Passage*, op. cit.   5. ibid.

argument is echoed by Paulme, who suggests that social science is male-centric, if only because the majority of its practitioners are males who are disinclined and possibly incapable of perceiving a view of female behaviour substantially different from the conventional 'Western' one.[1] Another argument that social science is male-centric is put by Betty Friedan.[2] Friedan is particularly anxious to demonstrate the sexually biased nature of Freudian theory (see her Chapter Five), and illustrates the important consequences which potentially follow a theory based on inadequate data and interpreted without objectivity about female socio-sexual behaviour. An additional impediment – and perhaps a more consequential one – to the use of Freudian theory to explain behaviour, is that the theory has been so influential as to constitute a feature of the very cultures it seeks to explain. Precisely in those societies in which Freudian and neo-Freudian analysts are numerically and intellectually powerful – for example, in the U.S.A. – lay folklore as well as professional theory is structured around the expectation that the behaviour Freud identified will appear. (While this is in one sense a tribute to the credibility and possible correctness of Freudian theory, it also constitutes a barrier to its disconfirmability. This does not mean Freudian hypotheses should not be used, but only with special care and consciousness.)

Given the argument I have been making, one would predict that there will be far fewer female organizations than male ones. Where they do exist, the relative obscurity of the female organizations and their apparent unimportance for the macro-life of the community is striking and provocative. I am not saying females do not aggregate (in Melanesia and elsewhere) for some purposes, such as childcare, gathering, and farming, or for simple gregariousness. But those female organizations which do exist bear much less direct relationship than do men's organizations to the political structure of their communities and the establishment of the dominance hierarchy. Nor do they appear to be as persistent over time. Even where female organizations are relatively well-established, such as among the Mende of Sierra Leone, it is the male *Poro* secret society which, 'In the political field . . . exercises an overriding influence which is both direct and indirect and only *Poro* members can have political office

1. See Denise Paulme (ed.), *Women of Tropical Africa*, University of California Press, 1964, p. 1.
2. Betty Friedan, *The Feminine Mystique*, W. W. Norton, New York, 1963.

in the chiefdom.'[1] The *Sande*, which deals with women's affairs, and the *Humɔi*, which is concerned with the sexual conduct of the community, do not formally impinge upon the political process in Mende society. The Head of the Humɔi society – a woman – may attend meetings of *Poro* high officials, but she is not permitted to participate. Significantly, even her role is symbolically restricted, because she is assumed to be invisible during meetings to all members except the Grand Tasso.[2]

Interestingly, one common way in which females acquire high office is by being close and politically active relatives of senior politicians who die. This is perhaps the most obvious and certainly the easiest way in which women have come to occupy high posts. Various cases come to mind: Mrs S. R. D. Bandaranaike of Ceylon, Madame Ghandi, daughter of Nehru, Mrs Maurine Neuberger, Eleanor Roosevelt, Jennie Lee (wife of Aneurin Bevan), Madame Sun Yat-sen, Lady Gaitskill, Lady Nancy Astor, Lady Iveagh, Lena Jeger. 'A curious fact of political life in Canada is that if a widow stands for her late husband's seat in a federal by-election she is almost sure to win.'[3] The explanation for this is commonsensical. But at another level the matter may be rather more complex. Undoubtedly part of the reason for the appointment of widows to high office is the sense of gratitude which the deceased politician's colleagues may feel for his efforts during his lifetime. Internal party equilibrium may be maintained by honouring the memory of an individual whose supporters remain important and ambitious. There is probably an element of 'pensioning-off' a widow whose husband's death might have left her financially deprived unless a post was arranged for her. More simply, the widow's experience during her husband's career and her contacts with his professional colleagues might draw attention to her possible talents in the political field.

But a more interesting if more fugitive process may be at work when either professional politicians or electors or both give political posts to female relatives of deceased dominant males. In many vertebrate communities females assume the status of their male mates; in primates the phenomenon is sufficiently closely related to small-scale human class structures for one ethologist to propose that

1. Kenneth L. Little, 'The Role of the Secret Society in Cultural Specialization', *American Anthropologist*, 51, 1 (March 1949), pp. 204–5.
2. F. W. Butt-Thompson, *West African Secret Societies*, Witherby, London, 1929, p. 72.
3. Jean Sharp, 'Widows Are Often Successful Running for Political Office', *Montreal Star* (22 December 1964).

comparable mechanisms operate in primates as well as humans.[1] For example, in Hutterite communities in Alberta, the post of Chief Cook – the highest female post – is normally filled by the wife of either the Preacher or the Boss, the two highest ranking males.[2] A Maratha princess of India traditionally had the responsibility of leading 'her troops in person when there was no husband or son to do so'.[3]

Perhaps females possess the 'releaser' which stimulates people to follow them mainly when they embody or share the 'charisma' of dominance of a closely related male. Otherwise they neither inspire the confidence nor channel the energies of potential supporters.

Thus, that females only rarely dominate authority structures may reflect females' underlying inability – at the ethological level of 'pattern-releasing' behaviour – to affect the behaviour of subordinates. However, this general handicap apparently can be overcome by those females who have obviously participated in the use of power through their closely related men. More than any other factor, this appears to lend efficaciousness to females' otherwise ineffective political efforts. Of course, this is similar to the general process of transmission of charisma[4] from one person to another which occurs in the development of dynastic political traditions. A retired incumbent's endorsement of an aspiring candidate is part of the same process of transmission. Female succession is only one factor in the complex process of maintaining social order. But it may be of vital significance to the understanding of this process to recognize that the division of labour along sexual lines predictably occurs in any community and that the dominant political roles in this division are disproportionately assigned to males.

Of course, many of the reasons for female non-participation in higher politics arise out of a variety of straightforward social situations, such as the complexities of the role of child-rearing, the legal propertylessness of females in some communities which must inhibit their freedom of political action, the fact that often they may not

1. William R. S. Russell, personal communication.
2. Vernon Serl, personal communication.
3. A. S. Attekar, *The Position of Women in Hindu Civilization*, Motilal Banarsidas, Benares, 1956, p. 22.
4. For a brief discussion of Weber's view of the biological nature of charisma and its relationship to human dominance patterns, see Tiger and Fox, 'Zoological Perspective in Social Science', in op. cit.

easily enter professions such as law[1] which may be a typical prelude to political careers, and the simple fact that females are generally less well educated and have fewer broad opportunities for political experience than males.

But I have been stressing that there are other underlying species-regularities involved. First, that women leaders do not inspire 'followership' chiefly because they are women and not only because of the consequences of those factors noted above; secondly, even if they want to, women cannot become political leaders because males are strongly predisposed to form and maintain all-male groups, particularly when matters of moment for the community are involved. The suggestion is that a combination of these two factors has been the basis for the hostility and difficulty those females have faced who have aspired to political leadership. This has been the basis of the tradition of female non-involvement in high politics, and not the tradition itself. Cultural forms originally express the underlying 'genetically programmed behavioural propensities'. In their turn, such cultural forms maintain – as tradition – an enduring solution to the recurrent problem of assigning of leadership and followership roles. In this connection, Margaret Mead writes about 'zoomorphizing Man'. 'Culture in the sense of man's species-characteristic method of meeting problems of maintenance, transformation, and transcendance of the past is an abstraction from our observations on particular cultures.'[2] This is then another way of looking at how broad political patterns may predictably emerge from the more detailed and programmed patterns of different behaviour of males and females.

Some females may indeed penetrate some high councils. They become ministers of governments, ambassadors, and so on. A few may receive assignments which are not 'feminine' in their implication, such as Golda Meir, former Israeli Foreign Minister, and Barbara Castle, U.K. Secretary of Productivity and Employment. It is important to know what happens to the 'backroom boys' under such circumstances. Do they retire to an even more secluded chamber? Does the lady become 'one of the boys'?

Formal conduct of business is one thing. Constitutional and other

1. Mead and Kaplan (eds.), op. cit., p. 73. 'Law is commonly the professional background of both state and federal legislators, but only 3·5 per cent of the lawyers of the country are women.'
2. Mead, *Continuities in Cultural Evolution*, op. cit., pp. 30–7.

legal constraints may permit successfully dominant females an effective role. But no one can control informal activity. Card-playing, hunting, fishing, all-male clubs, and so on may provide that further back room in which the outlines of policy and the distribution of power are determined. How pertinent are, for example, the hunting and fishing facilities which wealthy companies in the U.S.A., the U.K., Germany, etc., maintain for the entertainment of business colleagues? Paradoxically, the attention paid by many corporations to the wives of promotable executives underlies the dependency of females on the male hierarchy and their need for commitment to advance company purposes and not their own. Corporation wives – like wives of men in many spheres of activity – must be willing to subserve their own interests to their husbands' and their husbands' employers. They must also be willing to withdraw from conversations or events involving 'the men' or 'the Company'. Clearly this is an effect of social pressures and conventions; it does not occur unambiguously in all groups and in some – certain sectors of academe for example – women are less likely to be thus subservient to the male group. It is also clear that this pattern is as much a function of power as of maleness, and it can be argued that powerful *people* are being deferred to, who happen to be male.

On the other hand, the contention here is that this association is no accident. There is an extreme case which could throw light on the whole situation. Presently, in the formal sphere, one female or several can become members of powerful bodies. What would happen to these groups and their power should females come to predominate in them?[1] In a cabinet of fifteen persons, one, two, or even four females might be acceptable to the remaining males and the voters. But if there were nine or ten? Significantly, even in the Soviet Union, which has elected as many as 17 per cent of females to the Duma, the Supreme Council – which has the effective power – has occasionally contained one female, but more often none. Were a Cabinet to become dominated by females, probably its role would be circumscribed. We can predict that other – male – power centres would emerge to withdraw crucial powers from the female-dominated body.

Perhaps we can draw an analogy with the racial encounters in the

---

1. In the small Ontario town of Tweed, a female Reeve headed an all-female council – the only known example of this phenomenon in North America. The situation seemed reasonably ordered for several years. But in an election fought in 1967, several men ran on a straight 'sexual' ticket, and one was elected.

U.S.A., and with what happens when blacks move into white residential areas. What is virtually an all-white area becomes a predominantly black one. This is not because property values decline (often they increase), but because of some apparent caste-like response by whites who prefer not to live in close proximity to blacks. Undoubtedly there will be a number of social and economic changes in any neighbourhood when a new social group moves in. But the chief underlying reason for the exit of the whites appears to centre about status factors. George DeVos has made a cogent analysis of two kinds of exploitation of social groups by social groups: instrumental and expressive. The former is well understood – it involves money, jobs, consumer goods, etc. As De Vos makes clear, the latter is less well analysed.[1]

. . . expressive exploitations are related directly to the irrational and unconscious psychological processes and motives characteristic of man's complex mental structure. The motives behind such exploitation are less readily perceived than those leading to instrumental exploitation. . . . Expressive exploitation, although universal in one form or other, is most visibly institutionalized in societies that are rigidly segregated by birth or occupational groupings. Inherent is a biological and/or a religious concept of unalterable inferiority which distinguished one group of men from another. In external group or cultural relationships this patterning of belief is apparent in the justification of wars. Within a society, it justifies maintaining a fixed social order of dominance and subordination from birth to death.

DeVos sees the expressive exploitation of females as a marked feature of only some societies; in its less marked forms it occurs in most if not all communities. The racial or caste analogy may be instructive here.[2] When white people live among blacks they are

1. George DeVos, 'Conflict, Dominance and Exploitation in Human Systems of Social Segregation: Some Theoretical Perspectives from the Study of Personality in Culture', in Anthony de Reuck and Julie Knight (eds.), op. cit. See also Chapters One to Three of Andrew Sinclair, op. cit., for discussion of the racial analogy.

2. The American joke comes to mind: a white man goes to heaven and negotiates to meet God. After various trials he does meet God. God turns out to be a Negro woman, thus combining two improbable characteristics of the most dominant figure of all. Of course, the analogy cannot be taken too far; blacks have lived in all-black communities within which expressive exploitation occurred between classes or castes. Women cannot live in communities apart from men, and so far

held to acquire characteristics of the low-status 'impurity' which the prejudiced community at large attributes to blacks. In the same way, when males work in occupational groups in which there are many females, such as interior decoration, hairdressing, acting, or ballet, it is frequently assumed or alleged that they are effeminate.

The questions can be posed: Does a similar process occur when groups wielding power become predominated by females? Is female power low-status power? If so, can a community accept dominance of its powerful bodies by females? Based on the data and extrapolation from the results of experimental and accidental attempts to alter the sexual balance of power, the answer is a secure if tentative 'no, the male-centred dominant group recurs'. To recall my original analogy: it may be a species characteristic of *Homo sapiens* that the 'spinal column' of *Homo sapiens*' community must be very predominantly male. And to return briefly to black–white relations in America, the interesting argument has been raised that the effectiveness and significance of black protest politics is related to 'the masculinization' of black politics.[1] Namely, to the efforts of comparatively young black males to establish patterns of community organization and political action which supercede those possible in 'traditional' black American society – a post-slavery society in which disenfranchised and economically marginal males could create no communal political 'spinal chord' and in which females were inevitably the effective social and economic people around growing children. This has had numerous well-reported effects on black family life; the masculinization of black corporate life remains a relatively unresearched but crucial subject.

The upshot of all this is the contention that male dominance coupled with sexual dimorphism occurs cross-culturally; it may be a phenomenon rooted in the nature of *Homo sapiens*. Accepting the first half of the statement does not require accepting the second. Simply, a view of the close links between politics and socio-sexual role may provide a picture of political activity with a useful emphasis on the factor of maleness in determining the participants in and forms

there are no good major cases of communities which are finally female dominated. The perplexing pervasiveness of the myth of the Amazon women suggest that symbolic needs and/or fears continue to persist. And even the poor mythical Amazons couldn't really be women – they had to remove one breast to improve their archery.

1. See Christopher Lasch, 'The Trouble with Black Power', 10, 4, *New York Review of Books* (29 February 1968).

of politics. Harold Lasswell briefly notes that, 'Political life seems to sublimate many homosexual trends. Politicians characteristically work together in little cliques and clubs, and many of them show marked difficulties in reaching a stable heterosexual adjustment.' He also indicates that homosexual interaction in the military is an important factor requiring analysis.[1]

Lasswell probably overestimates the importance of the purely erotic aspects of homo- and heterosexuality and underestimates the social-organizational aspects. If it is true as I have been proposing that human males characteristically form all-male groups which tend to have political or quasi-political functions, and that they seek to exclude females from these groups, then this is one explanation for the male near-monopoly of high political office. It supplements the explanation which is based upon the possibility that male political dominance is a reflection both of human evolution and contemporary traditions and socio-economic constants. The implication of this for the study of politics is that it becomes possible – indeed necessary – to regard political groups which are unisexual as possessing sexual (non-erotic) bases.

In trying to find out about the Nazis in Hitler's party, for example, in addition to asking the questions: What kind of people were they? and, How did they live with others? another question is necessary too, since it promotes the collection of particularly pertinent data: what kind of *men* were they, how did they express their maleness, how did they interact with other men? Had they particular insecurities as *men* which drove them to identify so eventfully with Hitler and his theory? Why did Hitler marry Eva Braun just before his suicide? What happened in that very special male bond of senior Nazis? Again, I must stress that I do not imply that the foregoing comments invalidate the studies of politics which have been made and are being made. What is suggested is that an additional dimension of understanding may follow an appreciation of the special nature of unisexual political interaction. A study such as Eisenstadt's,[2] which is constructed with great skill on the basis of immense erudition, could be augmented by an assessment of the importance of sexuality in creating and constraining such diverse groups as William Whyte's Boston 'Corner Boys' and the Nyakusa age-villagers. On the basis of the argument about bonding and evolution, perhaps it is clearer why I

1. Harold Lasswell, *Psychopathology and Politics*, Viking Press, New York, 1960, p. 178.
2. Eisenstadt, *From Generation to Generation*, op. cit.

think the sex of politicians is extremely important, why the most dominant politicians are usually male, why the introduction of formal female political equality has not had more obvious structural and behavioural effects, and why an ethological view of the sexually based group dynamics of political interaction is useful for the cross-cultural understanding of political behaviour.

These are issues which are still justifiably controversial. Perhaps a brief personal note is relevant here, simply to indicate that the scientific argument I have been making and the data I have presented appear to lead to very different conclusions about the ease of extending female political influence than – as a citizen – I am predisposed to seek. In other words, my political bias is towards an expansion of women's participation in and effect on politics. But my sociological work suggests the difficulty of achieving this because more than just routine education and emancipation may be involved. Perhaps rather major restructuring of political society will be necessary before what may be a deep predisposition can be overcome in the name of equity. This is not to beg the question about the 'desirability' of achieving this equity. Nor is it any guarantee that my conclusions are correct, because my personal political beliefs and my scientific conclusions do not coincide. But perhaps it is of interest to some readers to be informed directly about this (finally methodological) matter of what a social scientist brings personally to an investigation.

WAR AND THE USE OF FORCE

Almost universally, war is an all-male enterprise. In various communities females participate in police activity. But they usually do so in clearly defined and quite specialized circumstances. It is not commonly assumed that this deprives females of liberty or rights (though some – often transvestite – females have always sought to join armies). Some Englishwomen tried to fight in the First World War, and indeed formed a regiment and were trained, but 'the participation of the English women was confined . . . to technical services'.[1] When Emily Pankhurst saw a Russian regiment of 400 women she called it 'the greatest event in the world's history'. Much the same pattern exists elsewhere. Even Israeli women, who are required to do military service like men, have not fought on the

1. Magnus Hirschfeld, *The Sexual History of the World War*, Panurge Press, New York, 1934, pp. 110–17.

front-line battlefield in formal Israeli battles such as the Sinai campaign or the recent 'Six-Day War'. The special garrison state situation of Israel and the uniqueness of its territorial claim are the basis for the rather extraordinary Israeli effort to involve females in military action. Particularly in the *kibbutzim* bordering hostile Arab states, the potentially dire outcome of enemy truculence is held to justify the readiness to use females in defence, though, to date, not in external aggression. I have heard at second hand one interesting exception to this. A Canadian soldier connected with the U.N. Truce Commission has noted that Israeli women are sent out on guerrilla raids in certain areas. Rather than engaging in battle with them, apparently many of their opponents surrender or retreat when it is clear females are involved. The theory is that this happens for essentially religious reasons: a man killed by a woman cannot have a desirable after-life.

In Chapter Seven, on the relationship between maleness and aggression, I will discuss what happens among males during aggressive interactions and what prompts such interactions. In order to continue this analysis of the role of the male bond in human communities, for the moment I simply wish to draw attention to the fact that internal and external use of force is virtually a male monopoly. Once again, this may seem to be nothing more than 'the rediscovery of the obvious'. But it may allow us to inform ourselves better about males and females in their social-organizational roles, and about the possible limits of plasticity within which communities and individuals must operate.

Of course, there is a real danger of tautological argument here: men are soldiers and policemen because soldiers and policemen must be strong because law-breakers and enemies respond to strength. Hence soldiers and policemen must be men. Thus soldiers and policemen *are* men. But there is a very rigid nature of the relationship between force and maleness which can be observed cross-culturally. This may also belie differences in male and female behaviour which pertain to the use of force and may also be relevant to other behaviour which may not explicitly require force but may involve the attitude and emotions accompanying its use. (As in Israel, females in a number of other countries, such as Russia, Yugoslavia, Vietnam, and Tibet, have participated in defence actions against aggression from without. I think it is justified to claim there is an important difference between militant action in defence of one's home or city or country, particularly when males may be elsewhere or out of action, and the studied trained organization of persons into regiments for the purpose of aggressive activity possibly out of the home territory.)

What is central to our purposes here is that in two crucial areas of social action – defence-aggression, and the maintenance of internal order by police – the dominant and most directly effective roles are assigned to men. For example, in police forces, females typically 'specialize . . . in work for which they, as women, are best suited; that is work with women and in particular with children and young persons'.[1] This situation is widely repeated in roughly the same form. Here is a small selection of countries:

Mauritius: women are clerical workers only.[2]

Malta: women deal with price enforcement, searching, questioning, and escorting women.[3]

Austria: women 'do not perform patrol duties but serve mainly in places of detention'.[4]

Czechoslovakia: women perform mainly administrative duties.[5]

Uruguay: women act as escorts for women and children, and question women and children.

As I have already noted, female members of the military typically are assigned to supportive branches of the various services. For example, in the Women's Royal Air Force, the posts filled by women may be in the secretarial, catering, equipment, technical, or education branches, among others. In these supportive tasks, considerable integration between the sexes may exist, but in the critical functions of the R.A.F. – those directly involving flying and combat – females are excluded. This is a situation roughly analogous to politics. In politics, many females will be involved in supportive precinct work, such as entertaining, canvassing, and fund-raising, but are very unlikely to be chosen as candidates by party selection committees and as we have seen are even less likely to reach high office:

> The decline in the number of women elected in the (U.K.) 1966 election was accompanied by a fall in the number of women candidates (80 out of a total of 1,707). . . . The reason is brutally simple. The Party selection committees (including most of their women members) prefer men.[6]

In commercial aviation, the role of the stewardess has become clearly distinguished from the technical flying role. She performs

1. James Cramer, *The World's Police*, Cassell, London, 1964, p. 23.
2. ibid., p. 220.   3. ibid., p. 218.   4. ibid., p. 253.   5. ibid., p. 273.
6. 'Slow March of the Matriarchy', *Guardian* (leader) (3 November 1966).

expressive rather than instrumental functions. The house magazine of a major American airline makes it plain that the stewardess must not give an impression of participation in the technicalities of flight:

> A significant value of a stewardess on board an aircraft is one of 'presence' – particularly presence with a calm, relaxed and reassuring attitude toward the entire process of flying. . . . The stewardess . . . should perhaps shade her announcements less toward competence and ability [sic] and more in the areas of friendliness and a more casual attitude.

Again, all this is obvious. Individuals 'know' this in the way societies appear to 'know' it. But under modern conditions, in theory, interchangeability between males and females should be possible. For example, a general assumption of North American education is that there must be equal treatment of males and females. In some parts of North America, legal action faces employers who discriminate against females. Presumably females could be trained to assume senior military and police posts, not just those within a special female division of an otherwise predominantly male organization. Nor must they engage mainly in tasks held to be appropriate to females. There are, after all, no jobs which are not also performed by men, with the exception of those directly involving reproductive physiology. On the basis of his analysis of the division of labour in 224 different societies, Murdock notes, 'while a number of occupations are universally masculine, none is everywhere feminine'.[1] Males do all jobs. Why cannot females become fighter pilots, tank commanders, or police chiefs? When men join armies they become dishwashers, laundrymen, and nurses. Yet when women join armies they do not commonly take jobs which are conventionally defined as masculine. Males can legitimately and with self-respect undertake work which in other situations could be considered feminine. What relationship has all this to the pronounced difference in male–female political participation?

1. George F. Murdock, 'Comparative Data on the Division of Labour by Sex', *Social Forces*, 15, 4 (1937). Compare also with Gladstone's remark in the House of Commons (3 May 1871): 'I scarcely ever see in the hands of a woman an employment that ought more naturally to be in the hands of a man, but I constantly see in the hands of a man employment which might be more beneficially and economically in the hands of a woman.' Given that traditionally females receive less pay for a job of work than equally skilled males, Gladstone presumably wished to 'feminize' a number of male tasks.

As I have proposed, organized aggression remains an all-male phenomenon, in part as a result of human evolutionary history. Similarly, that political order is largely a male concern derives from the same history. It is as much a result of evolution as the facts that males and females have different bodies, some different physiological processes, different life expectancies, different metabolic rates and patterns of temperature control, different sexual responses, different growth rates, different psychological reactions to various tests, different apprehensions of their environment, and different enthusiasms. I am saying something like this, in effect: 'Sexually active males respond to most sexually active females in situations of potential sexual congress with a relatively predictable set of physiological and psychological responses *which have social-behavioural correlates*. In the same way adult males and females seeking defence from without or the maintenance of peace and order within respond positively to appropriate males and negatively to virtually all females.'

This is culturally determined in the sense and degree that sexual response is culturally determined. It is held that white gentlemen prefer blondes. But to Pygmy people blondness implies ill-health. In Euro-America, the Pygmies' ideal steatopygic female would have little luck in the sexual market-place. At any point in time, any defined community recognizes certain physical configurations, sensual features, postural and gestural styles, and fashions in adornment as desirable attributes of total sexual appeal. The range of variation is enormous and arbitrary. Two attributes are important: it is a *range* to which there are limits; and, the variation within a community (or sub-community, such as the teenage one) is at any one time defined in terms of an ordinal scale such that some persons more successfully approach the ideal than others. Other things being equal, those who are more fashionable will be more attractive, both to others who are fashionable themselves, and to those who are unable or unwilling to be fashionable but have not 'discredited' the whole system of fashion.

Sexual selection occurs in terms of culturally mediated cues of status and desirability. These cues are based on a biologically founded propensity to respond to members of the opposite sex within a certain range of possibility. Does political response occur in the same or a similar way? In the most general case of sexual response, erotic and reproductive propensities are satisfied by contacts with the opposite sex. The hypothesis here is that in the most general political case, defence and needs for social order are satisfied most effectively by soliciting subordinate or co-operative relationships with adult males. Thus, females of all ages and pre-adult males will seek subordinate relationships with adult males who will protect them when the group is attacked and who will enforce social order when internal disturbance occurs. Adult males will either themselves undertake direction of the response to a specific difficulty or will attach themselves as co-operative followers to those individuals who apparently possess some plan of action and the legitimacy to carry out these plans.

The hypothesis contains the proposition that the defenders and policemen must be males. Females will not suffice, except to perform subsidiary and supporting functions. This is because females cannot act as 'releasers' for the behaviours appropriate to managing interferences to social order. This is the suggested reason for female non-success in politics, for female subordination in matters of war, police, and (under normal circumstances) defence of the immediate environment. The subdominant status of females arises, then, from phenomena amenable to ethological study, as well as to cultural study. And what can emerge from an ethological approach to females' political status is some greater sense of the '. . . non-cultural aspects of human social systems and in consequence . . . a sharper appreciation of the role of culture in human adaptation'.[1]

4

The foregoing hypothesis contains the idea that not only will males and females reject other females as potential leaders and defenders, but that males will reject females as colleagues. If this is so, two aspects of the proposition may be suggested. I have already discussed the first: males are predisposed to seek at least some unisexual group activity; this activity may take a wide variety of forms and may range from the College of Cardinals to gambling cliques to Oxford colleges to groups talking shop at parties. The second is related to this: it is a function of the ethological principle that behaviours accompanied by strong 'emotion' are likely to reflect situations which are very important to the survival of the animal and which have been important for a long time during its formative evolutionary history. The connection between unisexual aggregation, and the relation of emotional display to 'biological importance' of a behaviour pattern, is (1) that

1. Tiger and Fox, 'Zoological Perspective in Social Science', in op. cit., p. 80.

defence and maintaining the social order are clearly crucial to the persistence of human social systems; (2) that these behaviours are typically undertaken by males, usually without female full colleagues. Therefore we can predict (3) that on all occasions defined by a community as vitally important and during which strong emotion is experienced by community members aware of the overall situation a male or males will assume the most significant roles.

The hypothesis attempts to explain why certain social functions are performed by males and not females. I have suggested that the fact that males are stronger than females, that they are more directly socialized to accept and use violence, that they form the major structures of defence and police in all communities, all generally reflect a 'genetically programmed behavioural disposition'. The cross-cultural incidence of the pattern is the result of more than inter-cultural diffusion of practices and the maintenance of tradition.

The willingness to display 'followership' to males in situations of violence and disorder may be directly related to the apparently widespread unwillingness to appoint or elect females to posts of high responsibility. By analogy, the leadership structure of hamadryas baboon troops can be seen to be male-dominated. The management of crisis is normally the function of males.[1] While I am not saying there is a necessary connection between baboon patterns and human patterns (though it has already been noted that terrestiality may be central to the development of male dominance among primates), I am proposing that 'human nature' is such that it is 'unnatural' for females to engage in defence, police, and, by implication, high politics. For human females to do so requires explicit self-conscious provision of special facilities by a concerned and willing community.

This is undoubtedly a major hypothesis. But is it not less difficult to support than the contrary one – that human sexual dimorphism is exclusively cultural in origin and perpetuation?

Of course, it can be argued that dimorphism results primarily from males' unwillingness to yield their privilege and superiority. My suggestion here is that one must add to males' insistence on their sexual advantage their meaningful and persistent pattern of all-male

1. Kummer has described a situation in which a mature female assumed the dominant role in a troop boasting only an inexperienced and young male. Perhaps the exception supports the general rule that a female can take the leadership role only when there is a clear sign of male incapacity or weakness. See Hans Kummer, 'Tripartite Relations in Hamadryas Baboons', in Altmann, op. cit. It would be of interest to explore the politics of slave societies along these lines.

grouping. In other words, what the pattern of heterosexual relations fails to effect will be achieved by forces generated by a pattern of all-male association.

Women may seek high responsibility in war, politics, or police on an entirely equal footing with men. And men and women may be willing to accept their leadership. But an anti-female pattern of male bonding will make it more difficult – if not impossible – for ambitious females to reach the posts they wish. This depends on the importance to the community of the organization in question, on the time at which the behaviour occurs, and on the kind of emotional ambience which surrounds the behaviour. Thus, it would be easier in peacetime for a woman to become a Chief of the General Staff than in wartime. It is easier for females to become managers of social work agencies and retail shops than of steel mills, stockbrokerages, and aircraft factories. A woman is more likely to become president of a women's college than of a men's college. In situations requiring high loyalty, patriotism, sense of duty, danger, stately or aggressive relations with external groups, males will be decisively favoured for the pertinent offices. Maleness is a concomitant of the sense of moment, of matters requiring rigour, hardness – the unvarying and unimpressionable prosecution of ends by means. There is of course a carping folklore about 'women's logic'. While this may be just snide or whimsical, it may also (accurately or not) symptomize what men and perhaps women too have in a 'folk-wise' way decided about female patterns of thought and consistency.[1] Perhaps, indeed, the Don, and not *la donna es mobile*. None the less men are not commonly thought of as being as fickle as women, and in practice the sociological law remains effective still: if people define a situation as real it becomes real in its consequences.

I hesitate to enter a controversy about the comparative skills of males and females. Nor shall I comment here on the felicitous or unfortunate effects of greater female participation in momentous matters of communal life. It is a controversy, anyway, which eludes theoretical solution and must be settled empirically. Having provided some data on which the discussion can be based, I want to discuss the possibility that the sexual division of political and aggressive labour –

1. A typical joke – and jokes often reveal points of tension – about so-called female logic is the one involving the wife who bought her husband two ties. He disappeared to put one on. When he returned his wife complained: 'You don't like the other one.'

observable in virtually all communities – has direct biological roots. Here I must disagree with the influential formulation of the sociologists Parsons and Bales that socio-sexual differentiation is an 'example of basic differentiation which tends to appear in *all* systems of social interaction regardless of their composition . . .'[1] – a differentiation of the 'instrumental-expressive' kind. Perhaps most females do tend to assume 'expressive' responsibilities and males 'instrumental' ones. But it is appropriate to explore the more fundamental theory that the differences are, in fact, biologically based. The Parsons–Bales proposition relies heavily upon the effects of family structure and early experience in determining sexual–behavioural differences. If the primate data do nothing else, they alert us to the possibility that sexual differences are very much determined by biology. Within this framework extensive and complex learning takes place.

Distinctions made along the instrumental–expressive axis must be arbitrary. For example, the simple instrumental activity required in running a middle-class Euro-American home is extensive. The fact that middle-class male work and middle-class domestic work may appear so different does not necessarily mean that male work is instrumental and female work expressive. A case could be made that the work of the public-relations man is expressive while his wife's household efforts are instrumental. Perhaps, were males to manage households over a long period, *without regarding it as exceptional and without seeing their positions as temporary*, it would not occur to them they were engaged in merely 'expressive' tasks. While it may appear expressive to deal with children, the hard-learned psychological lore supposed to accompany the acceptable treatment of children renders even this activity an instrumental kind of task. In other cultures, females may do much of the instrumental work, such as vegetable farming among sub-Saharan African peasants, while males may gamble, drink, or simply aggregate and talk. It requires special faith in the nuclear family to base on it such an important theoretical conception as the instrumental–expressive dichotomy. Such an over-emphasis on the nuclear family reflects a limited conception of, for example, how much adult learning goes on, the importance of size and physiological sex in determining behaviour, and the role of 'emotional' states of communal crisis and moment in defining tasks as male or female.

It might, indeed, be possible to go beyond Parsons to define tasks

1. Parsons and Bales, *Family, Socialization, and Interaction Process*, op. cit., pp. vii–viii.

not as instrumental–expressive but as male–female. We have, after all, got males and females as actual referrents for the concepts of male–female, an empirical advantage which Parsons's and Bales's concepts cannot share by definition, since they are abstractions from social systems. There may even be point in using the dimorphism concept to speak of *communally important* and *privately important* activities. The expectation would be that males generally undertake the former and females the latter, though tasks and performers will vary considerably from any norms which are proposed.[1] But it is simply unacceptable for Parsons to claim that the instrumental–expressive dichotomy rests solely on the fact that mothers must take care of children and consequently that men, who are 'exempted from these biological functions', 'should specialize in the alternative instrumental direction'.[2] This claim reflects a general over-emphasis on the importance of early family experience in particular and family life in general, and a very limited view of the relationship between biological cause, learning, and family. Parsons goes so far as to say: 'If, as some psychologists seem to assume, the essentials of human personality were determined biologically, independently of involvement in social systems, there would be no need for families, since reproduction as such does not require family organization.'[3] The primate field data, and such experimental data as Harlow's,[4] adequately undermines this particular argument.

Margaret Mead outlines several kinds of socio-sexual difference which may be rooted in biology:

> . . . a fair case can be made for considering that female behaviour, or possibly female species-characteristic behaviour, is more readily involved in all manufacture which is a simple supplementation of the capabilities of the body by manufactured objects, that is, containers and clothing, and by the preparation and dispensing of prepared food, and for considering that male behaviour involves

1. For a full discussion of the instrumental–expressive concept in a wider perspective, see Laurence Kohlberg, 'A Cognitive Developmental Analysis of Children's Sex-Role Concepts and Attitudes', in Maccoby (ed.), *Readings in Social Psychology*, op. cit.
2. Talcott Parsons, 'The American Family: Its Relation to Personality and to the Social Structure', in Parsons and Bales, op. cit., p. 23.
3. ibid., p. 16.
4. Harry F. Harlow and Margaret K. Harlow, 'A Study of Animal Affection', in C. H. Southwick (ed.), *Primate Social Behaviour*, D. Van Nostrand, Princeton, N.J., 1963.

cooperation with outside objects, other human beings, animals (e.g. hunting dogs or draft animals), and material objects of wood or stone or metal, which can be brought in relation to and can be used in the human situation. Perception of the possibilities inherent in the surrounding world for alteration to transcend the limitations of the human body may be seen as more likely to arise from male models. This correlates with all we know at present about activity ratios between male and female; the male's greater strength, greater activity, superiority in handling spatial organization, and so on, and the female's use of her own body as a theater of action.[1]

This view is a very sophisticated development of Robert Briffault's early proposition of 'psychical development of the race [which] takes place along two lines . . . masculine and feminine',[2] but Mead herself is aware of the limited available information to serve as a basis for this kind of generalization. For example, she comments: 'there may be in human males a hitherto hardly tapped instinctive response to very young infants, which originally functioned only to ensure protection but now functions to ensure active participation'.[3] Even though the care of children is almost universally female, there may be an adult male–infant bond which exists, at certain times and for certain purposes. One is reminded of politicians' enthusiasm for baby-kissing, and that among the Japanese macaques,

. . . paternal care is a form of behaviour typical of leaders and sub-leaders. . . . It is plain that paternal care itself is a sign of interest in the central part of the troop, and the males which display it are trying to establish their social position indirectly through the medium of their activity in the central part. . . . An adult male protecting an infant usually becomes much milder and behaves as if femininity were strengthened in him. But there are also a few males who become still more aggressive. We have records of the process by which one of the sub-leaders attempted to move into the central part of the troop. The fact that by hugging an infant

1. Mead, *Continuities in Cultural Evolution*, op. cit., p. 97.
2. Robert Briffault, 'The Origins of Love', in V. F. Calverton (ed.), *The Making of Man*, Modern Library, New York, 1931, p. 504.
3. Margaret Mead, 'Cultural Determinants of Sexual Behaviour', in W. C. Young (ed.), *Sex and Internal Secretions*, Vol. 2 (3rd edition), Ballière, Tindall & Cox, London, 1961, p. 1461.

he succeeded in being tolerated by the females and leaders is, with his rising in rank, a very interesting phenomenon.[1]

Indeed, when one considers the importance which political bosses appear to attribute to the advantages of being a 'family man' and not a divorced or single person, one may well speculate sympathetically on Mead's hypothesis about adult male–infant linkages, and on the general relationship of political and familial behaviour.

I have tried to avoid giving the impression that there is any necessary antithesis between familial and political–defensive–aggressive behaviour. In some cultures, a relatively sharp distinction is made between family relationships and political relations. This applies particularly to North America and parts of Europe, where females may expect considerable familial behaviour from their husbands at the same time as a formal distinction exists between public and private lives. In general, so long as the male bond is not actively threatened by the intrusions and requirements of family life, it is possible to maintain a view of the harmony rather than conflict of 'the two spheres'. In America, England, and some Muslim countries, this may reflect a general cultural preoccupation with publicly recognized assertion of virility. This precludes various kinds of public display of tenderness. However, men such as war heroes, politicians, sports heroes, who have established themselves as virile, may indulge in public tenderness more easily than persons in less evidently virile occupations, such as poetry, teaching, hairdressing, etc.

I have discussed male dominance in political, defensive, and aggressive organizations and argued that in these areas male dominance is species-specific. Closely connected with male dominance in power-aggression structures is a pattern of male bonding which is a co-determinant and/or reinforcement of male dominance. It may appear that I have strayed from my original intention to discuss male bonding by focussing as I have upon the ways in which males dominate structures involving force and power. But, inevitably, in considering organizations concerning themselves with dominance, the process of dominance within them must be logically stressed. Of course, it is possible to claim that male dominance of organizations results chiefly from the fact that males are stronger and bigger, and that the notion of male bonding is unnecessary and misleading. But I do not accept

---

1. Junichiro Itani, 'Paternal Care in the Wild Japanese Monkey, *Macaca fuscata*', in C. H. Southwick (ed.), op. cit., pp. 94–5.

that the concepts of bonding and dominance can be separated in this way. Politics is by definition an intensely social process which must be seen as a group not an individual phenomenon;[1] in which, therefore, the importance of bonding is paramount. Since it is males who dominate politics, it is male bonding which is crucial. But now let us turn away from politics and force and violence and tough talk about such matters which too often are the agents of humiliation of the gentle human spirit, and turn instead to examine the male bond in work and at play.

1. Earl Latham, 'The Group Basis of Politics: Notes for a Theory', *American Political Science Review*, 46 (June 1952).

CHAPTER FIVE

Work and Play

Bertolt Brecht comments: 'A man is just the food he eats.' How human beings have found their food, clothed themselves, afforded their artifacts and entertainments and passions, and protected their relatively fragile bodies from hunger, cold, rain, tedium, and fear, has always been a subject of enormous and absorbing interest. Social scientists may forget – because most of them work in universities or other organizations which give them money on a regular basis – how much the question of getting food and warmth and tools, or money, is a recurrent question, as urgent and yet as dully repetitive as hunger, and how it may be as elaborately symbolic a matter as it is brutally real. In the way the ancient hunters of the Dordogne in France painted animals and hunting scenes on cave walls, and in the way Willy Loman in *Death of a Salesman* created fictional runs of triumphant luck in his selling expeditions, people have necessarily always troubled themselves about goods and money, and the future, and the connection between these realities.

Many mornings when I return to the manuscript of this book I am aware of the connection – albeit not immediate – between the sentences I must spin, the ideas I must catch, the data I must record, and the foods and property I make my own. It is easy to forget when one is well off how the world looks to the poor, to those unable – though they wish it – to find the work which will yield even a small reward. It is, for example, quite extraordinary that, with a few exceptions (and they were widely thought to be 'politically motivated'), social scientists in the United States neither predicted the revolt of American blacks against their real and relative deprivation, nor identified the extent to which America harboured tens of millions of persons critically underprivileged by the standards of that proud and wealthy community. So to understand the meaning of work for people at large, both in worlds where work means survival and where work means satisfaction and pleasure, may involve something of an imaginative foray. Any discussion of the economic life of man must be founded on the fact that possibly more than half of living people experience serious hunger all or much of the time. So should we find social-structural similarities among such unfortunate persons and those who are relatively wealthy – bearing in mind that wealth is obviously an important determinant of life-styles and traditions – this lends weight to any conclusions we may draw about species-specific behaviour in general and male bonding patterns in particular.

1

I have already referred to Murdock's paper[1] which suggests the pervasiveness and importance of the division of labour on a sexual basis. Such tasks as metal-working, weapon-making, pursuit of sea mammals, hunting, manufacture of musical instruments, trapping or catching of small animals, work in bone, horn, and shell, are almost exclusively allocated to males. Water-carrying, grain-grinding, cooking, gathering of herbs, and manufacture and repair of clothing, for example, are overwhelmingly feminine. This distribution of tasks is in itself interesting, as is the suggestion that everywhere some distinction is forcefully made between women's work and men's work. Relevant again is the observation that, 'while a number of occupations are universally masculine, none is everywhere feminine'. Undoubtedly, physical strength is a factor in these allocations. But is it not clear that water-carrying, which women do, is easier than boat-building, which men do. Or that manufacture of musical instruments should be male, while pottery-making should be female. Females are effectively excluded from performance of some male tasks, but apparently communities do not press to exclude males from tasks normally undertaken by females.

A number of writers have commented on the ubiquity among a variety of societies of the division of labour by sex;[2] Oswald Hall

1. George Murdock, 'Comparative Data on the Divisions of Labour by Sex', in op. cit.
2. Among the most prominent are Marion J. Levy, Jr, *The Structures of Society*, op. cit., p. 330; George Murdock, *Social Structure*, op. cit., p. 7; Margaret Mead, 'Cultural Determinants of Sexual Behaviour', in op. cit., p. 1451; Oswald Hall, 'Gender and the Division of Labour', in *Implications of Traditional Divisions Between Men's Work and Women's Work in Our Society*, Department of Labour of Canada, Ottawa, 1964,

indicates that, while the tasks assigned to males and females may vary from society to society,

> . . . the variability between societies does not imply any corresponding variability within each society. Within a specific society the division is likely to be highly specific and rigid. On the surface such systems would seem to be formidably resistant to change. . . . Societies develop elaborate systems of taboos and beliefs which control the distribution of tasks. . . . The taboos that rule a society in regard to man's work and woman's work are usually fortified by a set of deeply rooted beliefs about the innate characteristics of men and women.[1]

The evidence is sufficiently extensive and heterogeneous in its theoretical, disciplinary, and national origin to lend confidence to the notion that the sexual division of labour is a cross-cultural constant. We are encouraged to conclude that we are involved here with a phenomenon deeply rooted in the nature of human social life. Let us consider why this constant exists, and what the explanation reveals about the consistency and plasticity of social structures. I must stress again that we are dealing here with more than a casual matter. It is a feature of social life at the heart of man's survival, the understanding of which must involve an approach to 'behavioural bedrock' – to the fundaments of behavioural process.

The crux of my argument is that male bonding patterns reflect and arise out of man's history as hunter. I have already provided the

pp. 18–22; Talcott Parsons, in Parsons and Bales (eds.), *Family, Socialization and Intervention Process*, op. cit., pp. 22–5; Lowie, *Primitive Society*, op. cit., p. 72; Roy G. D'Andrade, 'Sex Differences and Cultural Institutions', in Maccoby, *et. al.*, *Readings in Social Psychology*, op. cit.; E. E. Evans-Pritchard, *The Position of Women in Primitive Societies*, Faber & Faber, London, 1965, pp. 49–55. Evans-Pritchard also notes the general phenomenon of male dominance, the relative rarity of matrilineality, and some of the difficulties arising from the emancipation of Englishwomen. In a general statement, he records that: '. . . I find it difficult to believe that the relative positions of the sexes are likely to undergo any considerable or lasting alteration in the foreseeable future. Primitive societies and barbarous societies and the historical societies of Europe and the East exhibit almost every conceivable variety of institutions, but in all of them, regardless of the form of social structure, men are always in the ascendancy, and this is perhaps the more evident the higher the civilization. . . . The facts seem . . . to suggest that there are deep biological and psychological factors, as well as sociological factors, involved, and that the relation between the sexes can only be modified by social changes, and not radically altered by them . . .' (pp. 54–5).

1. Oswald Hall, 'Gender and the Division of Labour', in op. cit., pp. 19–20.

basic evidence for the claim that man's major evolutionary specialization was an ability to hunt animals co-operatively, and that from this have stemmed manifold other behavioural systems and cultural forms. And, as I noted, it can be argued that male bonding was preadaptive, possibly part of man's primate endowment, and that hunting behaviour was a development of this given propensity. The validity of these propositions is immaterial here; what is directly relevant is the contention that

> Hunting is the master behaviour pattern of the human species. It is the organizing activity which integrated the morphological, physiological, genetic and intellectual aspects of the individual human organisms and of the populations who compose our single species. Hunting is a way of life, not simply a 'subsistence technique', which importantly involves commitments, correlates, and consequences spanning the entire biobehavioural continuum of the individual and of the entire species of which he is a member. Man evolved as a hunter, he spent over ninety-nine per cent of his species' history as a hunter, and he spread over the entire habitable area of the world as a hunter.[1]

What Laughlin does not say, and what I have proposed, is that hunting has necessarily been a male activity. Male co-operative hunting is, therefore, an 'organ' of behaviour, whose contribution to human survival is as amenable to study as the role of any physical organ (see Tinbergen[2] for a discussion of the validity of such an enterprise).

Little is known of the origins and trends in comparative human sexual dimorphism. However, it is necessary to assume that male and female physical differences reflect different history and different conditions of sexual selection. Let us review some of these briefly. Aside from the obvious fact that females are less able to hunt successfully when they are pregnant or nursing infants, other anatomical and physiological factors may have combined to exclude them from hunting throughout the period of human history. For example, it has been suggested that females are less able to endure heat than males and that 'relatively greater strain for females than for males is apparent

1. W. S. Laughlin, 'The Importance of Hunting in Human Evolution', paper presented to 'Man the Hunter Conference' at the University of Chicago, April 1966.
2. Niko Tinbergen, 'On Aims and Methods of Ethology', *Zeitschrift fur Tierpsychologie*, 20, 4 (1963), pp. 417–23. See also Tinbergen's essay 'The Search for Roots of Human Behaviour' (unpublished MS.), Oxford, 1965.

with rising environmental temperature'[1] – presumably this was a disadvantage to women hunting in tropical countries of southern Africa where *Homo sapiens'* basic physical, and possibly behavioural patterns formed. The differences in male and female growth rates are now well-documented.[2] So are differences in behaviour resulting from hormones – particularly behaviours related to energy level and possibly territorial occupancy and defence.[3] Masters and Johnson outline differences in the sexual response cycles of males and females.[4] The importance of psychosexual development suggests that there may be 'critical periods' in the development of gender identification among humans[5] which may be comparable to a similar process evident among primates.[6]

Controversies continue over precisely what differences there are between males and females, how much these are physiological and biochemical, how much psychosocial, and how much culturally defined. As a working principle, and because it is a suitably cautious formulation, let us accept John Money's observation: 'There is no intractable antagonism between psychodynamics or sociodynamics on the one hand, and physiodynamics on the other. One suspects that the developments in sex research yet to come will show the way to their increasing synthesis. . . .'[7] But for our purposes, the social-organizational implications of being male or female remain of prime interest; it is in this context that the division of labour and human hunting history are directly relevant.

As Steward notes, most ethnographic records indicate that men are hunters while women are food gatherers or collectors. Hunting large game requires an episodic expenditure of much time and energy. It does not permit hunters to spend predictable periods of time with their families, and, Steward argues, the evolution of socio-sexual

1. Bruce A. Hertig, 'Acclimatization of Women During Work in Hot Environments', *Federation Proceedings*, 22, 3 (May–June 1963), pp. 810–13.
2. G. A. Harrison, J. S. Weiner, J. M. Tanner, and N. A. Barnicot, *Human Biology*, Clarendon Press, Oxford, 1964, pp. 323–38.
3. John Money, 'Psychosexual Differentiation', in John Money (ed.), *Sex Research: New Developments*, Holt, Rinehart & Winston, New York, 1965, pp. 15–20; Hamburg and Lunde, op. cit.
4. William H. Masters and Virginia E. Johnson, 'The Sexual Response Cycles of the Human Male and Female: Comparative Anatomy and Physiology', in Frank Beach (ed.), *Sex and Behavior*, John Wiley, New York, 1965.
5. Money, op. cit., pp. 12–15.
6. Harry F. Harlow and Margaret K. Harlow. 'The Effect of Rearing Conditions on Behavior', in Money (ed.), op. cit.
7. Money, op. cit., p. x.

roles mirrored the evolution of physical ones.[1] These behavioural differences augmented the more ancient terrestial pattern where males defended the group. As an economic mode, in the human line hunting precedes other forms of economic organization such as pastoralism, agriculture, or urban-based industry. Presumably we may regard the selective pressures on human populations existing during the hunting phase of human history – about 99 per cent of it, as we have seen – as being of particular and crucial importance in determining the human genotype. 'To the sociability, intelligence, and manipulative abilities of our primate ancestors were added the co-operative hunting activities of the social carnivore, producing a unique and potentially formidable new type of animal – the hunting hominid. The evolution of this new breed was well under way 14 million years ago.'[2]

While it is a not wholly satisfactory extrapolation – if only because present-day hunters live in relatively difficult marginal environments and may endure harder lives than their early predecessors[3] – we may derive some sense of early hunting social organization from contemporary hunter–gatherer communities. We may assume, in line with Steward's comments, that hunters were all-male, and that to the extent that co-operative rather than solitary hunting predominated, a significant genetic factor in selection was the *group* of hunters as well as the individuals composing the group. In the reproductive situation, the genetic package was the male-plus-female, a unit which ensured the existential continuity of the species. So, in the hunting situation, it was the hunting group – male-plus-male-plus-male – a group which ensured the survival of the entire reproductive community. Thus was the male–male bond as important for hunting

1. Julian H. Steward, 'Hunting as a Factor in the Evolution of Social Structures', paper presented to the 'Man the Hunter Conference' at the University of Chicago, April 1966.
2. David R. Pilbeam, 'Man's Earliest Ancestors', in op. cit., p. 52.
3. See Richard B. Lee's paper presented to the 'Man the Hunter Conference' at the University of Chicago, April 1966: 'What "Hunters" Do For a Living: Or, How to Make Out on Scarce Resources', for pertinent data on the time-budgets and sources of nutrition of hunter-gatherers. Lee notes that extant hunter-gatherers have persisted chiefly because they live in undesirable and marginal environments. A related point is made by Desmond Morris (personal communication), who suggests that modern urban man is truly the natural man in evolutionary terms, and that 'primitive' peoples in remote places are somewhat aberrant. This is persuasive only in part; the argument fails to take the relative novelty of urban patterns into account. Presumably it is not yet clear what genetic implications there are in urban living.

purposes as the male–female bond was for reproductive purposes, and this is the basis of the division of labour by sex. I have already noted some of the reasons for this. Those who hunted alone would be less likely to kill large animals and thus less likely to reproduce. Secondly, those males who took females on the hunt might be (1) distracted from hunting by sexual blandishment, (2) certainly slowed down on a chase, because females are slower than males, and not specialized for effective bursts of high-energy-using activity, which males are;[1] (3) they might also be affected by the varying behaviour and mood of females in the various phases of their menstrual cycle and affect by what may be a greater female propensity to express particular perhaps ill-adapted emotions in states of crisis; (5) females would be less able and willing to engage in physical struggle with prey animals, and less able to defend the group from predators and possibly human opponents.

In other words, there would be a definite genetic advantage to those males who insisted on hunting in all-male groups. There would be clear disadvantages to those communities who permitted females to join the hunt. This could be one basis of the male bond. We shall return to this in a moment. From the whole community's point of view, female hunters would have offered no advantage. As I have indicated before, were they pregnant, they could miscarry, or be injured, or killed. The offspring of lactating females engaged in the hunt would be clearly deprived by their mothers' enterprise. Either they would have to be taken along or not fed, or be fed by other lactating mothers. The disruption in the mother–infant relationship might deleteriously affect the infant's survival and growth – the work of the Harlows under experimental conditions with primates suggests a way in which this might have occurred. Thus there were definite reproductive advantages in favour of females who restricted themselves to child-care, local gathering, and maintenance activities. Those females who hunted with males could not reproduce as numerously as non-hunting females; the female hunting 'propensity' would not be maintained or augmented in the genetic pool.

If this is so, and if the propensity lingers, herein may lie some explanation for the almost unanimous resistance in many countries to

1. I am indebted to Professor J. S. Weiner for this point. Professor Weiner's detailed research on temperature control and other pshysiological processes lead him to believe that human males are specialized for high output activity under tropical conditions. Also, see Hertig and Sargent, op. cit.

mothers with small children who work out of the home;[1] and for that related attitude – the apparent general distrust women have of non-reproductive females, either in the figure of the dry spinster of Euro-American cultures or the barren woman of Africa and Asia.[2] There is a contemporary version of the 'genetic impotence' of 'hunting women' – I refer here to females involved in relatively high-influence, high-status work. For example, among female executives in North America an unusually high proportion, about a third, are unmarried, while those who are married tend to have no children or a number lower than the average. By inversion, this may be taken as suggestive of the historical process which maintained or exaggerated the behavioural concomitants of physical sexual differences.

2

So far I have stressed the implications for females of the pattern of their exclusion from hunting groups. What is the significance of this phenomenon for males? Is there evidence to demonstrate its pervasion and its possible biological basis?

In a sense all the evidence must be impressionistic – impressionistic in the way we infer from how selection works in community life that broadly Darwinian principles of sexual selection apply in some measure to humans. Against this background I want to treat the following propositions: (1) that, when they can, males choose their workmates in processes analogous to sexual selection; (2) that the bond established generates considerable emotion; (3) that males derive important satisfactions from male bonds and male interactions which they cannot derive from male–female bonds and interactions; and (4) that the sexual division of labour is a *consequence* of males' wishes to preserve their unisexual bonds and not simply a result of physical and temperamental differences with females in any culture.

Robert Lowie indicates the importance of Schurtz in drawing attention to the significance of male associations (though, finally, Lowie concludes Schurtz provides inadequate evidence for his hypothesis that these associations are psychologically based). According to Schurtz: '. . . woman is an eminently unsociable being and refrains from forming unions on the basis of like interest, remaining centered in the kinship group based on sexual relations and the reproductive

1. P. Chombart de Lauwe, Introduction to *Images of Women in Society: International Social Science Journal*, 14, 1, UNESCO, Paris, p. 17.
2. Evans-Pritchard, op. cit., pp. 46–7.

function. Associations created or even joined by women on equal terms with the men are rare and must be considered weak imitations of the exclusively male association. Man, on the other hand, tends to view sexual relations in the light of episodes and fosters the purely social factor that makes "birds of a feather flock together". Thus the psychological differences between men and women lead to a sociological separation.'[1]

Lowie disagrees with Schurtz's conception of the psychological basis of men's clubs, men's houses, and secret societies. None the less he appears to believe that it is associated with the kind of phenomena with which we are concerned here: 'We may add that the activities of women are frequently not of a nature that calls for concerted effort in the same sense as, say, a warlike enterprise.'[2] This may be a species-specific characteristic, of course; none the less it is significant that Lowie sees unisexual aggregation where it does occur as a function of 'warlike' and hunting activities, and furthermore that the origin of political society lies in the men's group and territoriality.[3]

Lowie arrives at the 'conclusion that sex dichotomy is not a universal phenomenon springing spontaneously from the demands of human nature but an ethnological feature originating in a single center and thence transmitted to other regions'.[4] However, Murphy disagrees, in course of discussing his own hypothesis, that:

> Cultural forms are clearly projections of unconscious materials and processes. . . . Men's secret societies in such diverse locales as Africa, Melanesia, Australia, and South America exhibit regularities of such a high order that they long attracted the attention of anthropology. . . . Some special explanation of a sufficient causal – and functional – kind is necessary to explain their wide distribution in the face of the vast geographical discontinuities.[5]

Murphy attributes the occurrence of secret societies to '. . . projections of the classical psychological themes of sex antagonism and

1. Lowie, *Primitive Society*, op. cit., pp. 285–92. Interestingly, Money comments on the episodic nature of male sexual response: 'More than woman, man is in his erotic pursuits fairly promiscuously distracted from one love object to another, especially over a period of time, except perhaps when he is in the vortex of having just fallen desperately in love. The female is more steadfastly tied to a single romantic object or concept' – op. cit., p. 17.
2. Lowie, op. cit., p. 291.   3. ibid., p. 380.   4. ibid., p. 300.
5. Robert F. Murphy, 'Social Structure and Sex Antagonism', *Southwestern Journal of Anthropology*, 15, 1 (Spring 1959), pp. 89–90.

ambivalence, perhaps incomplete sex role identification',[1] an explanatory theme related to Eisenstadt's conception of them in terms of sex-linked age grades and the continuity of communal life.[2]

But, in as much as among the chief constraints of specific evolution are economic factors, and given the significance of hunting in human evolution, I choose to interpret male bonding (and such phenomena as secret societies and initiation, which will be discussed in the next chapter) as dependent upon economic–ecological rather than non-materialist psychological factors in evolution. The former explanation is at least as searching as the psychological one. After all, inherent in the latter must be some conception of human nature which derives finally from phylogeny – unless it is assumed once again that early family life is the source of all later conscious and unconscious behaviour. It seems preferable to me to derive psychological factors from economic constraints rather than the other way round, particularly when the data about hunting economy is as persuasive as writers in the field have come to conclude. Of course, sexual antagonisms and ambivalences exist. But it may be more useful to see these as *consequences* of economic factors which have led to broad genetic 'programming' of the anti-female tradition and the division of labour by sex.

My evidence depends on the interpretation of extant data. Heretofore this data has been interpreted in different ways, from other viewpoints, and yielding other conclusions. I take it to be the role of theory in part to provide a framework for interpretation, and since I support a special theoretical position, predictably my interpretations of data will reflect this. For example: initiation ceremonies have been regarded as, among other things, a function of infant sleeping patterns and post-partum sexual taboos,[3] and a way of assuring a male consensus in an 'organized symbolic structure' in societies in which certain forms of initiation occur.[4] From an ethological perspective such explanations are limited. In general, I agree with Frank Young's advocacy 'of the function of rituals for groups, not individuals',[5] but would extend his comment; let us seek under-

1. ibid., p. 96.
2. Eisenstadt, *From Generation to Generation*, op. cit., p. 24.
3. Whiting, Kluckhohn, and Anthony, 'The Function of Male Initiation Ceremonies at Puberty', in Maccoby, *et. al.*, op. cit.
4. Young, *Initiation Ceremonies*, op. cit.
5. F. W. Young, 'The Function of Male Initiation Ceremonies', *American Journal of Sociology*, **67**, 4 (January 1962), p. 391.

standing of the function of archetypal rituals for the maintenance of the species. Many initiation rituals (either formal, as among Plains Indians, or informal, as in how street gangs respond to newcomers) relate to the ability of initiates to do the work of the males in the group without letting the group down – these rituals appear to serve in part a functional equivalent in the spheres of work or war as courtship and marriage do in the sexual one.'[1]

3

In the next chapter I discuss in detail the nature and function of initiation ceremonies and secret societies in terms of this hypothesis. Let me briefly describe here the male bond in a variety of work situations.

Coal-mining is a demanding and dangerous occupation. For many persons personally unfamiliar with coal-mining communities, the novels of D. H. Lawrence – *Sons and Lovers* in particular – have rendered the human realities in a clear and memorable way. A sociological study of a mining town in Yorkshire suggests how the male bond maximizes safety and governs extra-work relationships.[2]

A very common phenomenon is for men to stick together through many different contracts for years on end, sometimes for a score of years and even a work lifetime . . . there tends to be a core around which the team is built. . . . The strongest and most permanent alliances are between pairs of men, though sometimes three men will stick together for long periods. . . . If one man is meeting with difficulties the collier next to him or another man

1. The relationship between sexual and natural selection was, of course, most assertively and significantly first sketched by Charles Darwin in *The Descent of Man and Selection in Relation to Sex* (John Murray, London, 1871 (first edition) and 1894 (second edition)). Another work whose importance to the understanding of the historical development of human hunting patterns has been undeservedly ignored, is Carveth Read's *The Origin of Man*, Cambridge University Press, 1925. This contains many propositions and analyses which might have been fruitfully examined in the period between the book's appearance and the present time had not the whole subject of evolution and its effect on society been obscured first by suspicion and then indifference or antipathy. Read's prescient anticipation of the ethological theory of which this study is a part is quite astonishing. While it is true that a science reluctant to forget its founders runs many risks, it is equally the case that a science too willing to forget its founders may overestimate the novelty of its concerns and findings in the eager clamour of redundant and derivative activity.
2. Norman Dennis, Fernando Henriques, and Clifford Slaughter, *Coal Is Our Life: An Analysis of a Yorkshire Mining Community*, Eyre & Spottiswoode, London, 1956. References are to this volume.

who is a quick worker will help him out, but if any individual consistently falls behind and needs help, the colliers exclude him from the team. . . . [A man] must be a good miner and his work-mates must feel they can trust him (pp. 44–5).

During leisure times, talk is usually about work. The local club is predominantly male, though the cinema is not. When the club is opened to women, as on Saturday nights, this is regarded as a special, somewhat festive occasion (p. 162). '. . . the interest and activities of the women in the Labour Party in Ashton are "social" rather than political in character and in addition are often typically "feminine" in Ashton terms' (p. 166).

The husbands of Ashton for preference come home for a meal after finishing work and as soon as they can feel clean and rested they opt for the company of their mates, i.e., their friends of the same sex. . . . Some husbands prefer to be outside the home when they are not working, eating or sleeping (pp. 181–3).

The club is called by Dennis, et al., 'the secret society of adult males' (p. 211). '. . . the group of mature men is a closed group which once entered entitles the member to certain definite privileges, among them obscenity, in given situations' (p. 214). 'The only context in which they discussed sex was a circle of jesting males' (p. 218).

The youth of Ashton form groups of about a half-dozen males. 'Fighting together is the . . . extreme of solidarity . . . in these groups of young men.' Near the age of twenty '. . . the attraction of the opposite sex becomes a real danger to the solidarity of the group'. Competition for males' time will begin even before marriage, and there is a 'bachelor night' before the wedding day (pp. 221–3). 'The whole life of the miner under the influence of his group of friends inhibits any display of tenderness and love in sexual relations' (p. 229). Women rarely have sexual satisfaction. Raising children is regarded as their task, while family discipline is not related to the needs of children but to the routine of the home (pp. 231–7). Fathers markedly favour sons; girls and boys are fitted early into roles which will prepare them for adult life. Softness is crushed out of boys early, though they retain strong attachment to 'mum', who remains possibly the chief focus of their sentimental lives (pp. 239–41).

Let us turn now to a study of a small Newfoundland fishing village.

Fishing is, in England at any rate – more hazardous even than mining. Cat Harbour, a community in Newfoundland, is very complex. Its social relationships occur in terms of a densely elaborate series of interrelated conceptual universes one important consequence of which is that virtually all permanent members of the community are kin, 'cunny kin', or economic associates of all other of the 285 permanent members.[1]

The primary activity of the community is cod fishing. Salmon, lobster, and squid provide additional sources of revenue. Woodcutting is necessary in off-seasons. Domestic gardening, and stints in lumber camps when money is needed, are the two other profitable activities. The community's religion is reactionary. Women assume the main roles in the operation though not the government of the churches in the town. A complicated system of 'jinking' – curses, magic, and witchcraft – governs and modulates social relationships.

Successful cod fishing in the area depends upon highly developed skills of navigation, knowledge of fish movements, and familiarity with local nautical conditions. Lore is passed down by word of mouth, and literacy among older fishermen is not universal by any means. 'Stranger' males cannot easily assume dominant positions in the fishing systems and may only hire on for salary or percentage. Because women in the community are not paid for their labour, there has been a pattern of female migration out of the area. Significantly, two thirds of the wives in the community are from outside the area. This has a predictable effect on the community's concept of 'the feminine'. An elaborate anti-female symbolism is woven into the fabric of male communal life, e.g. strong boats are male and older leaky ones are female.

Women 'are regarded as polluting "on the water" and the more traditional men would not consider going out if a woman had set foot in the boat that day – they are "jinker" (i.e., a jinx), even unwittingly'. (It is not only relatively unsophisticated workers such as those fishermen who insist on sexual purity. The very skilled technicians drilling for natural gas in the North Sea affirm the same taboo: women are not permitted on their drilling platform rigs.)

1. This account is based on the sophisticated preliminary report by James C. Faris, *Cat Harbour: A Newfoundland Fishing Settlement*, Institute of Social and Economic Research, St John's, Newfoundland, 1966. The report is preliminary in that it is not in finally published form, and retains an ambience of the Ph.D. thesis (for Cambridge University) on which it is largely based – an ambience chiefly of modesty. References are to this volume.

It would be, however, a rare Cat Harbour woman who would consider such an act, for they are aware of their structural position in the outport society and the cognition surrounding their sex. . . . Cat Harbour is a male-dominated society. . . . Only men can normally inherit property, or smoke or drink, and the increasingly frequent breach of this by women is the source of much gossip (and not a negligible amount of conflict and resentment). Men are seated first at meals and eat together – women and children eating afterwards. Men are given the choicest and largest portions, and sit at the same table with a 'stranger' or guest.[1]

Women work extremely demanding and long hours, 'especially during the fishing season, for not only do they have to fix up to 5 to 6 meals each day for the fishermen, but do all their household chores, mind the children and help "put away fish". They seldom have time to visit extensively, usually only a few minutes to and from the shop or Post Office. . . . Men on the other hand, spend each evening arguing, gossiping, and "telling cuffers", in the shop, and have numerous "blows" (i.e., breaks) during the day.'

Pre-adolescents are separated on sexual lines. Boys play exclusively male games and identify strongly with fathers or older brothers. Girls perform light women's work, though Faris indicates '. . . some often openly aspire to be male and do male things. By this time they can clearly see the privileged position of the Cat Harbour male . . .' (p. 100). Girls are advised not to marry a fisherman, and are encouraged to leave the community if they wish to avoid a hard life. Boys are told it is better to leave Cat Harbour than become fishermen. But the greater glamour of the role in the eyes of young males induces them to stay. The girls leave, necessitating the importation of females – and thus the fact that two thirds of wives are strangers.

At adolescence, girls come to adopt the behaviour of adult females. They experience less ambivalence about their sex than earlier, while boys take interest in ice hockey; fishing now becomes more of a chore. A male is not regarded as fully mature until he marries; 'There are few structural options for the unmarried adult' (pp. 102–3). 'Spinsters are unknown' (p. 104). 'On marriage, a man immediately "qualifies" for the evening shop gatherings. Bachelors, on the other hand spend their evenings in the "restaurant", where there is an occasional girl they may take out. Usually . . . they talk

1. Faris, op. cit., pp. 95–7.

among themselves, or . . . go to Wesleyville . . . where they can buy beer' (p. 104).

Arrangements for setting up fishing crews are complex and subject to a variety of kin and property factors. The ideal is roughly as follows: '. . . a man begins fishing with his sons. He holds the estate. . . . Sons inherit equivalent portions . . . but continue to fish together . . . [and] begin to save . . . to form a new fishing crew, consisting of father and sons' (p. 121). But, in fact, because a man may not have any or enough sons, and because brothers may not get on well, the ideal is not usually realized. These frictions and demographic circumstances may lead to composition of crews and work units on specifically non-kinship bases, though Faris does not indicate the precise nature of the ties which bind males in the variety of work situations in which they find themselves. Tension between wives of crew-mates may also lead to break-up, because the important 'support' role of females during the fishing period must be smoothly and co-operatively fulfilled (p. 126).

Let us turn to another society. The Cree Indians of the American plains lived by hunting – particularly buffalo – and by warfare.[1] Male and female work was clearly differentiated; males did the major hunting, though females sometimes participated in herding buffalo into corrals (p. 192). While the care of horses was entirely a male responsibility, females cared for and owned dogs – which were however not used in hunting (p. 196). Food collectively procured by men was collectively distributed; 'Berries and roots were the property of the women who had gathered them. Small game fell into the same category' (p. 204).

Hunting skill and success largely determined male status. Eminent hunters might inscribe pictographs of their major battles on their robes (p. 207). A male who hunted well could become a 'Worthy Young Man' and then a 'Warrior'. Joining the latter group was marked by expensive ritual and the bearing of insignia. 'Each band had only one Warrior society' (p. 224), and the Warriors acted as the police of the hunt (p. 226).[2]

1. David G. Mandelbaum, 'The Plains Cree', *Anthropological Papers*, 37, 2, American Museum of Natural History, New York, 1940. All references about the Cree are to this work.
2. Recall here my remark at the beginning of the chapter that male bonds form the spinal column of the community. This is particularly clear when collective hunting is more important than individual hunting. Lowie has commented on the general significance of the Warrior groups among the Plains Indians: 'Since the survival

The hunt, which was 'work', was closely related to warfare, which was more aggressive – though not wholly so because it provided spoils. Here we see the male bond in both its social control and external relations aspects. That the same group of individuals performed both functions is significant. The connection between hunting–work and warfare–aggression I take to be a crystallization and example of a general phenomenon discussed more fully later on.

'A boy often attached himself to a young man who was a good hunter and a brave warrior. The two were constant companions [much like the knight and his squire] and called each other "*niwitch ewahaken*", "he with whom I go about" ' (p. 244). While a boy might choose his own 'tutor' and companion, his parents normally chose his spouse (p. 245). Two men who were close friends might exchange wives (p. 246). The ritual of the Sun Dance, in which self-torture was inflicted, and the ritual of the Smoking Tipi, were all-male and were regarded as most important activities (pp. 269–88). While women constructed the common tipis for the community, all ceremonial ones were the work of men (p. 212). Occasionally, families might try to dissuade boys from warring, but general social pressures were greater than familial ones, and boys normally warred; those who didn't were given feminine names. During a hunt, there was banter about penis size, a favourite subject of ribaldry (p. 296). It is of interest that men could lead raids only if they claimed to have had a 'vision sanction' or if they had pievious experience of leadership (p. 295). When a warring or hunting party returned, a 'Happy-Dance' took place. During this event, women conferred their approval or disapproval on individual members of the party: successful warring was validated in social ceremony. 'It was the honor of being named and praised by the women that motivated the young men in their fantastic quest for scalps', and, 'A man's rank depended to a large degree on the courage he displayed in battle' (p. 299).

In Ashton and Cat Harbour, the relationship between male bonding and work is clear; among the Cree there is an additional factor – warfare – which contributes to the structuring of male relations. The

of the people might hinge on success in the chase, the directors of the undertaking issued orders that had to be implicitly obeyed, on pain of severe punishment by the police' (p. 14). 'While women were auxiliaries in some military societies, women's societies' *naturally* [my italics] lacked military and constabulary features' (p. 104). From Robert H. Lowie, *Indians of the Plains*, Anthropological Handbook Number One, McGraw-Hill for American Museum of Natural History, New York, 1954.

three cases, coal-mining, fishing, and hunting-battle, can be regarded as a contemporary reflection of the type of ancient hunting pattern and its accompanying sexual dimorphism. This is directly related to what is now presumed to be the most significant human evolutionary specialization. In isolation, these three cases prove nothing in themselves, and there are cases to be found in which behaviour and attitudes to work and battle differ from these. None the less the range and kind of evidence about division of labour on sexual bases and the reservation of certain defined tasks in each society for men only suggests the validity of pursuing the study of work along the lines I have outlined.

Even in situations where equality between males sand females in the labour force has been legislated the differentiating tendency persists. A recent report from the U.S.S.R. is worth quoting here at some length:

> Soviet women have the right to work alongside men with equal pay for equal work; but mounting protests insist that the women get too large a share of dirty, heavy and unskilled jobs.
>
> The gangs of earth-digging, brick-carting, snow-shovelling, and asphalt-laying women to be seen in most Soviet streets, with the men supervising or sitting comfortably in the cabs of their machines, are one of the first impressions to strike visitors.
>
> Giving statistics about the employment of women in heavy manual work, the Literary Gazette today called for additional legislation to protect the feminine labour force. In fairness, it must be noted that all the professions are open to women, and it is no surprise to meet women sea captains, judges or industrial managers.
>
> Nevertheless, a study carried out at a Saratov construction site showed that out of 1,212 persons employed in heavy manual labour 1,030 were women. Out of 136 diggers not equipped with mechanical aids, 119 were women. Conversely, in jobs where mechanical equipment was used only 138 of a labour force of 1,033 were women. There is the same picture in agriculture.
>
> One reason suggested by the Literary Gazette was that heavy jobs have much higher rates of pay.[1]

1. Kyril Tidmarsh, 'Right to do the Hardest Work', The Times (16 February 1967). For a detailed outline of the successes and failures of the Soviet government's efforts to achieve equality in the labour force among men and women, see Norton T. Dodge, Women in the Soviet Economy, Johns Hopkins Press, 1966. An outline of the government's position is Vera Bilshai, The Status of Women in the Soviet Union, Foreign Languages Publishing House, Moscow, 1959.

In the United States, not until 1963 were women legally entitled to equal pay for equal work.[1] Despite this development and various others facilitating equal employment, serious resistance to equality remains. It arises anew in occupations for which clear sex-assignment has not yet occurred – such as computer roles.[2] But Gross concludes that in the U.S. '. . . there is as much sexual segregation now as there was some sixty years ago . . . this phenomenon is very persistent.'[3] Considerable discrepancy between males' and females' earnings remains in the United Kingdom. For example, in 1966, averaging out for all industries, male wage-earners received £20 6s. while females had £10 1s. Among salaried employees, men earned an average of £26 14s., women £14 5s.[4] Even in Sweden which is commonly thought to have a relatively emancipated and effective female labour force, the situation is if anything more unfavourable to women than the English one. For example average hourly pay for Swedish women in all occupations in 1964 was 40 per cent less than for men. High-level posts and high incomes are very disproportionately retained by men, and there is no evidence of movement towards the equitable distribution of money and perquisites which Swedish social ideology would recommend. This is not to say there are no educational and other circumstantial reasons for these inequalities, but it indicates that they exist and necessarily will significantly influence patterns of social life.

In the U.S. there are some occupational categories such as teaching where females have traditionally had dominant roles, but as salaries in these occupations rise, the proportion of men may increase – in teaching from 25 to 30 per cent in a decade. Furthermore, 'the higher teaching and administrative posts are far more often held by men'.[5]

Again, in the U.S.S.R., where over 80 per cent of medical doctors are females, none the less women tend to concentrate on pediatrics and obstetrics while surgery is almost exclusively male. In sub-

1. 'Equal-wage Bill is Voted in House', New York Times (Western edition) 24 May 1963.
2. Elizabeth Faulkner Baker, Technology and Women's Work, Columbia University Press, 1964, pp. 426–7.
3. Edward Gross, 'Plus Ça Change . . . The Sexual Structure of Occupations Over Time', paper presented to the American Sociological Association, San Francisco, 1967.
4. British Information Services, Notes on Some Prices in Britain, London, 1967, p. 22.
5. Baker, op. cit., pp. 429–30.

Saharan Africa, LeVine finds 'conspicuous uniformities' in the differentiation by role in each of the major institutions of society, and on the basis of several tested indices suggests that females living in traditional-type differentiated communities are happier and display less evidence of ill-health than more emancipated women.[1]

4

I have been dealing here with a number of issues and patterns which I have discussed interdependently. It is now time to separate out the points I want to emphasize.

In connection with politics, I have claimed that human communities tend to be sexually differentiated, and that males dominate. Where females have some success in politics, this appears to result from a self-conscious process of planned change rather than 'organic' development.[2] An analogous pattern of control exists in economic affairs; there is an inverse relationship between the status of occupations and the participation of females. Where females begin careers at status levels equivalent to men, they are not as successful as men in the high-status tasks of their professions. A study of Radcliffe Ph.D.s compared with Harvard Ph.D.s indicated that the former tended markedly to turn to teaching and counselling of students rather than research. Males with the status of Harvard Ph.D., on the other hand, tended to gain scientific eminence and posts in large research-oriented university departments rather than in those smaller teaching-oriented college departments which women joined.[3]

In many countries, women's employment has expanded considerably,[4] and a wider range of possible posts is open to a greater number.

1. Robert A. LeVine, 'Sex Roles and Economic Change in Africa', *Ethnology*, 5, 2 (April 1966), pp. 186–9.
2. For a very recent example: 'Norwegian politicians are now actively supporting a campaign which, if it succeeds, is going to push a good many men out of political life, with the aim of drawing more women into it both at the national and the local level. On the average, less than 10 per cent of elected representatives are women. In the Storting (parliament) 14 out of 150 representatives are women. In local and borough councils, there are 900 women representatives and 14,000 men' – Women Wanted in Norway's Politics', *The Times* (23 February 1967).
3. Maccoby, *et al.*, *Readings in Social Psychology*, op. cit., p. 40. Pertinent queries of this and related material are raised by Rita James Simon, Shirley Merritt Clark and Kathleen Galway, 'The Woman Ph.D.: A Recent Profile', *Social Problems*, 15, 2 (Fall 1967).
4. For example, see Mead and Kaplan (eds.), *American Women*, op. cit.; Women's Bureau, Department of Labour, *Women in the Labour Force in Nine Countries of Europe*, Government of Canada, Ottawa, 1962; Viola Klein, *Working Wives*, Institute of

But it remains the overall pattern that women work for men. Even though women may formally control business through equities, their disposition of wealth and control is through the agency of male advisers.[1] And that work which females typically do is generally awarded lower status than work men do.

Males dominate females in occupational and political spheres. This is a species-specific pattern and is associated with my other proposition: that males bond in a variety of situations involving power, force, crucial or dangerous work, and relations with their gods. They consciously and emotionally *exclude* females from these bonds. The significant notion here is that these broad patterns are biologically based, and that those variously different expressions of male dominance and male bonding in different communities are what one would expect from a species highly adaptable to its physical and social environments, and where learning is a crucial adaptive process. To use Count's term, male dominance and bonding are features of the human 'biogram'. New archaeological data underlie the claim that hunting is at least 14 million years old and that man separated from other primates possibly 20 million years ago. It seems to me that this forces us to reassess completely our conception of work, politics, and

Personnel Management, London, n.d.; Department of Labour of Canada, *Women at Work in Canada*, Government of Canada, Ottawa, 1958; *Women and Top Jobs: An Interim Report*, Political and Economic Planning, London, 1967.

1. See the relevant comment of an investment broker on women's attitude towards management of capital; a clear male–female dichotomy is suggested: Albert Schwabacher, Jr, 'The Repository of Wealth', in S. M. Farber and R. H. L. Wilson (eds.), *The Potential of Woman*, McGraw-Hill, New York, 1963, p. 241. This lends some perspective to apparent resistance of stock exchanges to admit women members; the London Stock Exchange has recently yielded to sustained pressure and is prepared to give membership to females, but only on condition they do not gain admission to the floor of the House during business hours – a condition which obtains on the New York exchange as well – 'Stock Exchange May Admit Women', *The Times* (18 January 1967). One of the formal excuses for this curious condition is that during hectic trading Stock Exchange members may utter curses from which as gentlemen they should presumably desist in the presence of ladies. Gallant as this and similar reasons may be, it seems more likely that the floor of any stock exchange is really an arena for highly skilled predatory behaviour which rests on an overall co-operative pattern, and that this mixture of predation and co-operative professional bonhomie, men fear, will be significantly altered by the participation of females. If men are right in this assessment, it would no doubt be the final argument of women that if the system depends on the exclusion of women for its operation it is an unacceptable system given contemporary notions of sexual equality. The issue reflects neatly the underlying dynamics of some features of the general subject of male bonds threatened by female claims to join, and it may be exacerbated because stockbrokers are high-status persons – we have already discussed the relationship between high status and male unisexual organization.

sexual differences in this context. There are some fascinating clues. One of the most provocative is Kortlandt's finding that females throw missiles, spears, etc., with much the same motion proto-hominids use. Human males appear to be adapted to a throwing motion closely related to the one universally used by hunters in spearing game. The survival value of this sexually differentiated adaptation is of the order of sexually differentiated reproductive adaptations, though it occurred much more quickly; an estimate of about 400,000 years is fairly generally accepted as the shortest period within which this could have occurred, though it probably took longer. The importance of the new dating of man's first hunting and his separation from other primates cannot be overestimated. It very simply – almost brutally – means that even the three million years of the Pleistocene must be seen as a period of development of detailed adaptations of an already extensively hominized creature.[1]

Thus, the fishermen of Cat Harbour, the miners of Ashton, and the hunter-warriors of the American plains follow an ancient and demanding biological programme. It is not a programme as old as sexual reproductive behaviour or maternal or childish behaviour, but it is one which everywhere still excites commitment, emotion, action, a sense of contact with the chief passions of life. More important from the social scientists' point of view is the possibility that these male patterns lie at the heart of all community action and organization. Are the male bonds of politics, work, and war the behavioural mechanisms by which small-scale communities – perhaps of one adult male and females and young – link under certain circumstances to form the large communities in which many contemporary humans live? We have a hint of the possible processes involved from the primates, such as the hamadryas baboon, who live in small 'one-family' units under difficult forage conditions and combine into large communities when and where there is ample food and water.[2] My proposition, perhaps supported by data about political participation, would be that when human groups expand beyond, say, ten to thirty individuals, it becomes necessary to form some kind of bond of super- and subordination and some allocation of work and defence functions. This bond is typically male,[3] and is observable in the

1. See A. Kortlandt and M. Kooij, 'Protohominid Behaviour in Primates', *Symposia of the Zoological Society of London*, No. 10 (1963), pp. 61–8.
2. Vernon Reynolds, 'Open Groups in Human Evolution', in op. cit.
3. In his survey of the Euro-American literature, Nelson Polsby makes no mention of female local politicians. See N. W. Polsby, *Community Power and Political Theory*,

rudimentary political arrangements of rural settlements in areas sufficiently beyond the subsistence level to sustain secondary economic institutions. As Washburn has commented, 'Our ancestors lived in very small groups, and we have evolved to feel strongly about only a very small number of people.'[1] In fact, the 'gemein-schaft–gesellschaft' dichotomy, abused though it has been, may reflect the shift from the relatively small-scale group in terms of which the human has evolved to one in which 'impersonal' organizations must structure social life. I have indicated the extent to which these structuring organizations are led by males. The male bond and male interactions, therefore, underlie the anatomical and physiological growth processes of communities. The mother–child interaction does not 'prosper' in this particular sense (which may be why many mothering females resent their involvement in a process which does not seem contemporary in spirit or scope), nor does the male–female reproductive process. Even in education, resentment and allegations of ineffectiveness follow when classes become large. Any teacher is uncertain about the pedagogic value of seminars of more than fifteen to twenty individuals, and the seminar-type method of instruction and discussion presumably prevailed throughout most of the period of human history when collective education was practised.[2]

As I noted earlier, the instrumental–expressive dichotomy of Parsons might be more profitably rendered as the male–female dichotomy. 'Female' implies tasks involving specific interactions of a personal or quasi-personal kind, while 'male' implies activities on a larger scale, with potentially greater impersonality, with greater direct and active relevance to communal integrity and social domi-

Yale University Press, 1963. Long ago, Jane Addams, a Nobel Peace Prize winner, complained about the failure of women to gain power in civic government, while it was true that 'A city is in many respects a great business corporation, but in other respects it is enlarged housekeeping'; therefore women should be consulted. She made a similar point about immigrants in American cities. She found survivals of militarism in civil government (p. 31) and thought that as the war virtues waned, there would be 'the substitution of the ideals of labor for those of warfare' (p. 224) – Jane Addams, *Newer Ideals of Peace*, Macmillan, New York, 1907.

1. S. L. Washburn, 'Conflict in Primate Society', in op. cit., pp. 11–13.
2. What seminars they must have had in the caves of Dordogne and Spain as they painted their diagrams and schemes on walls and painted over them as the lessons progressed! For two discussions of the dynamics and size factors in seminar-type behaviour, see Roger Holmes, *The University Seminar and the Primal Horde*, London School of Economics and Political Science (unpublished MS.), 1966, and T. T. Paterson, 'Ritual in Industrial Societies, a Discussion of Ritualizations in Animals and Man', *Royal Society Philosophical Transactions*, Series B, Biological Sciences No. 772, Vol. 25, pp. 247–526 (December 1966).

nance. Parsons and Bales do not propose a conceptualization derived from scientific observation of the wider effects of the division of technical and emotional labour in family life. The one proposed here is based on a more general conception of the division of labour, rooted in the history of the species as well as in the discrete life histories of individual people and their families. It assumes additional instructive value in as much as it may aid in the development of analytical continuities between small-scale and large-scale social structures. By this I mean it may be possible to study social change, community fission (as, for example, among the Hutterite or Mormon communities of North America) and the development of specific economic, political, recreational, and possibly religious systems in terms of continuities and changes in male bonding patterns and female behaviour. Political independence and decolonization are two potential subjects for this treatment, as are the gregarious behaviour of delinquents and deviants and the relationship between sexual equality in education with differentiation in economic and political life.[1]

A NOTE ON SPORT

Washburn notes that, 'The basis for the majority of contemporary sports was the preparation for war, and the purpose of the sports was to render the individuals taking part in them physically and psychologically tough, so that they would be capable of and would enjoy the physical destruction of other human beings.'[2] Studies of some primates reveal that males play more roughly than females; further, unisexual play differs in form from that of heterosexual groups. From his ethological study of three- to five-year-old human children, Blurton-Jones concludes that

. . . there appears . . . to be a sex difference in the amount of

1. Parsons and Bales (eds.), op. cit. Frank Young, in *Initiation Ceremonies*, notes: 'male solidarity is redefined as community solidarity, as . . . female solidarity [is] . . . redefined as family solidarity' (p. 141); Young's general finding is that females do not typically form associations of a community-oriented kind, that initiation ceremonies occur much less frequently for females than males, and that when there are female initiations these are much more likely to be individual and family-oriented. Young's explanation for his findings is in terms of a sociological, drama-turgical conceptualization of social order, and he rejects a psychogenic explanation (Whiting's, most prominently) which is considerably more moderate than the one I am proposing here. There are none the less important convergences in the assessment of data, despite divergences in explaining their causality.
2. S. L. Washburn, 'Conflict in Primate Society', in op. cit., p. 11.

rough and tumble play by children, males playing more often than females. The same difference is well established in rhesus monkeys. . . . It looks as if this may be one sex difference in human behaviour which is not culturally determined, although it may result from differences in physique rather than direct CNS [central nervous system] effects of hormones.[1]

The notion that play and war are related is not a new one, and I shall be considering it in a general discussion of aggression. For the moment, it is enough to recall the comment: 'The battle of Waterloo was won on the playing fields of Eton'; Veblen's claim, in *The Theory of the Leisure Class*, that sport is a functional equivalent of war; and the general relationship found to exist between socialization practices and the sex of children – males are permitted greater display of aggression and may be encouraged in this, particularly outside the home environment.[2]

What is relevant about sport to our argument is that it is normally a voluntary activity (in the sense that there is no direct pressure such as hunger or strict governmental compulsion to engage in it; there are other informal compulsions interesting in themselves), and that the male bond is a central organizational feature of sport. Of course, in those sports and games involving bodily contact, inhibitions about extensive heterosexual body contact and physical differences in size and strength combine to make female participation unlikely. The only major sports in which males and females participate equally are tennis and skating. But general public interest is greatest in male sports. The popular team sports such as soccer, football, baseball, hockey, basketball, are virtually always male. Most female sport activity is amateur. In general, this may reflect the fact that in all athletic sports males are superior to females,[3] and that spectators and fans prefer males' superior displays of physical and perhaps even psychological skills. But it may be – and this is more telling – that spectators identify more readily with male than with female athletes, that the former perform more emotively, and that the fact and

1. N. G. Blurton-Jones, 'Some Aspects of the Social Behaviour of Children in Nursery School', in Desmond Morris (ed.), *Primate Ethology*, op. cit., p. 363.

2. Robert R. Sears, *et al.*, *Patterns of Child Rearing*, Row, Peterson, Evanston, Ill., 1957, pp. 402–5.

3. Ironically, the only sport in which females are superior to males is long-distanec swimming – a precisely inappropriate skill for a terrestrial mammal. Other sports involving running, throwing, jumping, hitting, etc., presumably express more directly some evolved human skills and our continued interest in them.

dynamics of 'teamness' are more excitingly and agreeably apprehended by watching males than females. I have no data to support this in any systematic way, except that a cursory survey of the world's major sports must lead to the conclusion that they are very much male-dominated – almost entirely so for sports involving teams of more than two persons. Where overt physical punishment is involved, as in boxing and wrestling, interest again focusses upon males. Female boxers are virtually unknown, while female wrestlers occupy an even more bizarre niche in the show business of professional commercial wrestling than their male colleagues.

(Commercial wrestling is almost entirely scripted. But it is necessary for all performers to maintain very excellent physical condition because the work is dangerous otherwise. Continual practice is necessary to ensure timing and skill in the various falls, jumps, holds, and twists which constitute the classical repertoire of the wrestler's ritual enactment of a confused but persistently recurring morality-play theme. The unusual size and great strength of most wrestlers are no doubt important mimetic stimuli for the strong reactions their audience displays. The importance of size in boxing is equally clear; thus the dramaturgical prominence of the heavyweight champion alongside the lightweight or even middleweight champion. It is the amalgamation of size, power, dramaturgical *savoir faire*, and domiance which has turned Mohammed Ali into a world figure occupying a position which curiously strikes me as the obverse of U Thant's, though his refusal to be drafted into the U.S. Army brings his symbolic role rather closer than before to the Secretary-General's.

(One of the more notorious displays of female wrestling occurs in Hamburg where, in certain night clubs in the city's forthright entertainment area, semi-nude women wrestle each other in a mud-filled enclosure. This is undoubtedly a sadistic spectator expression of the anti-female attitude, while at the same time there is a clear voyeuristic element. In a London striptease club I have seen an intriguing vignette with the straightforward title: 'The Flogging of the Christians in the Roman Era', which involved two girls being stripped and then whipped (with a presumably painless cat o' nine tails made with very light P.V.C.); the act includes some pushing and jostling and seems to reflect some relatively mundane sado-sexual fantasies of the virtually all-male audience. Parenthetically, given the considerable amount of sado-masochist pornography available in London – what is known in America as 'bondage' material –

there is surprisingly little sado-masochistic content in the strip clubs. This may suggest either the limited ambition and imagination of the producers of strip shows and the zeal of police and courts, or the fact that there is a division of labour and 'bondage' enthusiasts find their pleasures in emporia which are hidden to the general public, or more likely in private performances costing very considerably more. The average entry price to strip clubs is about 15s. while the cost of entry to a performance of intercourse is £5; undoubtedly a bondage demonstration would be at least several times that price.)

The Olympic Games are an exception to the general rule about the lack of interest in female sports, as are the lesser international competitions involving national aspirants – figure skating for example. The Olympic Games represent a highly ritualized, almost religious, attitude to the relationship between nationalism and athletic skill, and they are intended to generate inclusive rather than exclusive attitudes among the nations. It would be as unreasonable to discriminate on the basis of sex[1] as on the basis of race or nationality – except by segregating males and females in competition. Representation is also an important feature of international competitions – whole nations are represented by athletes. It is a curious paradox that the political unit of the nation is more self-consciously represented – in sexual terms – in sports than politics. It may be acceptable for females to participate in a type of competition which, like the Games, is ritually non-aggressive rather than beligerently aggressive. In any case, the attendance at events featuring females falls below the attendance at all or largely male contests, and the competitions

1. Because of the success of operations changing persons from male to female, there have been a number of cases of alleged invasion of female competitions by once-male, nearly male, or simply deceptive entrants. This has led to the demand for physical inspections of all females in important competitions, which some women have refused to undergo on the grounds that such inspections constitute an undignified violation of privacy and the spirit of athletic competition. This has raised another version of a general concern about relationship between biological and behavioural definition of gender. For a good discussion, see John L. Hampson and Joan G. Hampson, 'The Ontogenesis of Sexual Behaviour in Man', in W. C. Young (ed.), op. cit., pp. 1404–18. On the basis of their study of human hermaphroditism, they suggest, '. . . in place of the theory of an innate constitutional psychological bisexuality such as that proposed by Freud . . . we must substitute a concept of psychological sexual neutrality in humans at birth' (p. 1406). It is not clear that one can learn more about the behaviour of normally sexed persons from studying hermaphroditism than from studying the ontogeny of normal behaviour. Generalizing to the large group from a tiny deviant one is a hazardous business, though it is a procedure which provides irreplaceable insights and perspective.

most eagerly followed, such as the Decathalon and the Marathon, are between men.

I am proposing that sport behaviour is functionally equivalent to the hunting pattern with which the human male has been endowed by evolution. It seems that team sport is far more alluring to male than female participants, and that spectators and fans prefer male to female players. There is an interesting distinction to be made between individual play and team play; the former involves a complex psychological and physical encounter between a person and time obstacle or competitor. It is a defined encounter with epic implications. Sports heroes such as runners and jumpers are perhaps the quintessential heroes because they operate in a private, absolutely rigorous world where there are no excuses and a person's triumph or loss is his or her own, not his team's. I recall seeing on television the great race between the first four-minute-mile runners, John Landy and Roger Bannister, at the British Empire Games in Vancouver; the event was almost a paradigm of the drama of the human quest for excellence and of the strenuous application of will and trained skill to the resistances in the task to be performed. In the four minutes of the race was a summing-up of training, talent, the demand to win; the outcome was total – one man won, the other man lost. In racing or swimming or pole vaulting, the results and the competition are clear-cut and highly individual.

However, in boxing, for example, there is necessary interaction which may be hostile or co-operative. But an individual's skill is always a function of his opponent's and the struggle for dominance is intensely personal. Boxing rules function to depersonalize conflict and maintain ultimate amity between contestants though their intentions may be more or less brutal. The element of sanctioned brutality is increased in professional boxing where smaller gloves are used which permits greater damage to be done to contestants and increases the possibility of one inflicting on the other the minor brain concussion called a 'knock-out'. Professional boxing is another paradigm activity, this time of inter-personal dominance processes of a very intimate kind. The only measure of success is who a boxer beats; there are no impersonal times and records to which he may address himself. It is rather surprising to note the hostility of spectators and sports writers to expressions of genuine hostility and personal rather than impersonal rivalry, as, for example, when Mohammed Ali's opponent insisted on calling him Cassius Clay rather than Ali. Why it was anticipated that a highly trained and extraordinarily powerful young brave, selected by a process of applied violence to his fellow man, should be expected to be a proper gentleman as well despite provocation, suggests the curious ambivalence which exists about the legitimacy of boxing in a relatively humane civilization. In theory amateur boxing evokes less ambivalence. The quaint statement of a trainer of amateur boxers suggests the theory: '. . . a Britisher, more especially a boxing Britisher, cannot shake hands and think nothing of it; there always comes over him a certain feeling of warmth; and thus at the very outset he is, by this action alone, made to recognize that he meets a friend in friendly rivalry'.[1]

Team sports involve different processes. While there may be fellowship between teams, more intense immediate bonding occurs between team members than among players of the same game. The importance of the bond in team sports is well known, both to professional and amateur players, and to spectators. The role of coaches and trainers in manipulating the psychodynamics of team members is equally well known; so is the importance of being 'up' or eager before a game as a reflection (in part) of the interpersonal relationships among the players.[2] The use of colours, emblems, and characteristic names to create team identity and differentiate teams qua teams is a feature of this form of group behaviour. An intriguing aspect of the naming of sports teams – this applies particularly to North America – is the frequent use of huntable animals' names – the Lions, Bears, Tigers, Hawks, Cubs, etc. It is not clear what this means, though possibly it may bear some relationship to the ancient pattern of linking animal representations with hunting–aggressive endeavours.[3] It may also be somewhat similar to the existence of animal mascots among military units.

Amateur sport behaviour is really quite extraordinary. Persons who could otherwise enjoy comfort and leisure willingly engage in violent exertions which may involve considerable danger. This willingness to experience danger is a perplexingly un-rational manifestation. It may be distributed unequally in the population, again

1. J. C. Trotter, Boxing, Routledge, London, 1901, p. 97.
2. See Norbert Elias and Eric Dunning, 'Dynamics of Group Sports with Special Reference to Football', British Journal of Sociology, 16, 4 (December 1966).
3. For example, see W. J. Sollas, Ancient Hunters and Their Modern Representatives, Macmillan, London, 1924, pp. 399–427; Bridget Allchin, The Stone-Tipped Arrow, Phoenix House, London, 1966, p. 83; A. and G. Sieveking, The Caves of France and Northern Spain, Studio Vista, London, 1962, pp. 22–33.

perhaps on a normal curve basis, like intelligence. But this 'fool-hardiness' appears to engage the interest and enthusiasm of followers of a variety of endeavours from Grand Prix motor racing to travelling circuses.[1]

In team sports the group shares the risks involved. Team members will engage in conflict on behalf of their fellows – violence in team games is almost always inter- rather than intra-team. An often intense if ephemeral loyalty bonds players in a team. Even in sports which involve individual performance, such as swimming, track and field, or boxing, players often participate as members of teams – this is probably the most usual form of entry – and they perform in terms of loyalty to their team as well as their own individual success.

Obviously some females do participate in team sports and do share many of the same emotions. But it seems clear that team sports are more important for the socialization of young boys; that team sports are of greater interest to males than females;[2] that male teams are of greater interest than female teams; and that the syndrome of male team behaviour and male spectatorship bears some connection – representative, sublimative, or direct – to the hunting-male bonding factor in human history. Again, I emphasize the male–female difference because it is relevant to this book's general thesis that sexual differences are not only physical and sexual-erotic but elaborately social-organizational on a large scale. The sociologist Meyersohn has noted the importance of television sports programmes in providing a common link between U.S. males: 'Far more Americans hunt and fish than play baseball or box; yet the latter are the most popular sports programs. . . . Spectators get nothing "useful". . . . What they get out of it is this: a common interest is developed and perpetuated which enables virtually any American male to carry on intense conversations with any other.'[3] Presumably a similar function is

1. The early sociologist, W. I. Thomas, thought the search for danger was 'instinctive': 'There could not have been developed an organism depending on offensive and defensive movements for food and life without an interest in what we call a dangerous or precarious situation. A type without this interest would have been defective, and would have dropped out in the course of development' – W. I. Thomas, 'The Gaming Interest', *American Journal of Sociology* (1906), pp. 750–6.
2. A Canadian journalist has estimated the amount of prime time coverage given to sports on Canadian television (which includes sports news for ten minutes following general news of seven minutes), and asserts that, 'as a member of a sex that presumably has fifty per cent equity in the medium, I think TV programmers should understand that the category they have scheduled is Male Soap Opera' – Barbara Moon, 'For the Sake of Argument', *Maclean's Magazine* (5 October 1963).
3. Quoted in ibid.

served by televised and live spectator sports in other societies. In England, the bus-loads of club-colour-wearing fans travelling with their favourite teams not only watch their teams play (and have fun!) but participate in a pattern of male bonding which establishes presumably important modes of masculine identification and group affiliation. Spectators' relatively impersonal links with their teams become mediated by and personalized through the agency of the informal peer groups of supporters. Thus, the small-scale male group is re-created.

I am aware that this phenomenon is another special case of the general process of social affiliation which I discussed earlier.[1] It is difficult to avoid this interpretation of fans' response to team sports in some situations: that watching or hearing games may stimulate aggressive partisanship between adherents of different teams, and this may on occasion lead to violence or at least ritualized heckling and cheering. The fact that, other things being equal, teams play better on their home ground presumably has to do with the comfort of numbers and possibly some vaguely formulated but real territorial affiliation. The widespread incidence of spectator violence surrounding team sports is presumably an indication of the mimetic interactions involved in spectator sports. Thus, in a generalized way, sports reflect and interpret quite primitive patterns of activity and affiliation. Perhaps we can regard sport spectatorship as a phenomenon bearing the same relationship to hunting and male bonding as love stories do to reproductive drives and mate selection.

Yet, as Meyersohn has indicated, American men actually engage most in hunting and fishing. The desire of men in wealthy societies to re-create the food-gathering conditions of very primitive people appears to be an appropriate comment on the power of the hunting drives discussed earlier. Not only is hunting expensive in many places – think of the European on safari in Africa – but it is also time-consuming, potentially dangerous, and frequently involves considerable personal discomfort. Men do it because it is 'fun'. So they say, and so one must conclude from their persistent rendition of the old pattern. What is relevant from our point of view is that hunting, and frequently fishing, are group activities. A man will choose his co-hunters very carefully. Not only does the relative inti-

---

1. In *The Uses of Literacy*, Penguin Books, Harmondsworth, 1957, Hoggart describes the football day-outing in omnibuses which is a feature of working-class life (pp. 146–8). See also his description of working-class males' attitudes to and behaviour about sports (pp. 108–10).

macy of the hunt demand some congeniality, but there is also danger in hunting with inept or irresponsible persons. It is a serious matter, and even class barriers which normally operate quite rigidly may be happily breached for the period of the hunt.[1] Some research on hunters in British Columbia suggests the near-piety which accompanies the hunt; hunting is a singular and important activity. One particular group of males takes along bottles of costly Crown Royal whisky for the hunt; they drink only superior whisky on this poignant re-creation of an ancient manly skill. But when their wives join them for New Year's celebrations, they drink an ordinary whisky: the purely formal and social occasion does not, it seems, merit the symbolic tribute of outstanding whisky.

Gambling is another behaviour which, like hunting and sport, provides an opportunity in countless cultures for the weaving of and participation in the web of male affiliation.[2] Not the gambling of the London casino, where glamorous women serve drinks, or the complex hope, greed, fate-tempting ritual, and action of the shiny American palaces in Nevada, and not the hidden gambling run by racketeers. Rather, the card games in homes or small clubs, where men gather to play for manageable stakes on a friendly basis; perhaps – like Jiggs and his Maggie – to avoid their women, perhaps to seek some money, perhaps to buy the pleasant passage of time. But also to be with their friends and talk, and define, by the game, the confines of their intimate male society.

Obviously females play too, both on their own and in mixed company. But there are differences which warrant investigation, in the same way that the drinking of men in groups appears to differ from heterosexual or all-female drinking; the separation of all-male bars and mixed ones is still maintained in many places despite the powerful cultural pressures against such flagrant sexual apartheid. Even in the Bowery, where disaffiliated outcast males live in ways only now becoming understood, it has been noted that, 'There are strong indications that the heavy drinkers are more integrated and

1. Werner Cohn, 'Social Stratification and the Charismatic', *The Midwest Sociologist*, 21, 1 (December 1958).
2. I am grateful to Robin Fox for bringing to my attention the importance of gambling in many cultures. We hope to collect the data on the phenomenon and present it in a forthcoming publication. According to an American study, the two favourite activities of fraternal organizations are: (1) Receptions for new or retiring officers, and (2) card parties, this may suggest the chief concerns of members. See Report of Committee on Lodge Activities, National Fraternal Congress, quoted in Gist, op. cit., pp. 168–9.

more sociable than the light. The analytical problem lies in determining whether socialization causes drinking or drinking results in sociability when there is no disapproval.'[1] In the gentleman's club in London, the informally segregated working man's pub in Yorkshire, the all-male taverns of Montreal, the palm-wine huts of west Africa, perhaps can be observed the enactment of a way of establishing maleness and maintaining bonds which is given an excuse and possibly facilitated by alcohol. Certainly, for what they are worth in revealing the nature of popular conception of the social role of drinking, advertisements stress the manly appeal of alcohol – particularly whisky – though it is also clear that there are ongoing changes in the socio-sexual implications of drinking. But perhaps it is hasty to regard the process of change as a process of female emancipation which will culminate in similarity of behaviour, status, and ideals of males and females. The changes are still too recent to warrant this. Also, they have been achieved under sufficiently self-conscious pressure so that some arbitrary criteria have been forced on the direction of the change. Change does not necessarily lead to freedom, equality, and sameness. But we shall have occasion to review this vexing and critical matter in the final chapter.

In this chapter and the preceding one I have adopted a somewhat impressionistic and expository approach. I have outlined the ways in which males dominate females in a variety of important social subsystems – particularly politics and economics – and I have indicated ways in which we can see this dominance as part of a species-specific patterned propensity. Intrinsic to the notion of male dominance are, I have suggested, those bonds formed among the males, and I have presented some evidence for the claim that male bonding is, again, a patterned feature of the human behavioural repertoire.

I am well aware that the wives of high-status males dominate low-status males and that many male bonds may be porous to females or female influence. (Indeed, female influence, or the possibility of female participation, may be catalysing factors in the formation of male groups, notably in the areas of recreation and projective-symbolic behaviour.) I am also aware that my evidence could appear anecdotal and random because it is so general, and that a good case could be made for explaining the existence of what I have described (and more) as the contemporary expression of long-standing cultural habits and not of biological evolution. But the subject is large.

1. Pat Nash, *Homeless Men at Home* (unpublished MS.), 1965, p. 53.

Without apology I have treated it in an introductory and programmatic way. My educated hunch is that I have discussed sub-systems (such as politics, economics, and recreation) in a meaningful context – perhaps ultimately more meaningful than contexts which exclusively frame behaviour in cultural terms or deny the possibility of knowing, at this point in science, what species-specific patterns humans may display.

Now, having proposed some general hypotheses about the role of maleness and femaleness in defining social structures and the kinds of valences and ambivalences which exist between males and females in several important social sub-systems, I want to turn to some concrete cases of bonding and try to indicate the value of these hypotheses as additions to the array of existing explanations. So from the relatively open worlds of politics, work, and sport, let us make our way into the often bizarre and astonishing world of secret societies, initiations, informal male groups, and misogyny. It is not only that it is a world which may be fascinating (for so it seems to be to many people). But knowing this world may deepen our understanding of the special aspect of human history and its contemporary consequences which is my special concern.

CHAPTER SIX

Men Court Men: Initiations and Secret Societies

Politics need not always have to do with legal government. It is a process. It exists in sports, in science, in the world of folk-rock, in religious organizations, in business, among fashion designers and their publicists. There is also a demi-monde of politics which has not received due attention from students of political process in particular and social action in general. I refer to secret societies.

To understand how secret societies work, why people join them, what their social consequences are, and why they exist in the first place, should be an important task for scientists. But scientists come from intellectual communities where the overt is the good and where unabashed ritual, magic, and changelessly deep loyalties are suspiciously close to mental ill-health. Hence most scientists may overlook a phenomenon which is found often and in many diverse places. In this chapter I will try to identify cross-cultural regularities and discontinuities in the structure and action of secret societies, and discuss them as a specialized version of the general process of affiliation. The fact that secret societies are primarily male[1] I must take to be pertinent to the test of the male bonding hypotheses I have put forward. That initiations are frequently bizarre, cruel, and of profound significance to both members and aspirants suggest the im-

1. See Noel P. Gist, 'Secret Societies: A Cultural Study of Fraternalism in the United States', *The University of Missouri Studies*, 15, 4 (1 October 1940), p. 133; K. L. Little, *The Mende of Sierra Leone*, Routledge & Kegan Paul, London, 1951, p. 254; Camilla H. Wedgewood, 'The Nature and Functions of Secret Societies', *Oceania* (July 1930), p. 135; Murphy, 'Social Structure and Sex Antagonism', in op. cit., p. 90; Hutton Webster, *Primitive Secret Societies*, Macmillan, New York, 1932, pp. 1–21.

portance of the initiation process and the exclusivist and selective principle it functions to defend. The fact that membership is often voluntary perhaps underlines the important role of these societies in the social lives of their members. The usually unisexual composition of the groups emphasizes the special part they may play in members' and communities' socio-sexual equilibrium.

In the good open British political tradition, let me 'declare my interest' at the outset – such a declaration may be relevant to the ensuing discussion. I belong to no secret society and have not been a member of one. In general I tend to assume that openness is preferable to secrecy, and have generally regarded unisexual organizations of men, secret or otherwise, as oddly primitive, with a potential for so-called 'anti-social' behaviour. At my Canadian university I did not belong to a fraternity. It remains my belief that all-male groups are generally more likely to perform actions prejudicial to what, as a citizen, I regard as the good community. But during this study I have become increasingly aware that it is very possible that certain actions I think desirable are better done by all-male groups than by heterosexual ones. I had not expected to find as much material on secret societies as I did discover during this research. These data also led me to reconsider how much a person's reactions to male groups express some fundamental psychological condition, perhaps comparable to attitudes to sexual relations or to authority. Also – and here I can speak mainly in terms of Euro-American culture – it has come to seem that an abiding and tense concern with homosexuality has hindered social scientists from developing general notions about the positive value of male bonds, exclusive of any aggressive intent on which they may be focussed. To this, the study of secret societies and various similar kinds of men's organizations is directly pertinent.

1

In general, sociologists have seen secret societies, voluntary associations in industrial communities, youth movements, and some political opposition movements, as analytically separate matters. With the exception of Georg Simmel's seminal and yet still unsurpassed essays on secrecy and secret societies,[1] there has been little serious effort to assimilate analysis of these various types of social organization and

1. Wolff (trans. and ed.), *The Sociology of Georg Simmel*, op. cit., pp. 330–76. See also Nicholas J. Spykman, *The Social Theory of Georg Simmel*, Atherton Press, New York, 1966 (reissue of 1925 publication), for a useful summary and discussion of Simmel's work.

to see this particular form of affiliation as a discrete and predictable feature of human social behaviour.

Very extensive anecdotal literature on secret societies exists. The subject appears to be endlessly fascinating. New books emerge regularly, based on a tiresomely over-used body of original source material. But little attempt is made to provide explicit analysis. More often, as in Daraul,[1] a general statement of the interest and complexity of the matter precedes the standard recital of the facts about a representative group of the better-documented or more notorious societies.

There are some studies which provide both good data and some useful attempt at theoretical understanding.[2] While the points of view and explanatory schemes of these writers differ considerably, none seeks to relate this form of grouping behaviour to psychological or biological constants of 'human nature'. A major exception is Schurtz, whose *Alterklassen und Mannerbunde* describes an evolutionary scheme within which age grades and male groups form the component parts of the growth of 'higher development'. A less important analysis along these lines is Schmalenbach's.[3] Kropotkin regarded co-operative behaviour as a function of natural law. He sought to support his reading of Darwin, which stressed the group co-operative rather than

1. Arkon Daraul, *Secret Societies Yesterday and Today*, Muller, London, 1961, pp. 9–11.
2. For example, see Webster, op. cit.; F. W. Butt-Thompson, *West African Secret Societies*, Witherby, London, 1929; Charles W. Heckethorn, *The Secret Societies of All Ages and Countries*, George Redway, London 1897; Mervyn L. Wynne, *Triad and Tabut: A Survey of the Origin and Diffusion of Chinese and Mohammedan Secret Societies in the Malay Peninsula, A.D. 1800–1935*, Government Printing Office, Singapore, 1941; W. P. Morgan, *Triad Societies in Hong Kong*, Government Press, Hong Kong, 1960; E. J. Hobsbawn, *Primitive Rebels: Studies in Archaic Forms of Social Movement in the 19th and 20th Centuries*, Manchester University Press, 1959; Harry B. Hawthorn, 'A Test of Simmel on the Secret Society: The Doukhobors of British Columbia', *American Journal of Sociology*, 62, 1 (July 1956); R. F. Fortune, *Omaha Secret Societies*, Columbia University Contributions to Anthropology, 14, Columbia University Press, 1932; N. P. Gist, 'Secret Societies; a Cultural Study of Fraternalism in the United States', in op. cit.; Kenneth Little, 'The Role of Voluntary Associations in West African Urbanization', *American Anthropologist*, 59, 4, (August 1957); Wedgewood, 'The Nature and Function of Secret Societies', in op. cit.; Walter Z. Laquer, *Young Germany: A History of the German Youth Movement*, Routledge & Kegan Paul, London, 1962; Prince Peter Kropotkin, *Mutual Aid: A Factor of Evolution*, Heinemann, London, 1902; Stanford Lyman, 'Chinese Secret Societies in the Occident: Notes and Suggestions for Research in the Sociology of Secrecy', *Canadian Review of Sociology and Anthropology*, 1, 2 (1965).
3. Herman Schmalenbach, 'The Sociological Category of Communion', in Parsons, Shils, Naegele, and Pitt (eds.), *Theories of Society*, Vol. 1, The Free Press of Glencoe, Glencoe, Ill., 1962.

the individual–combative nature of biological selection. Like Schurtz, he argued that the male bond was an ancient and essential feature of human society.[1] As I have already noted, Carveth Read made the forthright proposition that man evolved as a pack-hunting carnivore – which he called Lycopithecus – and that the hunting bond was the basis of many of the central systems in contemporary human society.[2]

A major research effort of sociologists has been to understand the incidence of and behaviour in voluntary associations, particularly in industrial societies (though latterly a more catholic range of data reflects the increased physical mobility and comparative sophistication of social scientists). One of the chief foci of researchers has been the relationship of voluntary association to urban life; this has been based on the underlying conception that urban life is generally impersonal but made potentially personal through the mediation of voluntary and/or work organizations.[3] Another focus has been the establishment or testing of possible relationships between voluntary associative behaviour and characteristics such as class, educational level, race, etc.[4] Still another is the effort to relate participation in associations to personality characteristics which can be identified by standardized tests.[5] The work of Francis Hsu stresses the importance of culture in determining the rate, kind, and consequence of individuals' attachments to groups.[6] Hawthorn has reviewed and tested some of Simmel's theories about secret societies in the context of

1. Kropotkin, op. cit.
2. Carveth Read, op. cit.
3. For example, see Mirra Kamorovsky, 'The Voluntary Associations of Urban Dwellers', *American Sociological Review*, 11, 6 (December 1964); John C. Scott, Jr, 'Membership and Participation in Voluntary Associations', *American Sociological Review*, 22, 3 (June 1957); Kenneth Little, 'The Role of Voluntary Organizations in West African Urbanization', in op. cit.; Basil G. Zimmer and Amos H. Hawley, 'The Significance of Membership in Associations', *American Journal of Sociology*, 65, 2 (September 1959).
4. E. G. Murray Hausnecht, *The Joiners: A Sociological Description of Voluntary Association Membership in the United States*, Bedminster Press, New York, 1962; Howard E. Freeman, Edwin Novak, and Leo G. Reeder, 'Correlates of Membership in Voluntary Associations', *American Sociological Review*, 22, 5 (October 1957); Anthony M. Orum, 'A Reappraisal of the Social and Political Participation of Negroes', *American Journal of Sociology*, 72, 1 (July 1966); William M. Evan, 'Dimensions of Participation in Voluntary Associations', *Social Forces*, 36, 2 (December 1957).
5. David Horton Smith, 'A Psychological Model of Individual Participation in Formal Voluntary Associations', *American Journal of Sociology*, 72, 3 (November 1966).
6. Francis L. K. Hsu, *Clan, Caste and Club*, D. Van Nostrand, Princeton, N.J., 1963; see Chapter 7.

the political activities of the Doukhobor group, and the group's interaction with the larger community.[1]

I wish to discuss an approach to voluntary and secret society behaviour which is complementary to the above positions, but also idiosyncratic. It seems to me possible to claim that voluntary and secret society behaviour is – in its general form – a reflection of the same species-specific male bonding patterns referred to earlier. In this case, male bonding occurs in a relatively voluntary context, often without formal legitimacy from the community at large. The chief function of the societies for their members is to provide an opportunity for male affiliation under conditions both predictable and satisfying. The stress in secret societies 'above all other . . . [on] the division of labour and the gradation of their members with great finesse and thoroughness'[2] suggests the close links between social affiliation, the creation of hierarchies, and male bonding. The relationship between secret societies and the political order has been widely stressed, for example by Heckethorn,[3] Little[4] (for the Poro of Sierra Leone), and Simmel[5] (though Hawthorn[6] has indicated a useful revision of Simmel's formulation that: 'In general, the secret society emerges everywhere as the counterpart of despotism and police restriction, as the protection of both the defensive and the offensive in their struggle against the overwhelming pressure of central powers – not by means of political powers only, but also of the church, as well as of school classes and families').

Secret societies, in terms of my hypothesis, are the consequence of an effort of individuals – usually and mainly men – to create the social conditions for exercising their gregarious propensities, the expression of which may be (or may be seen to be) inhibited by their community. The clearest case of this is the political secret society. Another form is the religious secret society. Both share the characteristic that secrecy protects members from detection by authorities ecclesiastical and civil, and may also disguise the weakness or strength or the nature of members' activities. What is striking is that when a

---

1. Hawthorn, 'A Test of Simmel on the Secret Society', in op. cit.
2. Simmel, op. cit., p. 357.
3. Heckethorn, op. cit., pp. 4–5.
4. Kenneth L. Little, 'The Role of the Secret Society in Cultural Specialization', *American Anthropologist*, 51, 1 (January–March 1949). 'In the political field, the Poro exercises an over-riding influence which is both direct and indirect' (p. 204).
5. Simmel, op. cit., p. 347.
6. Hawthorn, 'A Test of Simmel on the Secret Society', in op. cit.

secret society operates within a culture from which (almost by definition) it seeks to dissociate itself, powerholders in that culture and other persons generally react to the society with great antipathy. The secret society has the capacity to stimulate aggression. So do official secret groups such as the C.I.A. or N.K.V.D. This is because the secret band is defined as a hostile group, potentially antipathetic to constituted authority in its unwillingness to yield to open authority and expose its workings. Though undoubtedly the function of secrecy is, as Simmel has so sensitively shown,[1] to create a line of demarcation between those who know the secret and those who do not, the bizarre and controversial history of secret societies suggests the additional possibility that a process of bonding and threat is related quite directly to processes of social life characteristic of much of human time and perhaps of prehistoric time.

Murphy has proposed, as I have already noted, that the diverse range of secret societies, men's houses, and so on are 'cultural forms (which) are clearly projections of unconscious materials and processes'.[2] My assessment of them is, rather, that they are relatively pointed and exaggerated examples of human aggressive-cum-male-bonding propensities. The isolation from females is one matter. The adoption of special dress, language, ritual, and moral structure by members of secret societies, and even by members of a men's hut, indicates the existence of a bonded group commitment and fellowship. This is a necessary condition and probably a stimulus for aggressive behaviour. As Lorenz has speculated, animals who bond are also animals who aggress.[3] The association may not be fortuitous. The mechanism of group formation is at the same time the mechanism for the stimulus of inter-group conflict. The conflict may be violent, symbolic, literary, or sublimated. But the process of group formation and then inter-group hostility is the underlying and significant one. A good analogy is with those youngsters who, having co-operatively formed teams to play games, then set about asserting one team's dominance over another. In some other species, the apparent connection between territorial, aggressive, hierarchical, and 'ganging' behaviour has been briefly discussed by Davis.[4] These various factors need not always be overtly present. For example, in some situations

1. Simmel, op. cit., pp. 330–44.
2. Robert Murphy, 'Social Structure and Sex Antagonism', in op. cit., p. 89.
3. Lorenz, On Aggression, op. cit., pp. 141–88.
4. David E. Davis, 'An Inquiry into the Phylogeny of Gangs', in Eugene L. Bliss (ed.), Roots of Behavior, Harper, New York, 1962, pp. 316–20.

secret societies such as the Ku Klux Klan may emerge to defend a way of life from threats to cultural patterns, values, etc., implied by groups living in the same territory but defined as alien. From the ethological point of view, secret societies and other more open forms of association may approximate the general process of ganging. It may be useful to inspect the behaviour in this light.

2

But why? Why not conclude that secret society activity is simply one kind of social pattern with no special meaning beyond the obvious? My ethological review of the matter stems from a more general 'hunch' (or immature theory) about the relationship of secrecy and bonding behaviour to the maintenance of legitimate social order. I have already outlined a conception of political order informed by material on primate and other animal social systems, and I tried to indicate profitable ways in which social scientists could look at human social behaviour as both programmed by heredity and constrained existentially by socio-cultural factors in any situation. The programmed aspect of behaviour especially preoccupied me – in as much as it is possible or desirable to separate the two dominant influences on behaviour, it is reasonable to seek information about both.

The outline of this theoretical overview of secret societies is as follows: humans are predisposed to live in relatively small-scale communities[1] where males control dominance systems. It has been suggested that significant cortical development was in fact a function of the elaboration of super- and sub-ordination responses[2] and that one feature of these responses is what Chance has called the 'attention structure' in a community.[3] Leaders must be seen, if not heard; every politician knows how essential it is for crowds to be able to simply *look* at politicians. In effect, John Kennedy was killed because he refused to use a protected car in Dallas on the grounds that he would be seen less easily by the people whose political approbation the unfortunate trip was supposed to elicit.[4] A similar process is at work when leaders such as the Pope or kings appear on balconies or platforms to enter into visual contact with their followers. In in-

1. Washburn, 'Conflict in Primate Society', in op. cit., p. 12.
2. M. R. A. Chance, 'Conflict in Animals and Man', in op. cit., pp. 32–3.
3. M. R. A. Chance, 'Attention Structure as the Basis of Primate Rank Orders', in op. cit., 1967.
4. See Graham Wallas, *Human Nature in Politics*, Constable, London, 1908.

dustrial society, it was probably the Nazis who were most skilled with the essentially ethological tools of political drama and spectacle. Non-industrial communities are, and were, equally adept students of the ethology of pageantry – the British National Theatre's gorgeous conception of Inca political pageantry in Schaffer's play *The Royal Hunt of the Sun* dramatized the power and effect of one great polity.

Communities are structured. Political order is more or less predictable or negotiable. But, at the same time, there is a strain towards non-structure, towards change, and towards the very elimination of even the concept of structure. Cohn has provocatively argued this case and his generalizations accord with not only human but to some extent with primate society as well.[1] Cohn's essential point is that in certain groups, such as of adolescents, and for certain activities, such as hunting, fishing, or warfare, social process is 'charismatic' rather than stratified. This is to say, it tends towards equality, lack of systematized allocation of privilege, rank, etc., and towards a free-flowing camaraderie which – significantly from our point of view here – is seen to have a 'homosexual tinge'. The other process of social stratification involves the unquestionable assertion of hierarchy, the recognition of social differences rather than similarities, and strong control over the universe of potential mates among the youths of various social classes.[2] Not only must stratification exist, it must also be seen to exist.

An excellent example of these two processes at work (though the author was apparently unaware of Cohn's formulation) is John Finlay Scott's study of the role of college sororities in the U.S. in ensuring class endogamy despite the 'charismatic' sexual possibilities available in large state educational institutions. This applies mainly to females whose chief interest in sororities is social and marital. Men who join fraternities appear to do so chiefly for potential professional reasons, though there is also a clear element of maintaining social class positions in the selection of specific candidates for specific fraternities.[3]

Fox and I have proposed that the question of 'charisma' may

1. Cohn, op. cit.   2. ibid.
3. See John Finlay Scott, 'The Role of the College Sorority in Endogamy', *American Sociological Review*, 30, 4 (August 1965). For a brief general discussion of this issue from a geneticist's viewpoint, see Theodosius Dobzhansky, *Mankind Evolving: The Evolution of the Human Species*, Yale University Press (paperbound edition), 1962, pp. 231–52.

possibly be approached from a biological point of departure;[1] we were encouraged in this enterprise by Max Weber's estimate of the relationship between biological and sociological analysis of such general processes as I am investigating here:

> In the latter field of phenomena [charisma and traditional action] lie the seeds of certain types of psychic 'contagion' and it is thus the bearer of many dynamic tendencies of social processes. These types of action are very closely related to phenomena which are understandable either only in biological terms or are subject to interpretation in terms of subjective motives only in fragments and with an almost imperceptible transition to the biological. But all these facts do not discharge sociology from the obligation, in full awareness of the narrow limits to which it is confined, to accomplish what it alone can do.[2]

It is possible to regard Weber's theory of legitimacy as a complex taxonomic system in the understanding of dominance behaviour. In such a system, 'charisma' is essentially a primitive attempt to rearrange dominance orders, or the correlative expression of an intense individual dominance drive of limited incidence in a population (as is, for example, high intelligence).[3]

Cohn and Weber thus express very similar conceptions of social order and the proneness to disorder or change of order. Cohn explicitly relates charisma to sexual motivation, and regards certain 'charismatic' groups as somewhat 'homosexual', though not necessarily erotic. ('Homosexual' refers to male camaraderie and ésprit rather than to specifically erotic contacts.) Weber ties the understanding of charisma to recognition of the limits of sociological analysis and knowledge of biological processes.

My view is that the whole issue is illuminated by seeing secret societies, men's houses, some voluntary associations, etc., as potentially 'charismatic' in circumstances in which there is impetus towards change in the dominance hierarchy. They are 'traditional', to use Weber's term, or 'stratified', to use Cohn's, in situations in which there is no such evident impetus and wherein the dominance patterns are established and legitimized at least temporarily. This

1. Tiger and Fox, 'The Zoological Perspective in Social Science', in op. cit., pp. 77–8.
2. Max Weber, *The Theory of Social and Economic Organization*, The Free Press of Glencoe, Ill., 1947, p. 106.
3. Tiger and Fox, 'The Zoological Perspective in Social Science', in op. cit., p. 78.

conception is based on the hypothesis that male bonding is a process with biological roots connected – in Lorenz's terms – to the establishment of alliances necessary for group defence and hunting. Simmel, Webster, Heckethorn, *et al.*, saw secret society formation in close relation to political opposition or subversion. This fits our general scheme.

When groups of men are satisfied with the allocation of power and its use and constraint they may create elaborate structures like the *Poro* of Sierra Leone or the societies of the Plains Indians. Initiation rituals, payments for promotion to higher grades, the extraordinary tribulations which candidates undergo – these are all features of a process of male-bond selection which is functionally equivalent and analogous to mate selection in the reproductive sphere. Indeed, the male bonding process, for which in these circumstances initiations are so important, may constitute a strong inducement to sever family-of-origin ties and circumscribe reproductive-family activity. An initiation ceremony may symbolize the actual break. 'An initiation ceremony, with its attendant physical pain and isolation from parents, demonstrates to the youngster that his nuclear family is no longer his sole protector, refuge, and security.' The strong emotion experienced by initiates generates identification with the group, while the fact that initiations are frequently done in groups not only cushions individuals from shock, but 'also produces an exceptionally strong bond among the initiates'.[1] A similar anti-family bond for adults is not uncommon; candidates for the Great Hung League in the Han Dynasty (about A.D. 185) uttered the following oath (before mixing their blood to affirm the contract): 'I swear that I shall know neither father nor mother, nor brother nor sister, nor wife, nor child, but the brotherhood along where the brotherhood leads or pursues, there shall I follow or pursue; its foe shall be my foe.'[2]

Christ's admonition that if need be his followers should reject all their familial ties in exchange for ties with his movement, is another significant example of male-bond selection. (The group of Apostles, led by Christ, is an illustration of the bonding phenomenon: the emphasis on symbolic eroticism, such as the washing of feet, touching of garments, etc., is revealing. So is the Apostles' attitude to females.)

1. Cohen, *The Transition from Childhood to Adolescence*, op. cit., pp. 110–13.
2. Given in Heckethorn, op. cit., p. 132.

It is clear from the work of Young, Eisenstadt, Cohen, and others how significant initiation ceremonies are for maintaining continuity in communities, and how closely linked initiation and age-grading are with establishing sexual and social identity among the young. This is particularly so in communities whose social patterns persist or appear to members to persist. It also applies to communities where social change only occurs normally within those limits of tolerance of possibility sanctioned by the legitimate leaders of the communities in question. Secret societies, men's houses, and initiation activities reflect one important way in which males are inducted into the groups within which they will work, fight, lead, follow, worship, or play.

But secret societies have also been the agency of more or less severe social change in many situations, and they have for long been the instrument of political revolutionaries. One general characteristic of secret societies, as I have noted, is that they excite the hostility of established authority. This may be simply the result of experience – governments know that in the past secret organizations have inconvenienced or overthrown established authority. Another simple reason is that governments require information about the activities of persons both within and without their territory; hence the elaborate detective and spying systems that virtually all governments maintain. Secret organizations constitute a challenge to – if nothing else – the professional skill of security agencies and must expect to have their secrecy threatened should the organizations become even slightly prominent and even mildly political.

But an additional explanation involves the very nature of the secret and the fact that the secret is maintained by and represented through a cohort of persons defined by contrast with the non-knowing community. At the risk of exaggeration, let me suggest that any group of persons who join together and agree to hold certain secrets, whatever these secrets are, and who permit their secrecy to be known or suspected, are committing an aggressive act which is bound to invite hostility and fear. In some communities secret societies are not only sanctioned but play critical functions in maintaining the *status quo*. In such communities they will be greeted by fear and respect. Thus, the women of Melanesia – supposedly terrified of the taboo *churinga* – sometimes try none the less to discover the secrets of the men's group, even though they can be punished by execution or by paying fines or being forced to have intercourse with all the men of the violated group.[1] In this and similar situations secrecy becomes a factor in maintaining dominance and social distance.

But where secret societies are not openly sanctioned – particularly by the dominants of the communities involved – the combination of secrecy and bonding appears to be an unambiguous inducement to hostility. In fact, a particularly easy way of exciting antipathy to a particular group in a population is to accuse it of involvement in a secret conspiracy. If the accused do not reveal the activities of the alleged secret group, this confirms that the conspiracy exists. If they do reveal something, it is proof that more remains secret. A recent and striking illustration of this phenomenon was the allegation that The Protocols of the Elders of Zion, now known to be originally a satirical document appropriated by anti-semites, represented a plot by Jews to subvert Christian communities. This, it has been argued, was an important initial factor in the Nazi justification of racial murder.[2] What was pertinent to The Protocols – that they were supposed to reflect a conspiracy – is common to many other situations; at least some members of any population seek in the spectre of conspiracy a persuasive and helpful explanation of the political and social worlds. The Orangemen, the Masons, the Ku Klux Klan, the Mafia, the Carbonari, etc., etc. – a long list of secret societies in communities with formally open political structures – have been held rightly or wrongly to be the protagonists of social disruption and the hosts of treason.[3]

In fact, secret societies have often indeed been the agency of political reform and revolution. For example, it is claimed that Asian

1. Johannes Falkenburg, Kin and Totem: Group Relations of Australian Aborigines in the Port Keats District, Oslo University Press, 1962, pp. 165–8.
2. Norman Cohn, Warrant for Genocide, Eyre and Spottiswoode, London, 1967.
3. There is an extensive literature on the reaction to secret societies. For example, Una Birch, Secret Societies and the French Revolution, Bodley Head, London, 1911; William F. Brainerd, Masonic Lecture, John Marsh, New London, 1825; Encyclopaedia Britannica, 11th Edition, Vol. 23, Cambridge, 1911, p. 886 (on the kylysti and skoptsi sects of Russia); Gershon Legman, H. C. Leam, T. Wright, G. Witt, Sir A. Tennant, and Sir W. Dugdale, The Guilt of the Templars, Basic Books, New York, 1966; Emerson H. Loucke, The Ku Klux Klan in Pennsylvania, Telegraph Press, New York, 1935; William Edward Smith, Christianity and Secret Societies, Meador Publishing Company, Boston, Mass., 1936; Charles E. Woodhouse and H. J. Tobias, 'Primordial Ties and Political Process in Pre-Revolutionary Russia: The Case of the Jewish Bund', Comparative Studies in Society and History, 8, 3 (April 1966); Norman Lewis, 'The Honored Society', New Yorker (8 February 1964); Hereward Senior, Orangeism in Ireland and Britain, 1795–1836, Routledge & Kegan Paul, London, 1966; Henri Le Caron, Twenty-five Years in the Secret Service, Heinemann, London, 1892.

secret societies have been involved in or responsible for the Taiping Rebellion of 1850; the Boxer Rebellion of 1900; and the Perak war in Malaya, 1874–5;[1] Sun Yat-sen[2] and the present government of China both used the support of extant secret societies – in China and abroad – in coming to power.[3] The so-called 'Red Hand' is described as having played a violent role in the conflicts over the independence movement in Tunisia. Hobsbawn has discussed the response to oppression of what he calls 'social bandits' (as opposed to 'millennarian' movements); among the former are the various groups of southern Italy, notably the Mafia, and the Terrorists of Bengal. In the American and French Revolutions, Masons were prominent.[4] Heckethorn cites the Internationale, the Fenians, the Communists, and the Nihilists, as revolutionary secret societies, while of political importance were the Mahdists, the Troubadors, the Vehm (of Westphalia in the thirteenth century), the Thugs and Assassins of India, the Chauffeurs of France, the Camora of Naples, the Communeros in Spain, the Carbonari of Italy, the anti-Napoleonic secret societies of France, the societies to which Mazzini of Italy belonged, the Irish societies, the Broederbund of South Africa, and the Ku Klux Klan. Less directly relevant to politics are the more or less secret guild societies of medieval Europe. These groups trained apprentices, protected guild members in situations lacking the predictable protection of the law (often under arms), and represented the trade's general interests. Occasionally this latter function was merged with overt politics; predictably this excited resentment more directly than the guilds' control of trade practices.[5]

Webster's view is that in communities where secret groups are legitimate the societies reflect the relative unsophistication of the political system and its lack of effective centralization.[6] This does not help to explain the processes underlying secret society behaviour, and in a different form represents a claim that political activity among individuals bearing some kinship relationship to each other is not really political but kinship behaviour. Webster also regards

1. W. L. Blythe, 'Foreword', in Wynne, op. cit., pp. xix–xxi.
2. Carl Glick and Hong Shenk Hwa, *Swords of Silence: Chinese Secret Societies – Past and Present*, McGraw-Hill, New York, 1947, p. 9.
3. A thorough review of political secret society activity in Asia is by Stanford Lyman, op. cit.
4. Hobsbawn, op. cit.
5. Henri Pirenne, *Early Democracies in the Low Countries*, Harper Torchbooks, New York, 1963, pp. 20–6.
6. See Webster, op. cit., pp. 74–80.

secret societies as characteristic of 'the primitive mind', a comment which presumably reflects the values of openness and democracy of his culture rather than his assessment of the relationship between the societies and human evolution.[1] It is interesting that few if any commentators say that secret societies are 'modern' as opposed to 'primitive'. Since many of these writers have assumed that a more or less unilineal progression from primitive to modern forms of social life can be identified – an assumption we must reject – possibly we can take their estimate that secret societies are 'primitive' as data to support the notion that these groups stimulate deep and persuasive emotions which symptomize their biological importance.

I am saying two things here: (1) That in communities where secret societies are legitimate the societies will play upon fear of the uninitiated (frequently because of the relationship supposed to exist between the societies, the community ancestors, and the gods)[2] and will serve as agents of social control. They will broadly support the existing political order. But also (2), where secret societies do not overlap with the authority structure or formally support it, they will be almost invariably regarded as hostile to the authorities and probably will be either kept under scrutiny or actively fought. This latter category includes the social bandits Hobsbawn describes, as well as avowedly criminal gangs who claim no other goals than self-enrichment by exploiting the weakness of others.

I am concerned here with the legitimacy of exploitative actions, not the fact of them. There is not a great deal of practical difference between the exploitation of Sicilian peasants for the profit of *Mafioso* and taxing peasants to support the high living of kings and nobles. Both systems are ultimately dependent upon the use of force and both offer no choice to the payers of tax. And of course legitimate and illegitimate systems may merge, as they have at certain times in certain parts of southern Italy. One of the more striking incidents was the facilitation by American occupation forces of the assumption of legitimate power by the Mafia after the Second World War, apparently because it was thought that the Mafia was the only organization sufficiently strong to prevent political gains by Italian Communists.[3] (The Italian film *Hands Across the City*, indicates the nature of collusion between some Italian politicians and illegitimate operators and the difficulty of breaking their alliance.)

Thus, in as much as such a dichotomy can be significantly

1. ibid., p. 106.　　　　2. ibid., p. 104.　　　　3. See Lewis, op. cit.

maintained, 'legitimate' secret societies reflect the social stratification process of community life, and illegitimate ones the charismatic process. At the same time, both manifest the male-bonding propensity: 'The admission of women is characteristic of the disintegration of the secret societies and their conversion into purely social clubs or magical fraternities.'[1] Females have created and maintained few secret societies, with the important exception of those supposedly connected with witchcraft and sorcery. A more typical pattern is for females to join affiliated organizations under the more or less careful supervision of the male counterpart. It does not seem to be true that males form affiliates of female organizations.

I do not claim that females have no organizations; obviously they join and are active in a great number of social and service clubs. But female organizations affect political activity far less than male ones do; in part, this reflects the fact that female groups are not typically secret, and that females generally exert less political influence than do males. Paradoxically, I am saying that on the one hand these societies represent 'non-rational' species-specific human propensities, and on the other, following Simmel,[2] that the self-consciousness and momentousness of the secret bond imply threat or power to non-members of the bond thus making a sophisticated statement of 'rational' social intentions. We can resolve this paradox by not opposing instinct to learning. Then, we can say that males consciously create secret groups for the gregarious and efficacious control of political, religious, and/or economic worlds, and for the enjoyment of male company under emotionally satisfying conditions. Such grouping exhibits the culturally learned and socially mediated manifestation of a broad biological feature of the male life cycle.

The proposal, then, is that secret societies (as well as comparable voluntary associations) are paradigm exponents of the male bonding pattern and its relationship to political order. The societies may relate closely to occupational solidarities. A particularly obvious case is the guild society. Individuals doing the same work co-operate broadly in

1. Webster, op. cit., p. 121.
2. 'The secret society . . . cannot allow its members to forget the distinct and emphatic consciousness that they form a *society*. In comparison with other associations, it is here the passion of secrecy – always felt and always to be preserved – which gives the group form, depending on it, a significance that is far superior to the significance of content. The secret society completely lacks organic growth, instinctive expansions . . . and all naïve, matter-of-fact feeling of belonging together and forming a unit' – Simmel, op. cit., p. 363.

the exploitation of their skills or property rather than competing without restraint. The importance of male societies to individuals undoubtedly varies from time to time and place to place. Likewise will communities vary in their tolerance or support of secret societies. I have indicated one way in which the kind of reception a community gives to political or quasi-political secret societies reflects the general nature of political dynamics in the community.

The political order's relationship to economic activity in hunting and other small-scale communities[1] offers a useful insight into the merger of political and economic roles. In more complex communities, secret and voluntary societies permit significant re-creation of the male social bond which proved so adaptive in millions of years of human evolution. An organization such as the Rotary Club (particularly in Britain) reflects the economic division of labour in any community by its membership and also permits the exercise of political skills internally and social-service skills externally. Here we may see a small-scale paradigm of male social interaction; the ubiquity of this interaction, even in situations – such as in working men's clubs in industrial communities – where no overt economic 'gain' results, suggests that the satisfactions are social. My effort has been to indicate how this social activity may permit the emergence of displaced economic–political solidarities in conditions where men's work lives and political roles do not provide adequate opportunity for solidly male interaction.

3

Of course, the argument rests on an assumption which cannot be easily tested. I am well aware of the possible tautology of any attempt to describe widely occuring behaviours as consequences of universal human propensities which themselves must by definition lead to the widely occurring behaviours. My method, it is clear, owes more to the enthusiastic shotgun than the slim sabre. Not that this particular approach is less acceptable than others. It simply requires for its scaffolding a wide variety of data, and these data may not seem to be directly related – such as male–female differences in political participation and the division of economic labour on sexual grounds. At the same time it is generally useful to reconsider sociological links

1. For a good and concise survey of political and economic patterns of some hunting peoples, see the 'Appendix' to Elman R. Service, *The Hunters*, Prentice-Hall, Englewood Cliffs, N.J., 1966.

between phenomena which may seem socially discrete. In this light I will turn briefly to initiation ceremonies.

The title of this chapter contains the phrase 'men court men'. I conceive of initiation ceremonies as factors in a process of selection which relates to political and economic hierarchies as sexual court-ship relates to reproductive hierarchies.[1] (I remind the reader here that I see social systems patterned in terms of specific propensities which are distributed in populations, presumably along the normal-curve line and conforming broadly to Darwinian principles of the relationship between individual differences and the survival of the species.) I want to examine the possibility that initiation ceremonies symbolize a concern men have with the qualities of courage, com-petence, and loyalty, of the young who will be their colleagues and successors. The concern of the males for the competence of the young men, I will suggest, is akin to the preference men have for women thought lovely by the community, or women who are talented, or powerful, wealthy, good mothers and wives, – in short, who are benign forces to involve in the homes of men.

At the outset, a distinction must be drawn. A human pattern which is possibly species-specific is a propensity to form hierarchies.[2] Initiations are obviously related to this tendency. It is not necessary to my argument to establish a practical difference between initiation into a work–defence–aggression complex and initiation into a status-

1. For a discussion of several of these ideas from a biologist's viewpoint, see J. Merritt Emlen, 'Natural Selection and Human Behavior', *Journal of Theoretical Biology*, 12 (1966), pp. 410–18. Emlen's argument is that there is a sound genetic basis for the proposition that initiation behaviour may be biologically patterned, and that the great recency of non-hunting human organization compels students of human evolution to regard possibly adaptive features of hunting organization, such as initiation-type selection procedures, as still effective in constraining contemporary behaviour.

2. Robin Fox and I will deal with the support for and implications of this statement in a forthcoming publication. There may also be a contrary process of equality-seeking which is similar to but not the same as Cohn's concept of 'charisma'. There seems to be rather more evidence of hierarchical as opposed to non- or anti-hierarchical behaviour, but this intriguing question must have more searching treatment than I want to give it here. Whether or not the propensity to form hierarchies is species-specific or not – and it is not such a bold claim to make given what is known about genetics and selective advantage – it seems reasonable to assert that humans are prone to make distinctions about each other, which is no more than to say they feel and symbolize about social relationships as they do about many other aspects of their environment. In this context my discussion of initia-tion as a quasi-biological device may seem more firmly grounded to those who would stress symbolic skills in seeking to understand human behaviour.

maintaining complex. But it may aid understanding if first I discuss initiation as a factor in allocating responsibilities associated with work and fighting. Then I will try to show what relationship there may be between initiation and maintaining personal or familial status.

In the previous chapter I described the importance of the male bond in human communities and suggested that its importance did not arise by chance, but by 'programming'. There were good biological as well as sociological reasons for trying to understand the function of this bond in the adaptation of societies to their physical environments, to other animals, and to other human beings. It has also been argued that 'universal physical changes in the human body at certain stages of development are accompanied by universal psychological effects'.[1] This is one of Cohen's assumptions. But on various grounds it may be seen as more substantial than an assumption. While the 'universal psychological effects' will vary between individuals and communities, we are concerned here again with similarities more than differences. Puberty is puberty: a real phenomenon, like eating or dying, about which it is possible to make generalizations. I cannot make generalizations about the individual's experience of puberty,[2] but possibly can about communal response to it. Presumably, if there are universal psychological effects, communities universally will contrive ways of dealing with them. The communal responses to such changes as occur at puberty or death, for example, vary enormously. But just as variation permits us to separate communities analytically, so must we also consider what common factors there may be as well as be able to describe and understand the differences.

Let us first set out a hard fact: observation and experience and extensive data allow us to say that men prefer to be surrounded by beautiful and available women rather than by aloof and unattractive ones – the sense of manliness is enhanced in one situation, depressed by the other. This is obvious. What is also obvious is that a profound and complex interaction occurs between the enviable man and his choice harem, and between the luckless other male and his less exciting friends. In general, men prefer attractive women and women prefer men who are attractive and powerful. To use the term without

1. Cohen, op. cit., p. 12.
2. For material on puberty, see Harrison, Weiner, Tanner, and Barnicott, op. cit., pp. 321–66.

perjoration, we are all sexual status-seekers, and this is an explicable and appreciable biologically based process.[1]

An analogy exists here with the relations between males; males will prefer to be with high-status males defined by their community as attractive rather than with the contrary. They gain status themselves from the positions of their companions. A group of men conscious of their status, power, and security differs in emotional tone from a group in the Bowery. Individuals possess self-respect or self-depreciation in terms of their group relationships and the status of their group. One of the functions of initiation ceremonies is, in these terms, the insurance of 'fit' or consonance between the males already in a group and the newcomers to it. A group of men is pleased with itself and with its status and quality. To affirm to its members and to outsiders that their recruits are worthy of membership, a process of initiation is contrived which involves stringent ordeals to test the courage and endurance of initiates. This proves or disproves their suitability and keenness to join. The initiation ceremony, then, is part of a male–male 'courtship' pattern tied to a tendency for males to seek status among other males, to form groups with them, and to value highly the corporate 'presentation-of-self' to the community at large. The implacable reality of this identification is suggested by the gangs in *West Side Story*: 'When you're a Jet you're a Jet' runs the song; the commitment is almost like a marriage. Significantly, Riff, who is unwilling to join in the gang's fight because his future wife wishes him not to, finally fights despite his peaceful intentions. In an interesting reworking of the Lysistrata theme, the conflict between the demands of women and the demands of men is one of the foci of this musical. The song 'Keep Cool' suggests the importance of self-control and corporate loyalty as the men prepare to fight. Robert Ardrey has suggested the significance of the musical in

1. There will be some who, for various reasons, prefer culturally unpreferred persons. The rich white girl and her poor Negro chauffeur of Richard Wright's *Native Son* is a case in point; many of William Faulkner's stories revolve about a similar deliberate violation of socio-sexual norms. This phenomenon seems closely related to Cohn's 'charismatic' process and can be seen as an implied comment about the coercive rigour of the stratification system at any time in any community. An important feature of the Christian ethic is the belief that it is to the weak, the deprived, the ill-formed, and the outcasts to whom Christians owe their first loyalty. Again, this is a charismatic process. When the churches – as they frequently do – align themselves with the rich and powerful instead of the poor and weak, the theological purists or idealists complain in disillusion about churches' participation in the secular process of social stratification.

describing the territorial habits of young men and 'naturalness' of the aggression and gang hierarchy; the play also reflects the tension between males and females over war, and illustrates the dynamics of male bonding with vividness and understanding of the meaning of bonding for the men involved.[1]

Initiation is a courtship in the same sense that privileged men are more likely to marry equally desirable women. The superior male groups can attract the best candidates, can insist upon the most rigorous entrance ordeals, and can provide the greatest satisfaction and rewards for the membership. The *Alte Herren* of the élite German student duelling society, the Deutsche Burschenschaft, 'who include such diverse figures as the CDU Minister of the Interior, Hoescherl, and the SPD Prime Minister of Lower-Saxony, Giederichs, not only finance fraternities but are said to find jobs for members and generally operate as a closed society. To be expelled from a fraternity can still mean social ruin: to belong means life-long protection and obligation.'[2]

A comparable process appears to occur in some North American fraternities. How potential members are selected by the various individual fraternities on a campus is of interest here. At a number of review sessions with candidates, sometimes called 'ding'[3] sessions, fraternities and potential initiates seek to match each other. There are variations in membership fees, standards of living, dress, entertainment, etc., between fraternities, which complicate the process of 'fit' between initiates' socio-economic position and the fraternities. 'Fit' is generally achieved, though there are individual cases of upward mobility involving persons who work part-time to maintain

1. Robert Ardrey, *African Genesis: A Personal Investigation into the Animal Origins and Nature of Man*, Collins, London, 1961, pp. 330–1.
2. Corinna Adam, 'Duels and Jobs for the Boys', *New Statesman* (18 June 1965), p. 952. It is still necessary to receive a scar in duelling to validate membership, though now it may be a tiny scar which none the less retains its symbolic value.
3. This is based on a study of fraternities at the University of British Columbia, which from other information appears to be not untypical of the North American institutions except in so far as the fraternity system is less rigid and somewhat less important to student politics than in most other similar institutions where fraternities are permitted. A new president of the university tried to have the fraternities removed from their buildings near the campus because the land was needed for other construction, but influential men in the city of Vancouver evidently blocked this move through the University Board of Governors, which is composed mainly of businessmen. Incidentally, the word 'ding' is also used as a slang synonym for penis.

those standards informally but firmly applied to all members of each fraternity. Welcoming entertainments mixed with hazing activities occupy initiates until the final initiation takes place. By this time both parties are more or less committed to the bonding.

The initiations themselves frequently involve partial or complete nudity of initiates, and in many there are homo-erotic implications of greater or lesser clarity.[1] One fraternity in the U.S. evidently brands its members. Another conducts this ceremony: the pledges are stripped and stand in front of an open fire in which several branding irons are conspicuously heating. Pledges are then blindfolded and asked questions such as, 'Do you really want to join the ***** fraternity? Why do you? Are you worthy? Are you willing to be hurt for the fraternity?' It is rare for an individual to withdraw his candidacy at this point. Then the candidate is told he is to be branded, the branding irons are withdrawn from the fire and plunged into a bucket of cold water to create a hissing noise at the same time as a cold iron is jabbed against the buttock of the candidate. He is then a member. Another fraternity strips pledges and ties bricks to their penises; after being blindfolded the pledges are asked to pick up and throw the bricks without knowing that the strings attached to their penises have just been cut. In Montreal I once encountered a group of about ten men wearing dinner jackets and looking drunk but exhilarated. They were carrying another of their number whom they were pummelling as they dragged him along the sidewalk at the busy corner of Peel and Sherbrooke Streets, near McGill University. A good burgher, I looked more closely and noticed he was bleeding from the face and tried to stop them from hitting him any more. The pledge protested at my action, saying, 'Leave me alone, I'm being initiated,' and one of his tormentors said, 'It's nothing, it's just fun.' Suddenly a car appeared and all eleven men pushed their way into it and veered away through a red light. Interestingly, when pledges are finally received into the group they may don a fraternity ring, usually worn on the third finger of the left hand (which is either unconsciously symbolic or a capricious tradition of no significance).

A professional colleague has described to me the following initiation he experienced in a fraternity at Cornell University. It is almost a parody of the symbolizations implicit in many initiations. Before the ceremony pledges are required to find a variety of objects with

1. I am grateful to Stanford Lyman for information and discussion on fraternity affairs.

sexual connotations. These are brought to the ceremony. Included are a five-inch nail and a bottle of Vaseline. Pledges are ranged in a circle facing in. Behind each pledge is a senior member of the fraternity. In a progression articulated with various vows and statements, the pledges remove all their clothes. They are handed their nails and Vaseline and told to grease the nails and pass the nails back to the seniors behind them. The room is now dark. Then they are told to bend over, in effect presenting their buttocks to the seniors. The right hand is placed on the right buttock and the left hand extended back to the senior, to receive the nail, but a can of beer is placed in the hand, the lights come on, the pledges dress, and a drinking party begins. It is difficult to avoid mentioning the superficial parallel between this ceremony and the pattern, among some primates, of dominant males briefly mounting subdominants; this appears to define or redefine status. By contrast, a female of the same university described a sorority initiation during which pledges wear white floor-length garments and vow to be true to the sorority and to the ideals of virtue – in particular, chastity. This formal idea was frequently denied informally by the parties held in the sorority to celebrate the deflowering of various members.

These are, of course, relatively mild ordeals. Military ones may be far more severe. For example, the training of novice U.S. Marines at one period in the 1950s culminated in a number of deaths through fatigue, over-exposure, and illness. Entrants to certain military academies will have their heads shaved and will be subjected to an elaborate hazing and fagging process by their seniors and by instructors. In one situation, entrants are required to stand stiffly at attention while any senior can punch the entrants' stomachs as hard and often as he wishes. Webster believes puberty rites and comparable rituals are not merely sadistic: '. . . it is more likely that in many cases what we regard as merely tests of courage and endurance were once of deeper significance and were imposed originally for religion or magical purposes'. Ordeals can include: depilation, head-biting, evulsion of teeth, sprinkling with human blood, drinking of human blood, immersion in dust or filth, heavy flogging, scarification, smoking and burning, circumcision and subincision.[1] In one American Indian group, aspirant braves were hung by thongs pierced through their pectoral muscles and could not utter a sound of complaint. In English public schools initiation rites humbled the will of the

1. Webster, op. cit., pp. 35–6.

newcomer and induced him to accept authority unquestioningly.[1] A pledge to an American fraternity was killed in his initiation ceremony. He was brought to the edge of a high cliff, turned around a number of times and told that if he trusted his fraternity brothers totally, he should step to the left. He stepped to the right and fell to his death.

The lists of punishments and humiliations suffered by candidates for initiation into societies around the world is an immense catalogue of ingenious perversities, rigorous ordeals, and bizarre demonstrations of subordination.[2] This is largely a male phenomenon. The initiations of females are generally less violent:

> . . . for females restrictions are generally at the level of minimal social recognition, whereas for males they go beyond that to the level of personal dramatization. This fact supports the generally held impression that female role recognition, in contrast to that for males, is more often accomplished by restriction than by prescription. This conclusion is further indicated that 'ritual performances of the initiate' . . . are proportionately less frequent for girls than for boys.

Young also notes that 'female initiation rarely involves an organized group', except that 'it is the family that is the point of reference, rather than the adult members of one or the other sex'.[3] In comparison with the grim ceremonies of male fraternities, sorority initiations are more socially than individually oriented, and involve considerably less harsh demands on pledges. For example, in a Canadian college sorority, the initiation consisted in gathering a list of names, addresses, and telephone numbers of twenty-five male

1. Rupert Wilkinson, *The Prefects: British Leadership and the Public School Tradition*, Oxford University Press, 1964, pp. 32–8. Wilkinson makes the interesting point that there is more internal dissension in the Labour than in the Conservative party because fewer Labour members have been exposed to the stern necessity of accepting authority which public school boys quickly learn. In the public school one 'could closely identify love of community with deference to senior office'. This is presumably a common function or attempted function of initiation-type processes, and it is a necessary concomitant of the testing–selection function. Groups do not normally select junior members who will oppose the group leaders' will. This is undoubtedly a major reason for the conservatism of men's groups to which Webster refers in which initiations are particularly important (op. cit., p. 60).

2. A good discussion is by Harold Garfinkle, 'Conditions of Successful Degradation Ceremonies', *American Journal of Sociology*, 61, 5 (March 1956).

3. F. W. Young, *Initiation Ceremonies*, op. cit., pp. 18–41.

students. In another, as they walked around the campus, pledges were required to wear haloes about their heads and large signboards giving their name, course, and telephone number. This is not to say that clitoridectomy and scarification where they occur are not painful and harrowing to individual females. But the overall social process involved does not typically seem to demand as great tolerance of fear, pain, loneliness, etc., as the process of male initiation.

One of the female initiations which is sometimes thought to be painful is defloration. An abiding and complex interest in virgins and their undoing remains as much a preoccupation today as in eighteenth-century London.[1] Any cursory study of contemporary 'hard-core' pornography reveals the concern with the first intercourse. This action is frequently compelled by a brutal male, sometimes in an orgiastic setting, and followed usually either by intense pleasure or loathing once the pain of defloration subsides. It is not clear if defloration implies initiation into a male or female world, though it is a significant rite of passage for the female in many cultures. Margaret Mead speculates that the variation in thickness of the hymen may have survival value and that the fact that the human is the only species to have a hymen indicates the possibility that 'the hymen itself may be regarded as discouraging complete sexual relations with immature males incapable of rupturing it or as making first intercourse . . . sufficiently conspicuous and recognizable so that social regulation is possible. . . . The existence of the hymen does . . . give a clue as to the functional value of prolonging the childhood period well beyond puberty.'[2] Cohen suggests that prohibition on childhood intercourse may reflect similar awareness of the danger which the crisis of intercourse and particularly orgasm may involve for the insecure ego.[3]

As Allen has proposed, it is necessary to distinguish between puberty and initiation rites. Secrecy is intrinsic to the latter and not necessarily to the former.[4] Cohen distinguishes between the social response to the first stage of puberty, which normally occurs between ages eight to ten – when the most important developmental changes happen – and the second stage of emergence of secondary sexual

1. See Fernando Henriques, *Prostitution and Society*, Vol. 2, MacKibbon & Kee, London, 1963, p. 146.
2. Margaret Mead, 'Cultural Determinants of Sexual Behaviour', in Young (ed.), op. cit., pp. 1464–5.
3. Cohen, op. cit., pp. 121–2.
4. Allen, op. cit.

characteristics. The first stage is the more significant for the individual and the community, and more care and attention will be paid to it than to the second. In the first stage the crucial break with the nuclear or immediate family takes place. In the second, the *rites de passage* into adulthood are marked by ceremonies of a more elaborate kind.[1] One signifies the end of social childhood, the other the onset of social adulthood and full or growing participation in the world of adults. Co-educational ceremonies are relatively unusual; only in communities such as America or England are bisexual *rites de passages*, such as school graduations, somewhat common. Even in these communities, segregated school systems or ritual patterns external to the school system (sweet sixteens, debuts, bar mitzvahs, etc.) may emphasize sexual role differences in a limited way.

Of course, it is predictable that at or around puberty boys and girls will be socialized into the socio-sexual roles appropriate to any community, and it is certainly difficult to identify the psychological and possible biological mechanisms which are at work during initiation periods. Conceivably there is a 'critical period' involved here. Perhaps the changes of puberty are accompanied by particular susceptibility to role models of the same sex in the same way as there is a change in response to sexually mature persons of the opposite sex. After all, there is no *prima facie* reason why pubescent males should not form biologically based bonds of the kind I have been describing if they also have a new capacity to relate to females in a relatively mature if ephemeral way. Initiation ceremonies may constitute a communal response to this new uni-sexual responsiveness – particularly of males, if the data about incidence, severity, style, etc., of initiation ceremonies is any indication. Socially sanctioned ways of bonding are provided which resolve any ambiguity adolescents may experience about their new roles.

In this sense, juvenile delinquency may be some adolescents' response to ambiguous adult roles in communities which lack articulated rituals of the initiation kind. While this is a speculative diagnosis, perhaps the failure to provide adolescents with explicit specially visible ceremonies of initiation may lead to subsequent behavioural disturbance, which results from deprivation similar to that described by Harlow for newborns. Of course, infants are in most ways far more impressionable than adolescents. But a number of appreciable biological processes occur at adolescence which may have effects on

1. Cohen, op. cit., pp. 47–60.

brain function and social behaviour.[1] Conceivably, establishing certain formalized peer group bonds and receiving sanctioned instructions about adult socio-sexual roles at the 'critical period' of adolescence are necessary to channel behaviour in an appropriate way. The much greater incidence of male as opposed to female delinquency suggests that there are important differences in the ease of socializing or 'initiating' males in communities which are so complex as to render quite useless initiations into predictable and sanctioned male careers.

It has been suggested that initiation ceremonies

. . . also appear to express an envy of the female role. For example, the initiation is often culturally perceived as a rebirth ritual in which men take a child and bring about his birth as a man by magical techniques stolen long ago from women. These techniques would lose their magical efficacy if women were ever to observe them. The need for the initiate to prove his manhood by bearing extreme fatigue and pain without complaint appears to indicate some uncertainty in sex identity.[2]

While this interpretation may be valid in part, I prefer Young's.[3] He sees initiation ceremonies fulfilling social rather than psychogenic functions, and his arguments more readily apply within the cross-cultural and cross-specific biological context I have sketched. Though Young does not accept a biological explanation such as I have outlined,[4] his argument and interpretation provide greater scope and coherence for the use of the type and range of data with which I have been concerned than the more explicitly psychogenic approaches of D'Andrade, Whiting, et al. This is not to say that psychogenic factors play no important role in the social processes under analysis here. Indeed, the bonding phenomenon and its relationship to the assumption of adult socio-sexual roles clearly expresses individual psychological development. There will be individual differences in this process just as in any other.

I have focussed on specifically *social processes* which none the less depend upon *individual development patterns*. This focus should permit

1. See David A. Hamburg and Donald T. Lunde, 'Sex Hormones in the Development of Sex Differences in Human Behaviour', in Eleanor E. Maccoby (ed.), op. cit., for discussion of the possible general effects of specific physiological events.
2. Roy G. D'Andrade, 'Sex Differences and Cultural Institutions', in ibid., p. 196.
3. Frank W. Young, *Initiation Ceremonies: A Cross-Cultural Study of Status Dramatization*, Bobbs-Merrill, New York, 1965.
4. F. W. Young, personal communication.

some resolution of the traditional disparity between the two approaches. I cannot pretend I have made the best possible case for using the zoological perspective in assessing initiation behaviour. This would require a monograph of its own and wider familiarity with relevant ethnography and theory than I have been able to acquire in the course of developing some more general conceptions and propositions. Though I have chided others and myself in advance for presuming to await further research as a solution to problems such as I have raised here, more to the point might be a detailed theoretical review of secret societies from a zoological viewpoint, and it is to this review that my part of the division of labour has been directed.

4

This chapter cannot conclude without my comment that I do not know what kind of biological mechanisms would operate should there in fact be a biological basis for secret societies, initiations, clubs, and so on. It is difficult to specify the central constituent of the bonding process. This is, of course, the critical gap in the argument. By analogy, I am saying something very much like: ape looks at bananas near cage, cannot reach them by hand or with either of two sticks in his cage, but *thinks* of the solution of combining the sticks and sweeping in the bananas. But I can identify no bonding phenomenon comparable to cognition.

I have already referred to suggestions that cortical–amygdaloid evolution was associated with pertinent patterns of hierarchy formation and the inhibition of intra-group aggression. Closely associated with this is the apparently general association of relatively intense emotional experience during initiations, in secret societies, and between members of formalized male bonds. It is a finding of ethology that strong emotion tends to occur during behaviours of biological importance: that is, behaviours which are basic to the nervous systems of the animals concerned and thus which in the logic of evolution reflect relatively early and crucial adaptations. Another clue may be the primarily male and generally unisexual character of the organizational forms with which I have been dealing. This need not only result from biological propensity but from the obvious need in any culture to differentiate the sexes, if only to surround the process of reproduction with reliable social structural supports. Another clue, already considered earlier, is the curious association of bonding with a concern for blood initiations, with nudity, with the attribution to groups of animal names and symbols, with the ability to kill in the initiations of some hunting societies, and (particularly in Euro-America cultures) with the drinking of alcohol.[1] All these phenomena may connect with the hunting history of man and with the relationship between male bonding and hunting behaviour. Raymond Dart has suggested that Australopithicines may have drunk the blood of the animals or conspecifics they killed.[2] Do cups and trophies given to winners bear any relationship to this kind of suggestion? I remember photographs of hockey players drinking out of the Stanley Cup awarded to winners of the National Hockey League Championships. I have already noted the symbolic importance of mugs to fraternity members and 'regulars' in clubs and pubs, and the considerable role of drinking in men's groups in many cultures. While it is very much a suggestion, is there some relationship between human hunting history and contemporary drinking behaviour – particularly of the 'clubby' and 'hail-fellow-well-met' variety? In the military, 'drinking level' is an important mode of social control of drinking and of establishing group norms. It is part of folklore that persons who drink alone are especially prone to alcoholism. Is it possible that group drinking facilitates male bonding among inhibited individuals (who also believe that alcohol eases the often complex process of heterosexual liaison)?

But these various factors, singly or together, do not combine to provide specific information about the specific mechanism of bonding. We do not know if the 'morale' of a group of fighting, working, or drinking men is reducible to mechanisms similar to sexual attraction between males and females. We cannot say if successful leaders stimulate 'followership' behaviour in essentially the same way that attractive females evoke sexual interest among males. Even more difficult is it to say that the series of behaviours discussed here rest on a definable physiological platform of action equivalent to thinking or digesting or loving. Indeed, various explanations have already been

1. The young boys in Golding's astonishing novel, *Lord of the Flies*, distinguish among themselves between the hunters who have killed, in this case the 'Beastie', and those who have not. Golding makes this a distinction which goes beyond the purely technical and which is connected to his general conception of man and society as expressed through the book. In the next chapter, on aggression, I will discuss the book in more detail because it is such a searching and influential symbolization of many of the processes with which I am involved.
2. Raymond Dart, 'The Minimal Bone-Breccia Content of Makapansgat and the Australopithicine Predatory Habit', *American Anthropologist*, **60**, 5 (October 1958).

WAYNESBURG COLLEGE LIBRARY
WAYNESBURG, PA.

advanced by others for the behaviours I have discussed, and some of these have the merit of considerably greater specificity and demonstrability than I can claim at this point in time and knowledge. However, the search for a biological mechanism for male bonding in secret societies and initiations may be no more arbitrary, quixotic, or unstrategic than the search for a specific mechanism at the base of 'identification' or 'sexual identity' or other useful comparable concepts. I have indicated here how social forms hitherto considered chiefly cultural as opposed to biological may in fact represent culturally variable items of a relatively non-varying biological scheme. If it exists, a reifiable cause must presumably await the results of the interdisciplinary research to which Hamburg and Lunde hopefully refer.[1]

A few writers, such as Kropotkin, Schurtz, and Read, contemplated the possibility that male bonding was an intrinsically biological matter. But, in general, the social forms I have been discussing have been considered expressions of cultural variability – the result of the interaction of individual choice, community traditions, and possibly economic system. In one sense this is understandable, given the fact that the groups in question may not 'do' anything to alter the physical environment or affect the social environment by changing rather than maintaining it. Indeed, part of my argument depends on the notion that male grouping behaviour in the forms discussed is a substitute for 'real' hunting or defensive behaviour. I realize this implies a concept such as 'social sublimation' or 'organizational displacement' – some phrase which contains the meaning of 'a social organization which exists in a society to serve as the communal vehicle for the manifestation of propensities of individual life cycles'. Given the difficulty of adequately demonstrating the existence of sublimation on the individual level – if, indeed, there is such a process – it is ambitious to propose that groups may reflect sublimation patterns.

On the other hand, it may be easier to identify functional equivalents in the social world than in individual worlds, if only because of the larger numbers of people involved and the grosser patterns involved at the social level. For example, aggressive propensities may become reflected through the Apostles in the Church militant rather than a direct attempt to achieve political change in colonial Jerusalem; the Ku Klux Klan is in a real sense a sublimated government-cum-army. As I have suggested, the antipathy to secret societies

1. Hamburg and Lunde, op. cit., p. 21.

in communities where they are not sanctioned is that it may be recognized that they wish to be the government and it is feared the wish may become the deed. Sports teams, neighbourhood gangs, drinking groups, and so on, are perhaps fairly evident 'social-organizational sublimations' for the old hominid pattern of ganging, hunting, triumphing, and politicking, set in terms of a very small and local milieu.

Secret societies and initiations are dramatic enough, but they lead us to the equally or more dramatic matter of fighting and aggression. Men may hang around a pub and drink and while away their time discussing sports or politics or cars or sex or shop. They are doing something. But it is not as impressive in the biological as well as cultural sense as when they are fighting each other, planning to fight, living in armed hate and fear of another group, or hoping to kill the other group to take its land or wealth or crush its ideology. There is a growing body of material on the corporate nature and possibly 'instinctive' basis of aggression. Perhaps we can turn now to consider the relationship between maleness, male bonding, and aggression. At the same time, we must bear in mind – and I will not be loath to strew reminders in the reader's path – that possibly the behaviours discussed in this chapter and the next are analogical vertebrae of the same analogical spinal cord to which I have attached so much significance and which I am not yet willing to return to its closet.

CHAPTER SEVEN

Man, Aggression, and Men

Perhaps the most gruesome of all commonplaces is that human beings have always killed each other. Faced by this, people have contrived a number of theories and displayed a variety of responses. Of the theories, the two most simple and most pervasive ones are: humans kill each other because it is in their nature to kill; and, humans kill because circumstances force them to – when social and psychic conditions improve, killing will stop. Whatever theory predominates in any community, virtually all nations – weak and powerful – fear that killing will continue. To forestall the victimization of their own citizens, all nations expend money on arms and the bearers of arms. Not only money, but remarkably enormous sums of money. During wars what appears to be limitless wealth is destroyed and the careers, bodies, and sensibilities of legions of soldiers are afflicted by conflict. The essential nature of peacetime communities may be altered to suit warlike purposes. For some luckless nations arms, violence, and destruction have marked the rhythm of life for years. For more fortunate nations, the manufacture and management of armed power is a critical function of government, and the symbolic violence inherent in standing armies or ready striking forces takes the place of actual conflict.

That war is so costly and so terrible and yet so difficult to avoid is at the heart of the human uncertainty about the roles of caprice, reason, and despair in influencing social action. Recently there has been a revival of an ancient interest in the possibility that conflict between peoples and between nations results from a species-specific propensity. A relatively enthusiastic public response and guardedly interested academic one presumably results from eagerness to know about war and aggression in a nuclear-and-missile age – an age in which almost all individuals are unable to determine directly the conditions of their own safety. Additionally, there have been attempts to discuss war and aggression in terms of new data and theories of human evolution and the bio-psychological processes underlying social behaviour.

In this chapter I consider the role which biological and experiential factors play in motivating, consummating, and inhibiting war and aggression. My central concerns are: socio-sexuality and the male bond, sexual differences in aggression, and the role of co-operation among males and among males and females in making aggression feasible.

It is possible to be concrete about empirical situations to exemplify theoretical positions. But it is not possible to approach certainty in any considering of the phylogenetic basis of human aggression. As Hinde has commented,

> . . . it is easy for the sociologist, the respectability of whose discipline has perhaps not yet gained general acceptance, to forget that biology, and indeed all worthwhile sciences, also will have their problems; not all data are secure, not all interpretations universally accepted. These dangers are nowhere more marked than in the study of man's aggressiveness.[1]

This being so, it is necessary to proceed cautiously from example to principle and from notion to proposition. It is also necessary to examine with both due process and some generous leeway the possible routes of investigation along which cautious detailed study will be worthwhile or not. Here, I will follow a theoretical path which connects maleness and aggression to see in what ways, if any, it is worth more elaborate attention.

1

A number of imposingly interconnected phenomena are involved in the study of aggression. Probably among humans, and among some other animals certainly, territoriality is an important factor in locating aggressive traffic and defining aggressive groups. There appears to be some relationship between hierarchy and aggression, between the life cycle and aggression, between frustration and aggression. Some cultures sanction overt aggression more than others; it is necessary to examine how aggression is learned, and in what circumstances,

1. Robert A. Hinde, 'The Nature of Aggression', *New Society*, 9, 231 (2 March 1967).

before affirming that there is a causal link between aggression, its inhibition, and other factors in learning. The complicated human process of symbolization and communication which is intrinsic to any war or street fight or diplomatic threat is not yet understood sufficiently well to permit clear statements about any biological features of the process of symbolic aggressive interaction. It is evident that human males and females differ in the way they participate in organized aggressive action. But it is not even clear how, why, when, and within what limits of variability males and females are biologically different.

I will restrict myself chiefly to discussion of maleness and the male bond in aggression. I define 'aggression' as a process of more or less conscious coercion against the will of any individual or group of animals or men by any individual or group of people. At its broadest, the process is similar to chopping a tree, damming a river, or uprooting a yam – it involves the intervention by human agency in a situation or pattern. In its more complex meaning, the definition implies the imposition of martial law, religious orthodoxy, the establishment of consumer needs through advertising campaigns, the killing of enemy troops, winning a game of football, promoting a pop song on to the hit parade, or fighting an election. There is no necessary element of ferocity, viciousness, or destructiveness; the only necessary condition is that there be 'willed agency'. I am clearly making a rather close association between aggression and change – indeed, between aggression and action and between aggression and forms of competition. Such a definition is possibly closer to the conceptions of existential psychologists than to ethologists. But this seems justifiable in establishing a definition of aggression which is appropriate for humans. Co-operative or individual social action in its various forms is integral to the distinct hominid way of life. Here, the reference is to a particular form of action which involves the person's or group's self-assertion against, or in terms of, its environment.

I seek a useful distinction between aggression and violence – quite a different phenomenon from my perspective. 'Aggression' is a social-organizational term referring to a process, while 'violence' describes an event which is only one possible outcome of the aggressive process. Aggression occurs when an individual or group see their interest, their honour, or their job bound up with coercing the animal, human, or physical environment to achieve their own ends rather than (or in spite of) the goals of the object of their action. Violence may occur in the process of the interaction. Violence is most obvious when it is physical; unless noted otherwise, the term here will refer to coercion involving physical force to resolve conflict between coercer and coerced. For example, laundries may compete by advertising, service, and prices to secure contracts for servicing restaurants; in my sense, they are aggressing against their competitors. But Mafia-controlled laundries in the United States may use 'muscle', window-breaking, arson, etc., to win laundry contracts from firms not employing these means of securing business. In this case, violence is an incident in the process of commercial (aggressive) competition.

Obviously it is difficult to create a hard and all-embracing distinction between violence and aggression. Is the group of hunters aggressive or violent who bring down an ungulate with poison arrows? Is the manager of an electric console aiming missiles aggressive or violent? What is the driver in a hurry who passes another driver in a hurry on a crowded highway? Each of these can be argued in terms of the distinction, but I cannot regard the terminology of the distinction as in itself especially significant. What is significant is the statement of difference between effective action which is part of a process of mastery of the environment, and that particularly intimate form of mastery which involves the violation of an organism's personal space and the infliction of physical pain. The reason for making the distinction should become clearer later in the chapter. Here I want to suggest that, conceptually, aggression must be dissociated from violence. This allows more general use of the term 'aggression' so that it refers to a process rather than an event. Sociologically it implies a mode and direction of social organization rather than an actual circumstance of intimate intrusion. I want to regard aggression as a 'normal' feature of the human biologically based repertoire, a type of behaviour intrinsic to man's being and to his effective interaction with his social environment. Violence is not necessarily part of all or any of these.

Let us use one further set of distinctions. Aggression can be directed against one of three broad phenomena: the physical environment, other animals, and humans. I will try to show how each category elicits different responses, and why systematic and predictable confusions between categories may arise.

Human aggression is in part a function of the fact that hunting was vitally important to human evolution and that human aggression is typically undertaken by males in the framework of a unisexual social bond of which participants are aware and with which they are concerned. It is implied, therefore, that aggression is 'instinctive' but also must occur within an explicit social context varying from culture to culture and to be learned by members of any community. I suggest that males bond in terms of either a pre-existent object of aggression, or a concocted one. Aggression-out results from the bonding of males, perhaps analogically in the same way that eroticism-within results from the continued association of most sexually active males and females. Men in continuous association aggress against the environment in much the same way as men and women in continuous association have sexual relations. I am not claiming quite the same thing as Lorenz – that social bonds are necessarily accompanied by inter-specific aggression[1] (a principle which applies cross-specifically) and that each individual has a fund of aggression which must be expressed either by intra- or inter-specific aggression.[2] Rather, I am suggesting that human aggression in its social organizational sense is a propensity of males. It is most efficiently and effectively 'released' or stimulated by association with other males. Put a healthy male and female or even several of each into a relatively isolated place, and if they are members of a culture which sanctions or but mildly inhibits pre- or extra-marital intercourse, there will be sexual congress. Similarly, put a group of males together and, once some dominance order is established, the group will either split into competing coalition units or seek some exterior object for collective 'masterful' action.

William Golding's novel *Lord of the Flies*[3] represents a prototypical symbolization of this process. A group of English schoolboys are shipwrecked on an island. They have to survive. First, a leader, Ralph, emerges who believes in essentially constitutional order and conducts group meetings under the symbolic aegis of a shell which becomes the repository for constitutionality in the way the Mace does

1. Lorenz, *On Aggression*, op. cit., pp. 186–7.
2. ibid., pp. 216–18. See also Hinde's criticism of Lorenz's 'energy model of motivation': 'while models of this kind have been of some value in certain contexts (notably, perhaps, to psychoanalysts), they are not accepted by the majority of students of behaviour. This is in part because behavioural energy is so often confused with physical energy. . . . Perhaps more important is that energy models imply that behaviour comes to an end because energy is discharged in action, instead of through the situation which it produces in the simulus situation' – Robert Hinde, 'The Nature of Aggression', in op. cit., p. 303.
3. Faber & Faber, London, 1954.

in the House of Commons. Various disagreements about survival tactics – particularly the care of the fire the boys create – lead to emergence of another leader, Jack, who becomes convinced, after leading the hunt and slaughter of a pig, that in predation lies the best defence against, and appeasement of, the 'Beast' – in reality a dead parachutist hung in a tree and imaginatively reconstructed by the boys. As a token to and against the Beast, a pig's head is mounted on a stick. The boys who resist predation are symbolically eliminated either in reality or in influence. One of the major charges against the constitutionalist Ralph is that he is not an enthusiastic hunter. Simon, who discovers the real nature of the Beast and comes to tell the others, is ritually murdered. The sensitive quasi-rationalist, Piggy, is also killed. After enquiring at an assembly about his lost glasses (which symbolize foresight – they are used for making the signal fire which will get the boys off the island), Piggy asks, 'Which is better – to have rules and agree, or to hunt and kill?' Then the conch is destroyed and Jack – the leader of the hunters who have by now painted themselves and who Golding refers to as savages – proclaims himself chief and rushes to attack Ralph, who has now lost his colleagues as well as the symbol of legitimate authority. Ralph escapes, to learn later that he is to be hunted the following day, 'like the beast'. He overhears the savages incanting 'Kill the beast! Cut his throat! Spill his blood!' Before he can be found and killed, the pack of boys is rescued, significantly by an English officer from a passing warship which had sighted smoke on the island. The officer says, 'I should have thought that a pack of British boys . . . would have been able to put up a better show than that. . . .'

Yet England is itself at war! Golding's nest-of-tables series of symbolizations indicates the universality of the general process of group fission, predation, blood-lust, which he sees in his myth-maker's way. Significantly, this island lacks females,[1] and the boys are young. Yet the English officer is sketched no differently from the boys; he wears epaulettes and a ritual uniform in the way the savage children tie their hair and paint their skin. In war, as we have seen, females are not involved in the battles and the decision making which guides them. By using children as his protagonists, Golding (an

1. In an interview, Golding has said that the structure of the novel was most carefully worked out, and that the unisexual cast of characters was deliberately chosen because it suited his purpose – that is how he saw the nature of man on his symbolic island. See William Golding's comments to Frank Kermode, 'The Meaning of It All', Books and Bookmen, 5 (October 1959), p. 9.

ex-school teacher) presumably seeks to comment both on the nature of children and on the nature of the adults growing out of children. In the last scene of the book, after the children have been found by the officer, Ralph begins to cry: '. . . with filthy body, matted hair, and unwiped nose, Ralph wept for the end of innocence, the darkness of man's heart, and the fall through the air of the true, wise friend called Piggy'. The naval officer is embarrassed by this weeping, and turns away, to rest his eyes on his 'trim cruiser'; he does not weep at the sight of this promise of violence; his socialization into violence is complete.

Golding's concern is to illustrate the inevitability of the movement from order to fissaporous coalition to violence, and the timeless obsession with sacrifice, gods, and blood. In as much as he suggests that the process is inevitable and in a way quintessentially human, Golding has adopted a sternly anti-sociological attitude in relating his book to reality. In reality, violence isn't necessary, nor indeed are coalition and hostility; this depends upon the social and economic circumstances in which people find themselves. After all, in reality constitutional government *is* possible. The nature of man *could* be that he is constitutional not predatory (even though predation is pictured in the novel as more attractive: 'There was the brilliant world of hunting, tactics, fierce exhilaration, skill; and there was the world of longing and baffled commonsense'). Just as the boys can become savages, so can they become parliamentarians. Even wars are fought in the light of some grandly inconsistent conventions about humane treatment of prisoners, civilians, and one's fellow warriors. But Golding's intention is not the definition of sociological reality but the extrapolation from this reality of an absolute *possibility* of human life. He is not telling a fable-story, but is ambitious to coin a myth: ' . . . a myth is a much profounder and more significant thing than a fable. I do feel fable as being an invented thing on the surface whereas myth is something which comes out from the roots of things in the ancient sense of being the key to existence, the whole meaning of life, and experience as a whole'.[1] His myth is anti-sociological because his intention is to define the surpassing of sociological reality – to assert a theme, not its variations. He is concerned, then, with species-specific patterns – in this case, one of coalition, aggression, violence, and the savour of blood. And while this is not in the nature of proof, it is suggestive that this one of his novels has had extraordinary

1. ibid., p · 9.

success and popularity, and has quickly become a part of the 'high mythic' life of many people.

A film was made of the book; Peter Brook was director. The shooting was done on an island and the boys were initially organized to duplicate the original conditions of the book as closely as possible. But the experiment in Stanislavskian acting had to be controlled. The children threatened violence, felt deep antipathies to each other, and created a situation very close to the book's which was prejudicial both to their own safety and the progress of the film. In fact, a mutiny took place, led by the boy who played Jack the Hunter-Chief. Though elaborate precautions had been taken to prevent trouble, much trouble occurred and the possibility arose of calling off the entire venture.[1] In an article, Brook wrote:

> 'Many of their off-screen relationships completely paralleled the story, and one of our main problems was to encourage them to be uninhibited within the shots but disciplined in between them. . . . Even the wise and calm Piggy came to me one day close to tears. 'They're going to drop a stone on you,' the other boys had been telling him. 'That scene on the schedule, Piggy's death. It's for real. They don't need you any more.' My experience showed me that the only falsification in Golding's fable is the length of time the descent to savagery takes. I believe that if the cork of continued adult presence were removed from the bottle, the complete catastrophe could occur within a long weekend.[2]

Part of Golding's intention was to deny the validity of the optimistic Victorian story of English boys on the paradisical island implied in Richard Ballantyne's novel *The Coral Island* (1857). In contrast to Ballantyne's version, even though there was ample food and shelter on the island, feuds, hunting, and savagery would occur none the less.[3] It could be argued that *Lord of the Flies* is a comment not about human nature but about English public schools (from which the boys derive) and the ethics of violent mastery, hierarchy, and concern about God which public schools are supposed to impart to students. For example, Jack, the leader of the hunters, is also leader of the school choir and thus would be concerned with religious worship,

1. William Golding, personal communication.
2. Peter Brook, 'Filming a Masterpiece', *Observer Weekend Review* (26 July 1964).
3. See Carl Niemeyer, 'The Coral Island Revisited', *College English*, 22 (January 1961), pp. 241–5.

communion, sacrifice, and an overriding sense of formidable higher authority. But it seems more likely that these are secondary factors and that the primary ones refer directly to the social events on the island. If these resemble the wider adult society, then we must take this to reflect an extension of Golding's view of human process rather than simply a comment about a particular form of schooling and a particular social class of a certain country.

I have dealt with the book at some length because it is meaningful to me and because so many persons evidently read it with the astonishment of a strange and compelling recognition. Economically and vividly, it portrays a conception of human amity and antipathy which could have arisen out of the data and theory with which I am concerned here. The novel is a complex 'ideal-type', to use the sociological term, and can serve as a benchmark for the understanding of the social processes with which it is concerned.

2

But is it really helpful to distinguish between aggression and violence, to see social processes as pertinent to either the physical environment, animals, or humans, and to stress the factor of maleness rather than the factor of human-ness?

Lorenz is basically concerned with violence; it is acts of destruction and imprisonment which indicate for him the failure of the human species to develop inhibitory mechanisms equivalent to those found in other animals. He appears to regard sport, academic ambitiousness, cultural competitiveness, etc., as benign sublimations of processes or the reflection of a special form of innate energy which properly and most satisfyingly culminate in the protagonist's violent destruction of the antagonist. But it may be more parsimonious to claim that the process of bonding-cum-anti-environment activity is *the* basic aggressive process; in some situations, such as hunting, violence is one predictable outcome of the process. In other cases, such as sport, novel writing, or running a laundry, violence may occur as a less predictable outcome of the process. This is not to say that violence is not 'normal' or a parameter of human behaviour; rather, that it is but one of a number of possible outcomes of the bonding process.

This argument involves several assumptions which have already been discussed, namely that male bonding existed among pre-hominids for political–defensive reasons, and that bonding-for-hunting was grafted on to and reinforced bonding-for-politics. (In this connexion, the political relationship between the maintenance of internal political power and creation or recognition of an external enemy or internal enemy-scapegoat is well known. One wonders if politicians who know that to wage war tends to solidify their régime are acting out an ancient pattern through which dominant early hominids maintained their places in political (and possibly reproductive) hierarchies. It is after all curious that leaders who have committed their people to possible personal disaster should receive greater approval than under more pacific conditions. For example, President Kennedy's popularity increased as the Cuban situation worsened and Americans were in greater and greater personal danger.)

I propose to re-evaluate the relationship between violence and social control. I shall discuss the following matters: (1) that the process which leads finally to violence is the same process which underlies a predictable, biologically 'normal' pattern of social aggregation; (2) that this aggregation occurs between males and is facilitated by a sense of 'emotional maleness' of members; (3) that the real or symbolic existence of an enemy or out-group strengthens the existing dominance hierarchy; and (4) that the emergence of violence depends upon a number of facilitating circumstances which are social in expression and variable from place to place, time to time, and group to group.

The violence of groups concerns me; the violence of individuals may well involve quite different motivations, personality characteristics, and facilitating circumstances. There have been suggestions that some forms of crime and delinquency may be related to genetic abnormalities in the sex chromosomes. Individuals with an extra male or female chromosome in their body cells are apparently more prone to violent and criminal activity than persons with normal cells. Men with an extra male chromosome commit more violent crimes than violent and criminal persons with normal chromosomes, and environmental influences leading to deviant behaviour are very much less significant for the former's deviance than for the latter's.[1] While these findings are suggestive, they are based on relatively few cases; international comparative evidence would be interesting. In principle, there is no reason to deny the possibility that the propensity to

1. See W. H. Price, et al., *Lancet*, 1 (1966), p. 565. See also J. P. Welch, et al., 'Psychopathy, Mental Deficiency, Aggressiveness and the XYY Syndrome', *Nature*, 214 (29 April 1967).

violence or deviance may be distributed in any population on a bell-curve basis, and that, as with other distributed characteristics, genetic differences in part account for differences in behaviour. This must only point up the importance of the environmental situation in affecting individual differences, not deny the complexity of the inter-action between an individual's native endowment and his life chances.

The violence of groups is normal, at least in the eyes of members of the groups concerned. In wartime, a community's influential members support group violence. But the violence of individuals unsupported by group norms may be more profitably seen as a different pattern of violent behaviour; the difference between the peacetime murderer and the wartime hero may be greater than the relatively straightforward difference in social circumstances sur-rounding actions of human destruction.

Does it matter if male bonding is a function of aggression or if aggression is a function of male bonding? It is impossible in practice to separate the two processes; they are frequently parallel in opera-tion, and in some circumstances internal bonding may simply be the necessary correlate of externalized aggression. This is broadly Lorenz's position. The statement 'male bonding is a function of aggression' is basically a statement about evolution; the statement 'aggression is a function of male bonding' is a descriptive one, in-herent in which is a subsidiary proposition that bonding is a necessary though partial cause of aggression. This is a tautology in as much as I have said that, by definition, aggression and bonding are closely allied processes and have then said that bonding is a partial cause of aggres-sion.

But it may not be tautological if it permits an analysis of aggression which incorporates both an 'energy model' of aggression and one based on social–environmental stimuli. This formulation avoids creating a model of man which emphasizes either an innate violence-proneness or an almost entirely socialized proneness to respond to social cues.[1] This is not to beg any questions about 'human nature'. There is ample evidence to support a one-sided view of man as either aggressive and violent, or as peaceful and co-operative unless pro-voked by circumstance to be otherwise. It is more difficult to identify the important factors in a system based on a synthesis of ideas about 'instinct' and our knowledge of the role of socialization and experi-

1. See Dennis Wrong, 'The Over-Socialized Conception of Man in Modern Sociology', *American Sociological Review*, 26, 2 (April 1961).

ence in behaviour. Furthermore, there is a paradox here – that co-operation among one group is directed towards the destruction of another. But the argument is that this is a feature of the 'biogram' of a complex culture-creating and culture-needing species in which political hierarchies and reproductive advantage have long been intimately related to group defence and the hunting of dangerous animals.

A comment is in order on the relationship between aggression and violence. Hall has noted that among animals aggressive behaviour is usually adaptive under natural ecological conditions of breeding, feeding, and defence.[1] Applying the same principle to humans, aggression refers to political behaviour, defence, and hunting. It has already been suggested why it may be reasonable and indeed necessary to assume that hunting and male bonding are closely allied phenomena. I have noted that it may be useful to see relations between humans and (1) the physical environment; (2) other animals; and (3) other humans as different types of relationship. The killing of animals involves what has been defined here as violence. Perhaps violence occurs in human relationships because profound confusions develop between killing people and killing animals. The process is the reverse of anthropomorphism. Erik Erikson has called the result of symbolically transforming people into animals 'pseudo-species'.[2] This is a process of clearly defining an enemy or prey as different from members of the in-group, attributing especially disagreeable characteristics to the out-group, and finally coming to an implicit decision that the members of the out-group are not really human and may be killed without any of the inhibitions (as expressed by laws governing homicide, for example) against killing one's own kind. This form of 'pseudo-speciation' is a direct function of the cultural patterns of different groups' antipathies to other groups. Thus, it is possible to decide that Germans may be killed freely during the Second World War and then not killed – indeed protected and co-operated with – when they become members of the NATO alliance.

Childhood is an important period during which cultural patterning occurs. A recent study indicates how war comics influence the English child's stereotype of foreign countries and their people.[3]

1. Hall, 'Aggression in Monkey and Ape Societies', in op. cit., p. 51.
2. Erik Erikson, personal communication.
3. Nicholas Johnson, 'What do Children Learn From War Comics', *New Society* (7 July 1966), pp. 7–12.

Language we might think amusing . . . becomes serious in the realistic war context presented by this kind of comic. The enemy is described, either by the comic itself, or by British characters, as 'deadly and fanatical; lousy stinking *rats*; brainless *scum*; *swine*; devils; filthy *dogs*; slippery as *snakes*; or slit-eyed killers' [my italics]. A sample of the frightening propositions lightly put forward should include 'these Japs aren't human beings' and 'the only good Germans are dead ones'.

American war comics define not only Second World War enemies for their readers, but add Koreans, Vietcong, and Chinese Communists. 'The East German appears as a particularly convenient enemy possessing simultaneously the hate-potential of both Nazis and Communists.'

An examination of American war comics will reveal that even the death noises or screams of alarm of Americans differ from those of their enemies. This suggests distinctions in non-verbal 'language' of a quasi-specific kind. It is relevant to our concerns here that the war comics were all directed to boys; none were for girls. The only war story in a study of girls' comics was 'War Nurse Vicki' in *Bunty*,

'Similar to . . . boy's comics . . . [it] deals with tending the wounded rather than the actual prosecution of the war.' Boy's comics concentrate most on war and sport, although there are remnants of the more juvenile fantasy themes. Nationality is prominently referred to and . . . violence and killing are quite common. Girls' comics also present a version of the real world: one of careers, girls making their own way, school and animals.

Obviously it is impossible to trace directly the shift from dealing with enemies as members of our own species to treating them as 'pseudo-species'. At best it is possible to seek indirect clues. It is interesting, for example, that in situations of ritualized aggression such as team sports, animal names such as the Bears, Hawks, Tigers, etc., are frequently given to teams. Perhaps this betrays a concern to create symbolically inter-specific aggression out of a con-specific interaction which may be troubling to the community unless given this gloss. Though the human war record belies this, it may be that con-specific aggression rests uneasily with modern communities, perhaps because of an association of predation with inter-specific aggression. Team names may also reflect territorial or occupational loyalties, more usually the former. Also, if animal team names indicate uneasiness with con-specific predation, perhaps using names such as Hawks or Bears is thought to stimulate team members to achieve the ferocity and effectiveness associated with such predators.

Totemism is another phenomenon which may be involved not only with macrosocial organization, kinship patterns, and so on, but also with inter-specific aggression. (Though 'the polyvalent nature of logics'[1] associated with totemism involving animals makes it essential to know the entire context in which totemic systems emerge before judgements may be made about specific meanings of specific totemic practices.)

I mean totemism here to refer to the attribution to animals of special characteristics, which then exert an effect on human action which is considered a significant effect and which has to do with the explanation of human nature and action. These may be characteristics of the animals themselves, in so far as there is a human interpretation of such characteristics, or they may be characteristics attributed by humans to particular animals for human social and psychological reasons. Very simply, the relationship between totemic patterns and regularized inhibitions about killing reflects an awareness of the distinction between violence and aggression. Humans thus indicate consciousness of the difference between lustily killing or maiming and (possibly) 'constructively' mastering the environment, and between killing for satisfaction and acting with a sense of responsibility to a natural order disturbed by the taking of life.

When orthodox Jews eat meat, they must use animals which have been ritually slaughtered. The ritual involves a knife which must be sharpened before each kill to cause minimal pain to the animal, and a prayer must be said which indicates that the ritual slaughterer (*shochet*) knows he is disturbing the 'natural' world but that the disturbance is constructive and basically provident in intention. If we juxtapose this symbolization of violence and aggression with the one Golding describes where the little boys chant, 'Kill the beast! Cut his throat! Spill his blood!' we may see in the comparison that distinction between inhibited violence (close to aggression in my terms) and outright violence with which totemism may be involved. In this sense, I am suggesting that human totemic relationship to the animal world reflects an attempt to manage the potential confusion between taking the lives of animals and taking the lives of people.

1. Lévi-Strauss, op. cit., p. 61.

So, the orthodox Jews turn violence into aggression when they deal with food animals and see manly strength in this transformation. The tribe of Jack the Hunter-Chief sees predatory violence as the proof of strength. Totemic systems are related to religious systems – both are systems of social control. A long prehistory exists of inter-relation between hunting, social control, and the depiction of animals. This points towards the functional social importance of the kind of 'polyvalent' interplay with which I am concerned. Bonding has to do with hunting, hunting has to do with killing. Yet bonding also has to do with social order and constructive (viz. aggressive, in my terms) mastery of the environment. Totemic practices then may signal an attempt somehow to control and place under public scrutiny a process of profound interaction between man with animal and man with man.

Hunting *is* the master pattern of the human species. Most humans at most times – with the exception of several thousand recent years – have needfully existed with awareness of their symbiosis with animals and their need to both kill and preserve them. It should not surprise us to find that the control of hunting – and consequently its social organization – are intimately involved with management of human propensities to violence. The creation of pseudo-species is, then, the converse of the creation of gods, yet part of the same process of extracting symbolic helps from the dilemmas of existential reality.

3

Let me recapitulate briefly. I have tried to suggest a distinction between aggression and violence in that violence is one form of participation in an aggressive interaction. Aggression is related to mastery, and involves compulsion of one person or group by another person or group. A separate category is aggression against the natural environment. This may become violent in my terms when improvident or wanton destruction of natural resources occurs. This can suggest a failure of social control of the interaction with nature by socially acceptable norms. The significance in Euro-American culture of this is considerable – a culture in which the notion is that man really is all-important and powerful.[1]

Another category is aggression against animals. Particularly where food-giving animals are concerned violence may be the outcome of human mastery of them. Because of the importance of hunting in

1. Richard Means, 'Why Worry About Nature?', *Saturday Review* (2 December 1967).

human evolution, it is possible that some special relationship exists between the use of violence and man–animal relationships. This leads in turn to the possibility that such phenomena as totemism and pseudo-speciation reflect confusion between violence directed against man and violence directed against animals. These phenomena may be related to processes of social control which must necessarily exist in communities of a species apparently lacking the clear-cut programmed stimulus to curtail aggression – an inhibition which many animals possess. We do have some ritual inhibitors of aggression, which – like begging-posture or bowing – may have some biological component. The reviewing of troops by a visiting head of state may ritualize the expectation that these troops will not interfere with the liberty of the visitor. Inspecting the troops on arrival and often upon departure may thus allay fears which even exalted visitors to a foreign territory may feel. The firing of a cannon salute presumably signals the arrival or departure to a large number of people. It may also indicate that gunpowder will not be directed at the foreigner, but instead symbolizes respect for his or her status. Parades of armaments on national days – the Fourth of July in the U.S., May Day in the Soviet Union – may be equivalent to the threat rituals of animals seeking to maintain or improve their status without engaging in actual violence. There appear to be postural and gestural relationships which approach animal ritualizations; for example, the role of being seated and forcing others to stand in asserting dominance, and the use of hand position to express hostility, subordination, acceptance, etc.[1] At the same time, it is clear that cultural differences exist in the use of space, attitudes to bodily smells, styles of movement, etc. Whatever biological constants there may be must be interpreted differently in different cultures.[2]

In both violent and aggressive action male bonding is the predominant instrument of organization. Females tend to be excluded from aggressive organizations such as armies where violence may occur, or even from the management of religious, commercial, or administrative groups in which aggressive mastery of various environments is the condition of persistence and growth. Of course, females engage in a variety of forms of organization, from charity

1. Elias Canetti, *Crowds and Power*, Gollancz, London, 1962; E. H. Gombrich, 'Ritualized Gesture and Expression in Art', *Royal Society Philosophical Transactions*, Series B, Biological Sciences No. 772, 25 (December 1966).
2. Edward T. Hall, *The Hidden Dimension*, Doubleday, New York, 1965; Robert Sommer, 'Studies in Personal Space', *Sociometry*, 22 (1959).

groups to hairdressing salons to berry-gathering cliques. However, it seems that they do not form groups which are expressly devoted to violent activity or to potentially violent action. They are excluded from hunting large and dangerous animals, a prototypical male work-pattern (whatever its relationship to political activity) where the association between aggression and violence is most marked and in which confusion between the killing of animals and people may be most likely.

I have suggested that the very existence of a male group may lead to an aggressive relationship between the group and the outside environment. This may be functionally equivalent to, and probably more powerful than, the development of a sexual bond – however ephemeral – between a sexually active male and female put in proximity. Aggression and violence, then, are not individually motivated behaviour patterns. They are 'released' or 'directed' by social activity, and particularly effectively so by the social interactions of males. Furthermore, the *gestalt* of a group's social interactions – which perhaps we can call its culture – and the wider social system within which the group exists, provide the models and sanctions for aggressive and violent behaviour. The claim, then, is that male bonding is both a function and cause of aggression and violence. These, in turn, are defined, mediated, and expressed through local-cultural social patterns. Let us examine this in more detail.

A distinction must be made between the aggression and violence of single individuals and that of individuals in groups. The distinction is best seen when human life is destroyed. Groups of soldiers, or individual soldiers or single civilians imbued with military zeal, may receive honour and rewards for killing 'the enemy'. The same action in peacetime is called murder, or possibly manslaughter if there were wrongdoing but no clear intent to kill. The war hero who performs acts of destruction above and beyond the expectations of the military *behaves* like the peacetime psychopath who climbs a university tower and slaughters seventeen people. But the context and meaning are entirely different and so is the community's response. Nevertheless each is killing a lot of people. Despite the fascination which adheres to 'unmotivated' murder as an act of free will – the real case of Leopold and Loeb for example, or fictional ones such as in Dostoyevsky's *Crime and Punishment* and Gide's *The Counterfeiters* – peacetime murder can never be sanctioned if it is the expression of a purely selfish or philosophical position. The only complete excuse is 'insanity', which is, functionally, the community's affirmation that the killer shares none of its assumptions for reasons of his mental malfunction or his inability to become engrossed by the web of those social interactions which impose social control. Either through relatively greater skill, courage, inability or unwillingness to be inhibited by the consequences of his actions on the enemy he kills, the hero successfully expresses his community's ethic of destructive mastery in time of war. The hero may behave in an exactly contrary way; by allowing himself to be destroyed he rescues or advances his countrymen's interest.

The Japanese *kamikaze*, or suicide pilots, were an interesting variation of this pattern. The men who volunteered or were conscripted were given great accolades by their fellow militarists and by the public; they were well-treated with pleasures of the senses and were very privileged persons in the community, though beforehand they were often the least prestigious and esteemed soldiers and fliers. They left for their staging posts as heroes. Once on their bases, they received very rigorous and spartan training and indoctrination about the sacredness of their self-destructive action. If they refused to fly their missions they were shot as traitors; there were three individuals in each plane, each strapped into his seat and each with orders to shoot any crew member who would betray the crew's trust. The deaths of the *kamikaze* pilots were publically glorified. Similarly firemen or policemen killed in duty receive public tribute and in particularly dramatic cases their widows may receive substantial sums by spontaneous public subscription.

The function of the death of heroes in establishing or reaffirming social bonds is clear. At the same time it is difficult to reconcile the memorials among the vast graveyards of north-west France with the kind of scorn for the generals responsible for the battle expressed in a stage production such as Joan Littlewood's *Oh What a Lovely War*. Undoubtedly the dominant persons in a country at war allocate glory and blame. It is Earl Haig's statue which stands in front of Edinburgh Castle to mark his leadership of England's First World War French campaign in which huge numbers of persons were slaughtered in pursuit of questionable military objectives. Not only will class factors determine in part who is a hero and who is irresponsible (particularly as reflected by military rank), but, of course, so will who wins a war. 'The destruction of Dresden in February 1945 was one of those crimes against humanity whose authors would have been arraigned at Nuremberg if that Court had not been perverted into a mere instrument of Allied vengeance.'[1] In this raid, 132,000 persons were killed after three bombings, the third of which was 'a daylight American attack in which the bombers were accompanied by hundreds of Mustangs flying low and shooting up the thousands of helpless survivors littering the parks and river banks. . . . In terms of annihilation, this was the most successful operation in human history. . . .' The military effect of the raid was negligible; Churchill's chief purpose in ordering it was evidently to impress Stalin, whom he was to meet at Yalta shortly, with the force and resolve of the Allies. Because of bad weather the raid was carried out after the Yalta Conference. The incidence of 'war crime' is clearly greater among the losers of wars.

From sociological and other studies we have learned how crime and delinquency may grow out of and characterize sub-cultures. These sub-cultures may express antipathy to the dominant culture and power system by criminal and violent action. Groups of people who are disaffected, jaded, or needy will more readily than 'respectable' groups sanction the mastery of the environment through criminal and violent means. The riots in Watts, Detroit, and Newark were a particularly dramatic example of this.[2] While crime may take place on an individual basis, the criminal's culture provides some general support for the criminal resolution of tensions arising from feelings of 'relative deprivation' and from straightforward deprivation. More complex and more significant for the large community is the formation of extensive criminal groups such as the Mafia. These groups develop clearly defined notions of the propriety of criminal conduct (or 'honour among thieves'), possibly with intense and well-enforced loyalties between members.

The issue concerns legitimacy more than social process. Friedenberg makes an analagous comment in a discussion of violence:

In the modern world, nearly all the violence that occurs is lawful violence; while a large proportion of that which is not is nevertheless committed by the civil, penal, or military authorities in the course of duty. The German concentration camps were lawful. Our own authorities maintain that American intervention in

1. R. H. S. Crossman, 'War Crimes', *New Statesman* (3 May 1963).
2. An excellent analysis of the Newark riots is Tom Hayden, *Riot in Newark*, Random House, New York, 1967.

Vietnam is lawful. Executions are lawful. . . . Most Americans would say that they disapproved of violence. But what they really mean is that they believe it should be a monopoly of the state. . . . At a still deeper psychological level, there appears to be a strong though mute tendency among us to accept violence as legitimate – or at least, not to mind it very much – if it is manifested by individuals who come on with a gung-ho swagger in real or imaginary green berets.[1]

In other words, if an individual is a member of a group which enjoys respectability, he may more legitimately interfere, hurt, or destroy others than an individual with no respectable support who performs the same action.

This is no more than to say that (1) normative systems vary from place to place and for different regions and groups of nominally integrated communities, and (2) that members of groups given power, or having or taking it, may be more able to avoid punishment for aggressive or violent actions than individuals undertaking similar actions should these actions be illegal or immoral in the community. The latter implies that members of *groups* are facilitated in their aggressive or violent activity, a general proposition which accords with the basic conception here of the group-based nature of aggression and violence. Of course, individuals commit aggression or violence; solitary activity, such as writing a book, is not conceptually different from group activity, such as running a railway. But individual violence and deviant behaviour may result from psychological processes different in kind from group ones. Violence and aggression do not simply reflect individual personality disorder, emotional inhibition, or instincts operating unilaterally, but they are features of *social* processes which result from and stimulate social interaction. It is the lonely criminal who steals without need, kills without specific cause, rapes without the glimmer of love, who is the most genuinely deviant. While legal systems deal with the individual as the unit of guilt and innocence, it is really the group which is at the heart of all but a small proportion of criminal proceedings.

(While I cannot assess its significance here, it is an interesting thought that humans appear to be the only species to have created a system of 'justice' based on the individual rather than the group, or

1. Edgar Z. Friedenberg, 'A Violent Country', *New York Review of Books* (20 October 1966), p. 3.

troop, or flock, etc., with no real means other than warfare in various forms to assign 'guilt' or 'innocence' to groups. A poor eighteen-year-old male who steals a car is himself found guilty, not the social group which sanctioned the theft, possibly thought it exciting, perhaps drove in the vehicle with the individual singled out for sanction. Of course, any group based concept of guilt would contradict fundamental Judeo-Christian notions of personality and rectitude and involve racist, caste-like, or nationalistic rather than universalistic criteria for the administration of justice. In warfare – racial, class, or national – we see one form of group-based 'justice'; it is doubtless significant that this form of conflict-resolution is commonly regarded as primitive, in comparison with judicial procedure.)

4

In a general argument about the role of the male bond in stimulating patterns of aggressive behaviour, I have suggested that group-based aggression and violence differ in kind from individual aggression and violence. This is to say that a particular characteristic of the male bond is its close interconnection with aggressive and possibly violent action. In turn, this is directly related both to the establishment of in-group, out-group boundaries as well as to what may be broadly called hunting patterns. The latter characteristic possibly accounts for the chief differences in the dynamics and activities of male as distinct from female groups. Inherent in the responsibility of males to their groups is a willingness to undertake aggressive action on the groups' behalf; the behavioural record does not indicate that females indeed recognize the responsibility to fight physically on their group's behalf. (Females may help defend when their community is attacked; Russian, Israeli, and North Vietnamese women are examples. But they do not normally appear on the front lines of predatory conflicts and extra-territorial wars.) A young Englishman was interviewed by a B.B.C. producer about violence and gang life and related fighting to peer group status.

> . . . if I lose face in front of me mates, well I mean that is it I mean I have got no right to say anything, I have got no right to say well, no right to walk into a pub and say that is my girl sort of thing. I might be out with my girl one night and someone starts something, I mean what can I do. They can all turn around and say we

might as well have a go at Tony's girl, I mean he won't do anything about it anyway. So I just can't afford to lose face. . . . There
is a lot of us hang about together you know and they are pretty
terrific, they are not like average blokes, I mean they would help
each other out but what they all depend on, if you can't fight for
yourself you can't fight you are not fit to fight with them. . . . I
don't think I could lose face, I would rather get hurt and be put in
hospital than refuse to fight whether the geezer, whether the
bloke is ten times bigger than me, I mean the thing is you have
lost such a terrible lot not to be able to fight. I mean how could
you walk out, how could you speak to them I mean you just could
not, I mean they could always just throw that back in your face.
You could never argue a point with them after that because they
would say he would go to one extreme but he won't fight so we
win the argument anyway. . . . One day (a bloke) refused to fight
two people . . . and every time he says anything now they say it
is all right we remember the time you refused to fight. And
his standards have got so low now that he would not fight anyway.
I mean everybody was scared of him but now even the littlest one
of them says you are a load of rubbish. And no one likes him and
they won't let him, they just won't, no one will talk to him, but
if we ever go out he is never included, never included in anything
we do or say.[1]

In war the soldier who refuses to accept an order to fight may be
executed; the small boy among his friends who fears fighting is un-
favourably regarded by his peers. The traitor is an extreme case; he
treats with the enemy while appearing to enjoy solidarities with his
co-nationals. Of course, the process of bonding involved in nationalism may be of a different intensity from the bonding involved in
fighting; in circumstances in which fighting an external enemy is held
to cement internal bonds it may be similar. For example, in a
message to a ceremony at the Vimy Ridge memorial to the Canadians
who were killed in the First World War, the Canadian Prime
Minister, Lester B. Pearson, wrote:

The battle of Vimy Ridge was not only a feat of arms. It was the
birth of a nation, and it is appropriate that as we celebrate the
centennial anniversary of the creation of our country, we should

---

1. I am grateful to the British Broadcasting Corporation and to the producer, Anthony
Isaacs, for permission to quote from this interview.

recognize the one event which above all made it a nation half a century later. In all more than 66,000 Canadians died in that war. . . .[1]

External attack usually solidifies an attacked nation – for example, Pearl Harbor, the Battle of Britain, the bombing of Dresden. The scapegoat, too, helps to maintain the bonds of communal loyalty of his oppressors. Possibly, as Lorenz has suggested, 'the bond of personal friendship was evolved by the necessity arising for certain individuals to cease from fighting each other in order to combat more effectively other fellow-members of the species', and that (following Tinbergen) inhibition of aggression within the group leads to re-directed aggression to individuals outside of it.[2] This explanation may be appropriate for some human aggressive processes in which both males and females may be involved. But there is an additional bonding-cum-aggression process among humans which is specifically related both to maleness and to hunting. Human bonding along in-group, out-group lines has always been recognized as a predictable feature of behavioural systems. We must recall the phenomenon that armies are generally male, and that other agencies of aggressive– violent mastery are composed of males. Perhaps this is not only because females may be less able to perform successfully aggressive encounters with either natural, human, or animal environments, but, more significantly, perhaps the presence of female colleagues in groups would uniquely and effectively diminish the group's ability to perform its 'function' in those encounters regarded as important for group survival.

This is not to say that an aggressive war-like response to challenge is necessarily preferable to a conciliatory, passive, or 'cowardly' one. For example, in the early 1960s some Americans vocal if not numerous argued that one was 'Better Red than dead'. The continuing conflict in the U.S. between 'hawks' and 'doves' over the conduct of the Vietnam war suggests the vehemence with which members of a single if complex community dispute the role of violent aggression in achieving communal ends. In view of the antipathy to the Vietnam war, and its high costs in money and life, it is nothing less than as-tonishing that educated, wealthy, and informed leaders of a modern-ized community see violent aggression as the preferred response to a

---

1. 'Canadians Return to Vimy Ridge', *The Times* (10 April 1967).
2. Lorenz, 'Ritualized Fighting', in Carthy and Ebling (eds.), op. cit., p. 45.

presumed challenge to the balance of power. I imply no comment about the validity of the U.S. government's assessment of the relationship between its aims and its practice, nor on the activities of the persons and groups against which the war is presumably mounted. What is remarkable is the direct economic and personal sacrifice which the war exacts from the community and individuals. It is estimated that the money cost of killing a single U.S. enemy is $400,000 while the conduct of the war costs at least $2,000 million each month (£830 million). At the same time, another U.S. 'war', the 'war on poverty' in the U.S., was voted £1,365 million in the first two years and three months of its existence, and proponents of the programme in the U.S.A. experience great difficulty in securing sufficient funds to begin alleviating the situation of an estimated 34 million American poor by the official standards of their community.

The contrast between government largesse for the Vietnam war and relative parsimony for the war on poverty is striking enough to indicate the sense of priorities of the leaders of the community. It also contradicts criticisms frequently made about America to the effect that it is a materialist, selfish society; the expenditure of vast sums to defend, at least ostensibly, a quasi-moral position rather than on local prosperity is presumably one index of the relative importance of 'spiritual' as opposed to 'material' goals. Of course, it is clear that the low status of the persons to benefit from a poverty programme is as much a factor in developing a sense of priority as the high status and political influence of those soldiers, businessmen, politicians, and ideologists who may directly or indirectly benefit from an aggressive if expensive foreign policy. At the same time, as behaviour, the Vietnam war is an extraordinary display of the role of aggression in human affairs.[1] The confusions surrounding the Vietnam and other wars illustrate the point that human aggressive activity is not a simple 'instinctive' reaction but a complex symbolic enterprise.

At the same time, it would be interesting to know the extent to which less complex and potentially more 'instinctive' social relationships among the relatively small group of men making policy and operating decisions about the Vietnam war determine the course of

---

1. For a discussion of the relationship between the Vietnam and poverty wars, see Martha Gellhorn, 'A Tale of Two Wars', *Guardian* (14 April 1967). It is also interesting that a programme of government action against the human suffering, disaffection, etc., involved in poverty should be called a 'war'. Perhaps correctly it was originally thought that such a description would encourage more enthusiastic response among legislators and people than a less militant name.

the war. In a memoir of his military service, Alfred de Vigny commented, 'It is one of the bad sides of the military life that one is constantly straining to play the strong man.'[1] Conceivably such strenuousness underlies the difficulty of changing from bellicosity to conciliation among groups of men who feel themselves uniquely and finally entrusted with the security of their community at the same time as they must seek to maintain their resolve and reputations as leaders of courage. And in affirming their strength, they must cultivate strategic insensitivity to lesser cruelties in the name of some higher conception of general communal well-being.

That military activity demands strength is a notion worth examining. I have already discussed the role of co-worker selection in mining, fishing, hunting, etc., and the context within which initiation procedures gain biological significance. It has been suggested that heroes of a lonely action and civilian killers may be persons involved in a qualitatively different process than persons who kill together and are brave in groups. An emotional current, or perhaps an aesthetic excitement, adheres to manly militant strength – which seems biologically equivalent to the sexual excitement between men and women. The hero-leader of a flight of American fighter planes described an action in Vietnam in this way:

> 'This time we went looking for MiGs. We outflew, outshot, and fought them . . . to make a wonderfully long story short – they lost. We went in over an area just north and west of Hanoi and I think we sighted each other at about the same time . . . the MiG pilots seemed aggressive, quite willing to hassle. Within minutes, the sky was filled with dogfights. We countered their attack, mixed with them and fired our air-to-air missiles. My flight downed three of their aircraft. We didn't lose anybody,' said former West Point football All-American and husband of film actress Ella Raines. . . . 'Our purpose was to go up there in fighters and engage an enemy air force. And we were tickled when we saw they were airbourne and wanted to do a little jousting. . . . It's hard to explain the ecstasy, you might say, of engaging and destroying some of their first-line of air defenses.'[2]

1. Alfred de Vigny, *The Military Condition* (trans. by M. Barnett), Oxford University Press, 1964, p. 116.
2. 'U.S. Sets Out to Destroy North Vietnam Air Force', *New York International Herald Tribune and Washington Post* (4 January 1967).

The willingness to participate in fighting effectively is an important component of the sharing of the 'ecstasy'. In the U.S. military it was found that a major source of troop tension arose from the fact that soldiers could have no hand in choosing their officers or in moving to another group if they could not respect their current leaders.

A soldier knew that he might lose his life unnecessarily because of the lack of skill or judgement of his superior and there was little, if anything, that he could do to prevent it. There was much talk about men who had shot or planned to shoot their officers – an indication of the tension that prevailed.[1]

The British and to some extent the Canadian attempts to place recruits into regiments based on local territories was one strategy for easing the tensions that individuals felt when they did not know the people with whom they had to live and possibly die.[2] The discovery that soldiers fight in terms of the sanctions and patterns of their immediate social group rather than the formal ideals of their army and country[3] supports the particularistic – or intimate – rather than the universalistic – or bureaucratic – conception of combat and underscores the importance of relatively primitive bonding phenomena as opposed to rationalized ideological ones. While the ideology may or may not be important for individual or large groups, it appears essential that it be mediated by social relationships which make concrete, channel, and reward or punish specific responses to small groups' interpretation of community ideology.

Of course, in fighting as in other activities, human beings act in terms of social stimuli and are subject to the influence of the people with whom they have direct social contact.[4] But, as well, where bonding occurs a special, coercive, 'creative', outward-looking group *gestalt* arises which demands and rewards strength and in

1. Eli Ginzburg, *et al.*, *Breakdown and Recovery* (Vol. 2 of *The Ineffective Soldier*, 3 vols.), Columbia University Press, 1959, p. 54.
2. ibid., p. 53. But 'when men from the same area participate in a battle in which the casualty rate is high, the impact on their communities can be devastating'.
3. Edward A. Shils and Morris Janowitz, 'Cohesion and Disintegration in the Wermacht in World War II', *Public Opinion Quarterly*, 12 (1948).
4. An interesting example of this is Davis's finding that U.S. college students judge their personal status and potential for success not in terms of their standing in the U.S. population as a whole but directly to their position in their immediate college environment: '. . . success is judged by relative standing in the social group, not by standing in the total population', James A. Davis, 'The Campus as a Frog Pond: An Application of the Theory of Relative Deprivation to Career Decisions of College Men', *American Journal of Sociology*, 72, 1 (July 1966).

which it may be easier to regard moderation as weakness than in groups where the bond does not exist. So in *Lord of the Flies* the constitutionalists lose control of the group and those who advocate killing and external attack take over. In a group's apparent division into 'hawks' and 'doves', or toughminded or tenderminded, it is the latter who are most readily accused of weakness and lack of deep loyalties to the wider community. I am alluding here to an aesthetic of action, of a style of commitment to the group and response to the group's problems. There is a manly style and there is a feminine style. Like the American Indian communities who decide that a male is either a warrior or a *berdache* – in effect a woman – societies make distinctions between males and females and maleness and femaleness.[1] As Mead makes clear, cultures may vary between themselves as to how extensively maleness and femaleness are differentiated, but some socio-sexual distinctions are always present. One would expect differences between cultures in this as in other regards, for genetic perhaps as well as for cultural and ecological reasons.

Typically, maleness involves physical bravery, speed, the use of violent force, etc.[2] While there are enormous inter-cultural variations in the definitions of maleness and femaleness, some core characteristics remain widely attached to males and females in most cultures. Males more than females incline to tough mastery of the environment and a creative rather than reactive interference with physical and social realities. When the masterful activity is undertaken by a group of men, the pressures for bravery, toughness, self-proof, etc., are normally increased. The dares which young boys issue each other and their effort to achieve decisive drama in their play foreshadow the patterns of adult mastery which in part comprise the adult manly style. Clearly the socialization of boys differs among cultures in the encouragement given to aggressive and violent display, and there are great variations between individual boys as well as between social classes.[3] But the generalized conception of maleness, represented in such projective materials as films, advertisements, literature, and in the sexual composition of the controlling organizations of societies – especially manifestly aggressive and/or violent organizations – suggest that the central concern and capacity

1. Margaret Mead, 'Cultural Determinants of Sexual Behaviour', in Young, op. cit., p. 1451.
2. Margaret Mead, *Continuities in Cultural Evolution*, op. cit., pp. 96–7.
3. Robert R. Sears, *et al.*, *Patterns of Child Rearing*, Row, Peterson & Co., Evanston, Ill., 1957, pp. 252–9.

of males for toughness, bravery, confident assertion, violence, and related phenomena is probably species-specific.

This is understandable in phylogenetic terms, as well as through functional analysis of contemporary societies.[1] Carveth Read saw the development of the hunting life as a superposition of wolf-like gregariousness upon a basically primate pattern of consciousness and society (see his pp. 48–61). Though we now know that human hunting and separation from the other primates occurred much earlier than Read thought, there remain sufficient physical similarities to see behavioural similarities as representative of divergence from a common original pattern. Read did not stress sexual differences in behaviour, though his conception of human evolution and contemporary behaviour does not appear to permit the interpretation that males and females can interchangeably perform social roles other than explicitly reproductive ones. Margaret Mead notes the possibility that human warfare has a direct biological basis and that warring is a male occupation, stimulated when most intense by

> . . . protectiveness toward women, children, land, and ideals. . . .
> It is probably . . . that the young male has a biologically given need
> to prove himself as a physical individual . . . in the past the hunt
> and warfare have provided the most common means of such
> validation.[2]

Young males seek self-validation. In addition I am suggesting: (1) that validation involves a process of attachment to specific male peers and superiors who become defined as the 'significant others' with respect to whom the individual seeks validation; (2) that the process of attachment itself facilitates the effort of validation and in fact leads to a demand that satisfactory evidence of maleness be prerequisite to group membership; and (3) that the combination of the process of attachment and the need for validation leads to a cumulative group 'feeling' which – particularly under the stimulus of external threat or the perception of a possible advantage – tends to increasingly bold and effective activity. The latter characteristic, as much as misinformation, prejudice, inertia, etc., may lead to 'escalation' of conflicts between groups of males for whom conciliation without triumph means invalidation of their maleness. 'Honour must

1. Carveth Read, op. cit., outlined an early position which remains relevant to contemporary study.
2. Margaret Mead, Introduction to *Male and Female*, Penguin Books, Harmondsworth, 1962, p. 23.

be served', even though the escalation involves danger and the loss of property, time, and opportunities for other rewarding activities. And validation does not occur only once. The need for validation recurs throughout the different stages of the male career, and is expressed by the different symbols of success, achievement, power, goodness, etc., which are appropriate to the various age categories as defined by individual cultures. Ceremonies of initiation or *rites de passages* chiefly signify changes in criteria by which individuals are judged and ranged, not the cessation of the process of validation altogether.

Thus I am relating the control of human aggression – at the level of schoolboy fights and bar-room brawls as well as possibly on the international scale – to the control of the dynamics of male groups and the maintenance of male self-respect and confidence. With only half a whimsy I suggest that one reason for the removal of women and children from the battlefield is that, as well as protecting them, the absence of women and children permits males to fight without the inhibition they might experience were children to cry and wander about, were women to complain about the danger to children, themselves and their men, or all the participants. In addition to Lorenz's notion that bonding evolves as a concomitant of aggression, it may be necessary to assume that the process occurs primarily and most significantly among males, and that the control of aggression is essentially a question of the extent to which males with power and sense of their manly status may retain their self-esteem and maintain their positions without recourse to actions which involve destruction and pain for some other group, and probably their own as well.

This phenomenon is connected not only with defence and politics, but also with a propensity for men to engage in hunting or hunting-type activity. This makes the management of aggression considerably more complex than the fairly straightforward rather mechanical model sketched above may suggest. The focussing of a group on a specific goal – which is functionally equivalent to a prey animal in the dynamics of the group – suggests that perhaps male bonding requires a consummatory stimulus. Such a stimulus 'cuts off' the aggressive impetus, as does the killing or escape of a prey animal.[1] Outright

1. Berkowitz calls this 'the competition tendency'. See his very useful article, 'The Concept of Aggressive Drive: Some Additional Considerations', in L. Berkowitz (ed.), *Advances in Experimental Social Psychology*, Vol. 2, Academic Press, New York, 1965.

victory is one consummation, loss is another. Possibly the drinking of alcohol by groups of men is somehow associated with triumph or consummation rituals. Dart has noted that certain fossil remains among Australopithicine settlements suggest that the skulls of the defeated were used for the drinking of blood by the victors in conspecific battles.[1] (It is also to be noted, for what such an observation may imply, that the prelude to much Scandinavian drinking, the word '*skol*', translates into 'skull'.)[2] The significance of drinking to men's groups, the importance of inscribed personal drinking mugs, etc., may be taken as one index of the relationship of drinking to male affiliation. In some cultures, where a variety of inhibitions prevent the warm expression of male-affiliative sentiments, the role of drinking may be unusually important in permitting affiliation to occur at all. Drinking certainly functions as a means of validation. Rules governing entry of minors to places of public drinking are fairly widespread. But perhaps it is most markedly in North America, and possibly in Scotland, that there is such a strong popular correlation between manliness and the ability to drink a great deal of alcohol. Why the ingestion of a mild poison should be regarded as the test of the manly virtues is curious, except in so far as response to alcohol may belie an individual's response to other circumstances involving noxious food, odour, sights, etc. A comparable situation is the smoking of cigarettes and the frequent association of smoking with manliness, both in life and in projective materials such as advertisements and films. It is particularly interesting that smoking is so frequently depicted in advertisements in association with hunting or fishing, or with some 'tough' enterprise. The derision may be recalled which greeted one company's attempt to characterize its product as 'the thinking man's filter'. The implication was: manly men did not think. On the other hand, there is a clear popular association between pipe-smoking and intellectualism.

The relationship between cigars and the concept of manliness is intriguing also. Is it simply because cigars are expensive and prized that they are handed out by new fathers to their male friends? Or lurks there some deeper if obvious significance in the gift of a rigid phallic-sized object to be orally enjoyed? Is this a symbolic celebration by the male group of a man's virile success, in the absence of cultural

1. Raymond Dart, 'The Minimal Bone-Breccia Content of Makapansgat and the Australopithicine Predatory Habit', *American Anthropologist*, 60, 5 (October 1958).
2. Alex Comfort, personal communication.

patterns which permit men with manly self-conceptions to enjoy the activities of each other in the tender sphere of women and babies? Walter Pople has speculated that conceivably the pleasure humans derive from smoking reflects an evolutionary history in which the smell of smoke meant security, warmth, and possibly food.[1] That we should seek to re-create this pleasure by means of little portable fires which yield much fragrant smoke is not wholly improbable. Of course, there are a vast array of cultural differences with respect to smoking, but the persistance of the habit despite its now certain potentially disabling effects may indicate something about the role of smoke in human evolution and consequently of fire.

Another curiosity is the special willingness of males to cook on an outdoor barbeque grill which involves charcoal smoke, heat, and a sense of the rich reality of the culinary operation underway. Barbequing appears to present no threat to men who might avoid cooking boiled cabbage in their wives' kitchens. Neither does cooking in hunting or fishing camps. While I have no data to support this beyond the observations I have made, it seems that men prefer steaks while women prefer salads – rather than the other way round. Perhaps women enjoy steaks more than men appear to enjoy salads. Have we here a reflection of the hunting–gathering dichotomy, even in a supermarket culture? Incidentally, does the relationship between fire, food, hunting, and success have anything to do with the popularity of restaurants and occasions in which the cooking fire is visible and nearby? Is this also why *flambé* dishes particularly connote festivity and well-being? And why dining by candlelight or dim light is regarded as 'romantic'.[2] In some situations, drinking may be more closely related to consummation – to the hour of triumph or feast (among orthodox Jews, for example, drinking is associated only with feasts). Carveth Read regards the feast as a direct relative to early man's hunting, and even suggests that 'the origin of laughter and the enjoyment of broad humour . . . may be traced to these occasions of riotous exhilaration and licence'.[3] Lorenz describes the adaptive value of gluttony among hunting peoples after a large kill; it is clear that among persons with secure food supply this is now an ill-adaptive behaviour.[4]

1. Personal communication.
2. See John Pfeiffer's article, 'When Homo Erectus Tamed Fire, He Tamed Himself', *New York Times Magazine* (11 December 1966). I am grateful to Pfeiffer for the observation about steaks, salads, and socio-sexuality.
3. Read, op. cit., pp. 60–1.   4. Lorenz, *On Aggression*, op. cit., p. 218.

What is of interest here is the possible connexion between feasts, drinking bouts, stag parties, etc., with consummatory features of processes of male affiliation after aggressive or violent enterprise. The literal or symbolic sacrifice of animals or other humans may also function as consummation of a process of bonding and exercise of power and mastery. Typically, of course, religious sacrifices result from the decisions of male leaders. Where sacrifice and/or torture (of either humans or animals) have political implications, these are necessarily a function of male-dominated systems. The catalogue of bloodletting, cruelty, sadism, and cavalier disregard for the suffering of others is so extensive as to suggest that these crudities may result not from something as private as 'instinctive cruelty' or the fact that man is 'evil', but as a direct consequence of a process of male bonding which is deeply related to the *social* nature of human beings and which is linked both to political structure and the hunting method of ecological exploitation. Again, if hunting is indeed the master pattern of the species, one may presumably expect that, like all biological patterns, some consummatory stimulus must be available. Perhaps sacrifices and various other forms of killing-the-prey provide this consummation. Thus the argument about the concept of pseudo-species and its relationship to the use of animals for totemic purposes can be seen in this context as an additional clue to understanding the otherwise perplexing and apparently profitless ceremonies where ritual tasks are sanctioned – tasks which in other circumstances would be condemned as heinous and unnecessary. I am suggesting, then, that the phenomena of human cruelty, blood-craving, sacrifice, and pseudo-specific killing and abuse are directly related to the sense of personal manly validation individual men feel in terms of their male groups, and that perhaps the chief effect of intercultural difference in this matter is to specify object, instrument, and mode for the validation of individual maleness and group power in different cultures. While it is clear that females may participate in the situations I am concerned with and may, in some cases, act more cruelly and viciously than males, females do not often contrive, manage, and justify the social structures surrounding the violent and aggressive violation of the rights and health of coerced persons.

Hannah Arendt's term 'the banality of evil', used in her description and discussion of the trial of Adolf Eichmann, implies inter cultural differences in moral order and the essentially routine prosecution of policies once they are clearly stated. Evil becomes an incidental by-product to a process of activity involving personal reputations and corporate bonds. If only because they sought to destroy the records of genocidal activity, it appears many Nazis were aware of the illegality (if not immorality) of what they were doing. But the social pressures of the military machine were such that even individuals who could withdraw from the more flagrant violations of war law were loath to do so. Again, it is presumably significant that the Nazi movement was an essentially male organization. While a substantial number of infamously cruel women presumably took their cue from the male structure, even their behaviour seemed to be more private and arbitrary than the relatively smoothly bureaucratized male variety.

A visit I made to Dachau made clear the tidiness, regularity, and internal logic of the concentration camp and crematorium system. That the system involved human destruction of a fantastic and monumental order at the same time as it was genteely orderly and self-justifying suggests that the term 'inhuman' cannot be used to describe it. If anything, this was a devoutly human feat; the photos of the genial faces of the officers in their mess alongside the faces of the prisoners propose a contrast different only in degree from the legion examples of minor or gross human invidiousness. That the degree of difference is great is a comment on the specific people and set of events in question rather than on the process of social differentiation between captors and sacrifices which was most bewilderingly reflected in the German camps in our time. Even in the camps of U.S. troops, clear and superior conditions for officers caused U.S. soldiers bitterness and distress to the point where some reflected on the similarity of U.S. and German military conditions.[1] There is no question of equating the two types of camp. But what is of interest is the effect of social permissiveness in creating social divisions within communities of two cultures which differed dramatically in – and indeed were fighting about – their central approach to equality and human fellowship.

5

This is not to say that all men will feel equally strongly about their male bonds in aggression; some will perform in terms of their bonds with strenuous loyalty, others with fear, apathy, or outright rejection.

1. See Samuel Stouffer, et al., The American Soldier, Vol. 1, Princeton University Press, 1949, pp. 364–79.

Unless there are mitigating circumstances, in wartime deserters will be shot. Despite this sanction, men still desert, particularly under conditions which they regard as hopeless, or unconscionably uncomfortable, or the product of careless or incompetent leadership. The acute dilemma this presents to a military structure as well as the individuals within it is suggested by Joseph Losey's film *King and Country*. An allegedly shell-shocked young man walks away from his First World War unit and is subsequently tried for desertion and found guilty – finally in fact because an impending offensive seems to demand the boost to morale which the execution of one of their number is thought to provide troops under pressure. Stephen Crane's *The Red Badge of Courage* is another study of the problem of the deserter. It is clear that all individuals will not voluntarily elect to join aggressive organizations such as armies; as Andreski has indicated, the existence of the draft suggests this: 'If human beings were in fact endowed with an innate proclivity for war, it would not be necessary to indoctrinate them with warlike virtues; and the mere fact that in so many societies, past and present, so much time has been devoted to such an indoctrination proves that there is no instinct for war.'[1] (It can also mean that the inhibitions against intra-group warring are so necessary and strong that a process of disinhibition is required before more 'instinctive' intergroup responses can be released. For example, recruits learning bayonet use are made to utter an animal-like howl as they plunge the bayonet into the man-dummy. Apparently this helps to relax inhibitions.) Only with the advent of democracy in its various forms has the mass of the population been subject to extensive direct taxation and the legislated requirement of military service. As a consequence, draft-dodging is a common enterprise; the burning of their draft cards by American pacifists and opponents to the Vietnam war represents an open – and aggressive! – form of antipathy to participating in aggressive action.

Conceivably, in addition to experiencing different socialization, males are endowed with differential propensities for both male bonding and aggression in the same way that intelligence, metabolic, or sexual activity rates may be distributed in any population. Some men are more bellicose than others. Of interest here is the manner in which the bellicose are able to impose their will on others in times of crisis, and how, once even the gentle join the fray, they are likely to

1. Stanislav Andreski, *Elements of Comparative Sociology*, Weidenfeld & Nicolson, London, 1964, p. 125.

participate with more or less loyalty to their social group and possibly some conception of the overall purpose of the series of activities which comprise war. The stimulus which pacifist groups provide to militant ones is significant too: Dutch sailors were only mildly discouraged from fighting with 'Provos' in Amsterdam and giving them impromptu haircuts, while the 'Hell's Angels' motor-cycle gangs have been tacitly permitted to beat anti-war demonstrators the California police could not hurt for fear of legal retribution.[1] Because members were permitted to remove their badges and other identifying marks and enjoyed the clear support of political authorities, during the Democratic Party Convention of 1968 the Chicago police force was able to express brutally and bloodily its opinion of anti-war demonstrators. Groups representing charismatic tendencies in community life are apt to be sharply disciplined by the forces of social stratification. This is particularly evident, it seems, when the proponents of social stratification patterns are also at odds with external opponents, for example during a war. Chance has indicated[2] that an important feature of participation in hominid and near-hominid political structures is the ability to inhibit aggressive responses to one's peers and superiors in the interests of long-run success in a particular community. Such inhibition does not appear to operate as effectively in restraining individuals – securely sanctioned by their own group – from aggression and violence against others outside the group.

In other words, participation in a bond in which internal aggression is inhibited facilitates aggression against the outside world. This is not to imply that there is a strict mechanical transfer of 'aggressive energy' from internal aggression to external. But an essential component of successful viable bonding is ready proneness to aggress externally.

The logic of my argument then is: males are prone to bond, male bonds are prone to aggress, therefore aggression is a predictable feature of human groups of males. To reduce opportunities for such aggression is to tamper with an ancient and central pattern of human

1. Friedenberg, op. cit., p. 3. In early 1967, Paris *gendarmes* took to cutting the hair of beatniks they apprehended. The response to long hair by men is intriguing, as is the sexual significance of hair in general. It was no doubt far from the intention of Dutch sailors or French police to play Delilah opposite the Samson of pacifist beatniks. But one cannot help speculating upon the significance of the phenomenon, particularly in view of the widespread practice of head-shaving recruits to 'total institutions'.
2. Chance, 'Social Behaviour and Primate Evolution', in op. cit.

behaviour. In view of the importance of hunting and quasi-hunting behaviour among human males, perhaps it can be suggested that bondless aggressionless males are in a real sense equivalent to childless females. Of course, childless females are viable and many choose their condition and enjoy its benefits. At the same time, it seems reasonable that they also do not experience for good or ill a crucial characteristic of human females and may be held to have lacked participation in a massive biological activity and its psycho-social consequences. In the same way, friendless inhibited males are not only friendless and aggression-inhibiting, but possibly do not experience the male equivalent of child reproduction, which is related to work, defence, politics, and perhaps even the violent mastery and destruction of others.

This is not to say that, if my hypothesis is correct about the relationship between male bonding and aggression and violence, it is necessary to assume that hurtful and destructive relations between groups of men are inevitable. As population can be controlled, so presumably can social relationships be governed by constitutional agreements, awareness of mutual interest, and the tutored insertion of mediating influences in potentially antipathetic interactions. It may be possible, as many writers have suggested, to alter social conceptions of maleness so that gentility and equivocation rather than toughness and more or less arbitrary decisiveness are highly valued. This might lead to different notions of successful participation in male groups so that leadership and rewards are allocated to less truculent individuals who are less committed to the vindication of their power and legitimacy. But as far as political leadership is concerned, we must recall that the process of selection of leaders and the careers of successful politicians, as well as the necessary association in practice of political success with male-group effectiveness, may make this difficult to achieve in the foreseeable future.

And the critical issue of the nature and role of military leadership cannot be easily avoided either, given that the effective purpose of military organization is the rapid and unquestioning provision of armed force to defend against aggressors as well as to aggress against and possibly destroy persons regarded as enemies of the sovereignty in question. That there is no clear correlation between a society's bellicosity and its support of equality of females suggests that not for a while may it be likely that the interposition of females in male-dominated organizations will lead to cessation of potentially destructive relationships between different 'bonds'. As I have suggested before, it is also necessary to see the control of violence in terms of the fact that aggression is a concomitant of constructive and benign activity as well as of destructive and malignant.[1] This adds significantly to the burden of those who would devise means of managing the relationships between males which, I have suggested, are potentially so intimately connected with forms of activity no longer adaptive to human survival. Obviously this can be done – as the dangers of playing football were mitigated by the regulations produced at Rugby in 1845[2] – in situations which do not involve critical issues of prosperity and survival. That disarmament is difficult to achieve is well known, and may suggest the complexity of any attempt to substitute apparently soft safeguards of the peace for conspicuously hard ones. Prohibiting hard measures may affect internal dynamics of peace-keeping defensive organizations and yield difficulties similar to the ones of infertile married couples. Such a process must present an additional latent hazard of considerable social importance to those who seek peace through organization, not force, and communication, not confrontation.

6

I have emphasized the relationship between maleness, the male bond, and aggression and violence because I think too little attention has been paid to a central characteristic of human organization and the sex-linked role of individuals in organizations. I have tried to stress the possibility that consequences of male group interaction which may be socially 'harmful' are directly a function of processes of group dynamics which are predictable and indeed 'healthy' in that they are species-typical; and that the 'harmful' results of male bonding derive from the same process as the 'healthy' ones. At the same time, the possible basis of male bonding in real or quasi-hunting and defence may give some greater urgency to some harmful activities, or at least render it likely that many male groups will seek activity permitting re-creation of the processes and satisfactions in terms of which human males have evolved until several thousand years ago.

My concern has been to indicate what relationships I think there

1. See also Anthony Storr, 'The Psychology of Aggression', New Society (11 October 1962). For a fuller statement, see Storr's Human Aggression, Allen Lane, The Penguin Press, 1968.
2. See Norbert Elias and Eric Dunning, 'Dynamics of Group Sports with Special Reference to Football', in op. cit., pp. 394–5.

are between maleness, male bonding, and violence and aggression, and the process of these relationships. The management of this process, for whatever social purposes and goals, is another matter. This I am not particularly qualified to discuss here, except to note the importance of understanding how explanations of human conduct must relate genuinely to the underlying biological principles and characteristics of behaviour. If what I have suggested about aggression and violence is correct, it makes the problem of peace-keeping more not less difficult than if aggression is seen as private, the result of frustration, or a response to wholly social stimuli. If aggression is profoundly connected with sexuality – which is important to individuals – and also connected with social groups – which nearly all of us need and like then dealing wisely with aggression and the potential for violence is very difficult. It is just as well that this be fully realized.

CHAPTER EIGHT

Some Concluding Remarks

By now readers have had many opportunities to draw their own conclusions about the cogency and implications of the book's arguments and data. In this final section I review analytically the propositions offered here, stress those I consider most pertinent to the main themes, and suggest some possible consequences of this work for the study of society and the management of social affairs. I have deliberately refrained from calling this section a 'Conclusion' or 'Conclusions'. It would be simply too optimistic to imply that a *quod erat demonstrandum* happy ending can follow a book in sociological-biological theory. None the less it remains my responsibility to generalize about the general, having done so about the specific, and to round out the argument by indicating where it might proceed from here.

1

First, recapitulation. I have been primarily concerned with two matters: first to discuss the extent to which biological and sociological analyses are united and useful for understanding human behaviour; secondly, to describe a social phenomenon, the male bond, and aspects of its role in human communities and other primate communities, its relationship to certain kinds of group, and its possible rootedness in human evolution. To this end I outlined some features of sociology–anthropology and biology which were amenable to co-operative use and some which appeared to preclude any immediate oecumenical success in this field. I did affirm that whatever theoreticians in either camp may say, the kind of new data which has emerged suggests that at the moment the 'lumpers' are in the ascendancy while the 'dividers' must improve their defences – should they really wish to maintain the isolation of their respective disciplines. It is obviously too easy to say only that there is a predictable pendulum effect in the earnestness and success of attempts to relate biology and social science and to claim the pendulum has begun to swing back in to a point it left in the 1930s. None the less it was my intention to illustrate the movement of the pendulum through discussion of male bonding. Hence I have tried to identify a biologically based human process which is best understood by using jointly new data from natural and social scientific effort.

As one indication of this effectiveness, I sought to describe the role of the male bond in three human communities and in two primate communities, suggesting the points of difference and comparability among these. In all these ethnographies the notion was stressed that, instead of regarding relations between politicians, warriors, sentries, etc. (either humans or their primate equivalents), as relations between people (or primates), it might also be useful to see them as relations between males. This necessarily involved emphasizing differences between males and females. Such an emphasis is routine in primatology. But in the study of humans the assumption has been that, with the exception of childbirth and immediately associated activities, the roles of males and females are more or less interchangeable and that, furthermore, constant biological differences are far less significant than malleable cultural ones. My emphasis on sexual differences in social behaviour underlay a review of data about political, economic, military, recreational, and other forms of social organization. Hopefully, this defined the importance of biological sex in determining and accompanying social-organizational behaviour. I paid particular attention to political organization, because both in humans and other primates this form of organization is relatively notable; in primates, and probably among pre- and early humans, it was an important concomitant of breeding success and hence of evolutionary change.

In relation to this, secret societies, initiations, and various forms of recreational activity were discussed in some detail. These, it was claimed, could also be held to bear some clear relationship to maintaining political order and defining status hierarchy. There were definite sexual differences in participation, type, and extent of this behaviour; I argued that this was central to more general political and socialization processes. I tried to suggest the importance of male bonding in human communities and its possible biological basis and significance. In the latter connexion, the proposition was put that ceremonies of initiation reflect a pattern of unisexual selection for work, defence, and hunting purposes comparable to sexual selection for reproductive ones.

I also sought to show the relationship between male bonding and aggression. Here the central point was that aggressive behaviour is directly a function and/or outgrowth of corporate male interaction. This allowed an assimilation of theories about man's 'inherent aggressiveness' with observations that aggression is an intensely co-operative process – it is both the product and cause of strong affective ties between men. Some comments about 'pseudo-species', totemism, human–animal relations, and religion's function in social control were suggested as evidences of a further relationship between male bonding and these significant phenomena. As before, consideration of sexual differences in these areas yielded some speculations about the partly biological basis of aggressive behaviour.

In a discussion of the evolution of human male bonding, I tried to relate extant social patterns and somatic differences to available data and discussions of human evolution. It was also necessary to consider the possible connexion between the evolution of the brain, patterns of political and personal 'equilibration', and the significance of social hunting in establishing the human type. The existence of physical sexual differences as well as behavioural and social–organizational ones was held to be relevant in assigning relative value to particular theories of human evolution in general and the hypothesized evolution of the male bond in particular.

THEORY

I restrict myself to those theoretical consequences which follow from the hypothesis of the male bond rather than to a more general attempt to relate biology and social science.

The argument's most significant consequence is the establishment of an additional intervening variable between individual social existence and social process. Indeed, the link between the individual and the social, if the matter can be separated thus, is a dependent rather than independent variable. Individuals may have sexual needs independent of particular sexual stimuli, but my proposition is that the male bonding propensity can only be elicited (or released) and manifested by real social contact with other males. It is, in this sense, a refinement of the obvious need of human gregariousness to manifest itself by association with other people, but it possesses the additional characteristic of relating to specific sub-systems of society described earlier. This does not mean that symbolic stimuli are unimportant. Obviously, war comics, novels about politics, adventure stories, films of various kinds, storytelling, etc., may all stimulate the desire to engage in male-bond activities, and may indeed permit some consummation or 'catharsis'. There are two points to be made about this:

(1) Individuals will presumably react to male-bond symbolic stimuli in terms of their own experience and the canons of their own culture (which would explain differences in types of aggression and cooperation depicted in, say, American upper middle-class and working-class magazine literature). This implies that some cultural preparation is essential for the use of symbolic stimuli, and illustrates the intrinsicness of the interaction of propensity and learning in this matter. Of course, given the symbolic component of any interactions, one would expect the distinction between symbolic and actual male bonding to be difficult to make. I recall Shaw's comment that 'Love consists in overestimating the difference between one woman and another' – a clear recognition of the relationship between sexuality and symbol. Presumably a comparable process operates in unisexual male bonding.

(2) It is not clear that the Aristotelian notion is ethologically acceptable; that drama, for example, allows public catharsis of private emotion. There is some evidence that seeing violent action makes it more likely that children will themselves commit violence than if they do not observe violence.[1] The catharsis notion depends upon a mechanical or energy conception of human needs and propensities, whereas the ethological one employed here depends upon an interactional model in which both stimulus or releaser and behavioural pattern are necessary for the pattern to operate.[2]

Such phenomena as political loyalty, work-group morale, the treatment of spies, the emotionality of initiations, the ribaldry of anti-female pornography (in some strip-shows, for example), and the role-model links between old and young males, may be viewed as activities on their own and as exhibiting a common factor – the male bond. Just as anxiety about status can affect a theatre group acting in a play, or sexual attraction might affect the relationship of a

1. See L. Berkowitz, 'The Concept of Aggressive Drive: Some Additional Considerations', in L. Berkowitz (ed.), *Advances in Experimental Social Psychology*, vol. 2, Academic Press, New York, 1965.
2. For an interesting essay on the relationship between drama and ethology, see Irving Wardle, 'Evolutionary Stage', *New Society* (May 1967).

male and his secretary, so the patterns of male bonding might operate in a Cabinet in which certain individuals more easily than others formed bonds which affected formulation of policy and allocation of government revenues to particular Ministries. This may be no more than to say that certain individuals possess 'political sex-appeal', or are more affable and trustworthy than others. But a constant or recurrent core characteristic of such relationships will be the process of male bonding. This concept enables us to separate out components of relationships between males in various circumstances. It becomes possible to add to the bonding 'infra-structure' of male relationships the other various distinctive features of these relationships. To know the non-cultural permits a more sensitive understanding of the explicitly cultural, and of the specification and elaboration of a basic but diffuse valence.

In the same way that psychiatric insights permit us to recognize in some religious behaviour, for example, the expression of sexual preoccupations or frustrations, it may be possible to associate aspects of political, economic, religious, etc., behaviour as much with the process of male bonding and the validation of social maleness as with the actual concerns of particular groups or organizations. People place ads in personal columns to contact other people who wish to join groups for intellectual discussion, artistic appreciation, etc. It is neither unkind nor unfair to see that these ads reveal not only a wish to talk about something but also a wish for social contact, a wish strong enough to overcome the formidable barriers of anonymity. In the same way, we can look at the behaviour of frustrated Nazis in the early days of Hitler's movement, in the disciplined aggressive cadres of the Black Muslims, or the cells of the Ku Klux Klan, and we may see an attempt by men feeling relatively deprived to establish themselves as full and effective men in significant and dramatic groups. Not only political unrest, and not just anomie, and not only class conflict or racial *hauteur* is here, but also the expression of a need to be a man among men. This yields privileges and duties and goals and the experience of a sense of strength and personal moment unattainable elsewhere in communities withholding from the unfortunate the complicated pleasures of corporate competence and mastery. Without fail, such posts always attract men in all places to share in these special pleasures.

For social scientific theory, a more general consequence of the male bonding hypothesis must be an addition to the list of 'universals' (in so far as any such list could be agreed on). Thus, in addition to sex, food, shelter, social interactions, etc., one would specify the need to male-bond. This is as important to the social and emotional standard of living of both individuals and communities as the provision of security in childhood, the opportunity for the young to learn, and the maintenance of some social order. Several policy implications of this are discussed in the following section. For social science the effect could be a clearer prediction of needs if not behaviour of males through their life cycles, and of the corresponding groups and institutions which – if this analysis is correct – communities will have. (There will obviously be a wide range of variation; I am concerned with central tendency.) Of particular interest will be the consequences of the attempt to assimilate such propositions into psychiatric and psychoanalytic theory. Especially in these areas is there an awareness of the need to relate individual to community through a series of intervening variables which tie social institution to personal biologically based propensity or need.

If the male bond in fact inheres in a wide range of dominating systems such as economics, politics, and religion, we can conceive of these systems in a cybernetic or servo-mechanical way. I mean by this that it will be possible to identify a reciprocity of system and individual so that social circumstances are at the same time symptom and cause of further action in the system. For example, let us say the Ku Klux Klan is aggressive because – as many writers on aggression would claim – they are in various ways frustrated. Simultaneously, the very act of bonding may relieve certain frustrations but also stimulate the undertaking of further aggression. The act of bonding may have creative or imperialist or predatory consequences once the group has overcome or minimized the difficulty to which it first addressed itself. It will then surpass that original stimulus by redefining the goals and meaning of the group to incorporate its newly developed strength and scope. Similarly, where (in my terms) bonding does not occur satisfactorily and the group is beset by strife and disunity, fission will result in the creation of small bonds – in the extreme case, of none. These may retain some, all, or more of the original objectives of the whole group but approach them explicitly in terms of accusations of impiety, compromise, error, or corruption. Such expressions of disunity frequently mark the inter-sectarian struggles of groups once united, but – like the Mensheviks, Bolsheviks, Trotskyites, or Christians, Jews, Essenes – latterly reduced to affirming the value of the smaller purer bond by exposing the falsity of other groups claiming allegiance to the larger purposes of the original enterprise. The severe acrimony which may accompany such contention suggests, that like a woman scorned, those who have their trusty alliances torn often despise more those once close to them than the general enemy against whom the alliances formerly inveighed.

PRACTICE

If this hypothesis is true, and if understanding is encouraged to guide behaviour, what are the consequences for social policy resulting from the attempt to relate insight to action?

These can range from the provision of facilities for male association on housing developments, to the diagnosis of psychological and psychiatric illnesses of men unable to enjoy or find bonds with other men, and, paradoxically, may help to solve the problems of those extreme effeminate homosexuals whose eagerness to attract other males may as clearly betray a craving for male bonds as a confusion about sexual identity and a desire to be female. There are many subjects which can be treated. But I will deal primarily with four: education, politics, aggression and its control, and – briefly – architecture and town planning.

What is the relevance of male bonding – as a process – to the educational system? This is necessarily bound up with the general question of sexual differences. Boys and girls mature at different rates, develop different skills at different times, and may express different interests. But in many, if not most, schools – certainly in America and Western Europe – boys and girls attend the same schools and often compete against each other for teachers' attention, grades, and prizes. School boards and teachers may find this administratively and morally easier, but the interests of individual students and the community at large may be poorly served. Do boys in coeducational classes develop differently than boys in all-male classes? Is the bonding mechanism a factor here? These questions are amenable to research based on the widest possible conception relationship between educational practices and community social life.

The evidence is only impressionistic, but there is some suggestion that males who attend all-male schools – particularly where these schools are also associated with high social status – develop mannerisms, traits of character, social and other skills, etc., which appear to advance the boys' adult careers in a marked way. Of course, the combination of high initial status at school entry and the creation and maintenance of 'the old boy net' (which is really a spatial conception of male bonding) prejudice the issue formidably. At the same time, one may ask whether the intensity of social bonds formed in all-male schools, where dominance through high status is implicit, underscores the relative rigidity of class structure of communities such as the U.K. and at the upper levels of the U.S.A. and Canada. In other words, the public (that is, private) school system is as much a part of the political as the educational system. It allows corporate socialization of young males who are offspring of dominants and who expect dominance for themselves. Their strongly forged links with similar individuals co-operate to produce a cadre of distinctive, mutually supporting persons, widely (and correctly) regarded as privileged. One is reminded of the studies of Japanese macaques and of other primates indicating that offspring of high-status females tend to achieve higher status than male offspring of low-status females. When this kind of support is augmented by the support of the peers who form a bond in play groups and possibly latterly in the adult community, it is clear that participant individuals are very advantageously placed in the struggle for dominance and – implicitly – breeding success. While the direct analogy to the human situation is not logically acceptable, it remains interesting that the public-school phenomenon should so directly link male bonding, initial status advantage, and ultimate high status in the community's structures of dominance. That boys derive their status from their fathers extends the primate analogy, and enhances the significance of male relationships.

Obviously high initial status and attendance at a prestigious public school provides advantages to females as well as to males. But in girls' public schools much more emphasis is placed upon the graces, skills, and socio-sexual preoccupations appropriate to attracting and marrying high-status males. Elaborate systems of party-giving and reciprocal institutional hospitality with high-status boys school and cadet corps students augment private parties and dances given to ensure appropriate mating milieux; this is an important service to ambitious parents of girls. Similar considerations may apply to some parents of some boys. But, in general, girls appear to prepare for high-status marriage while males prepare for high-status work. Of course, these are not static patterns, and it is by no means universal that girls' schools are more concerned with marriage than work and hence with social rather than explicitly academic excellence. In one Canadian school of very high social standing, academic success has become as important, if not more important, than immediate social success. This is a change which has occurred over the past decade and is attributable chiefly to the fact that the men in the marital 'catchment area' of this particular school must now demand university-trained wives because of changes in the occupational and political worlds. The school thus produces girls who can pass the difficult university entrance exams. The general status patterns have not changed, because the school remains very expensive and socially exclusive. What have changed are the criteria on the basis of which desirable males choose their mates and, of course, on which some girls base their choice of schools. I do not imply that passing university entrance exams is better or even more difficult than performing the range of activities which were appropriate earlier, but am simply saying that as the demands of community life change, the methods used by dominant people to maintain their status must change as well. This must necessarily include the specific devices used to distinguish between females occupying different places in the hierarchy of already high-status institutions.

A realistic assessment of respective life-chances of males and females is involved here; we must stress the social-functional differences in the all-male and all-female school. We must also suggest that public (private) schools – unlike their coeducational counterparts – maintain the status of particularly the most elevated families in a direct and concrete way. Perhaps unisexual schools are particularly conservative in relation to social class and occupational achievement. This may directly reflect the style and intensity of bonding which occurs in all-male as distinct from heterosexual schools.

Let us recall the earlier discussion of social stratification and charisma. The argument is that a unisexual school system, coupled with high-status support for certain institutions within it, tends strongly in the direction of stratification rather than charisma. The males' stratification problem is linked to the world of work and power. The females' problem is tied to the crucial matter of who it is possible to marry. Normally, females will seek males favoured in the stratification system, favoured in good part because of their school and possibly university attendance, and because of their links with other males who will provide, if not actual jobs, at least business propositions and clients and perhaps shared and reflected glory.

Other social institutions frequently organize themselves on the basis of comparable social networks. But I am concerned to stress the particular importance of unisexual institutions in maintaining high social statuses for already dominant groups and persons in any community.

The reasons for this may be intimately tied to the primate infrastructure of male bonding and breeding patterns. While the genetic effects of such patterns in a large-scale community will have no appreciable immediate effects for the community's genetic pool (except in so far as certain 'aristocratic' physical traits may be marginally selected for), it will none the less have considerable effect on the nature of leadership of any community and its overall relationship to the distribution of talent. There is a demonstration effect of life-styles, morals, conceptions of social value, and so on, from higher status to lower status persons.[1] If the high-status ideal is the male who has attended an all-male school, who is versed in the 'manly arts' such as sports, hunting, possibly war, who is fond of all male activities such as clubbing, fishing, and hunting, then presumably the conception of masculinity in the community in question will depend in good measure upon this image arising out of all-male schooling.

I do not want to press too far the relationship between male bonding and the educational system. But given the importance of social learning in expressing and organizing any species-specific behavioural patterns, one would expect significant differences between all-male school systems and heterosexual ones, particularly in the kind and intensity of links formed between males. It is not by chance that this matter relates directly to the maintenance of privilege of high-status groups. It reflects the link between bonding, 'equilibration', and superior positions in social hierarchies. Therefore, the compatibility of public-school systems with flexible democracy, for example, as in England, is perhaps a question even more perplexing than researchers, politicians, and educators have heretofore recognized. This is because the public-school system is a generalized expression of core human patterns. The system is not only involved in training social and technical skills, but also with conceptions of maleness and of male loyalty. Change or retention of the schools must have wide-reaching effects extending well beyond the educational system itself to include such phenomena as conceptions of hierarchical propriety and the sexual division of labour, principles

1. See the revealing essay by George Orwell, 'Boys' Weeklies', *Inside the Whale*, Secker & Warburg, London, 1940.

of colleague and mate selection, notions of societal firmness and flexibility, and the nature of the career.

A consequence of this particular emphasis on male groups and sexual differentiation for the content of educational programmes must be greater recognition of these sexual differences, in both individual and social-organizational behaviour. Obviously, much of the difficulty in this area results as much from prudery as from misinformation or ignorance. All the same, it is clearly to the advantage of both sexes for the males to learn not only about the physical events of the menstrual cycle but also about the behavioural and temperamental changes of its different phases. It is curiously anomalous that, while young males may be taught about the tax system, about the value of exercise, or about the poetry of Browning, they are unlikely to receive systematic knowledge about the specialized patterns of behaviour of members of the sex with whom the great majority will spend a good deal of their adult lives. More realistic and analytic treatment of the different typical careers and life-chances of males and females might alleviate what appears to be frequent disharmony between what many females expect about their working and married lives and the extent to which communities help them to meet these expectations. In particular, some objective discussion of the anti-female tradition and the nature of male exclusion of females from various male groups could simplify or clarify the problems women may feel who seek careers in predominantly male organizations. This would be especially pertinent for females entering politics. To date there has been relatively little change in the political role of women. Understanding the resistance to females could lead to self-conscious changes in electoral and political practices to facilitate women's entry into the political world. Changes of such a kind would have to be introduced because of information about the nature of human society rather than as an admission of female inferiority or incapacity. There need be no element of condescension implied by an attempt to increase the representativeness of political bodies. The very recognition of the problem – if so it is defined – in this form could be an important step in its solution.

But it is simply prudent to point out that historical evidence weighs strongly against the optimistic feminists in this matter. Particularly in terms of 'access to a public forum', as Robert Murphy calls it, or the 'attention structure', as Michael Chance calls it, females may suffer relatively inflexible disabilities; they may simply not provide the 'releasers' or generally satisfactory images of power, discretion, foresight, etc., which induce communities to follow their leaders.

At times of war and national crisis this may be especially pertinent.[1] If female involvement is to increase even in times of crisis more forceful measures than those which presently exist will have to be undertaken, if only because the inducements now available appear to produce relatively small effect. A more serious problem is whether or not it is 'desirable' – given various assumptions about the good community – for women to have high political office. I put this question in the same sense as the following question: is it desirable for men instead of women to rear children? Obviously considerable admixture of roles is possible in many spheres, but given cross-cultural data about the political role of females, it may constitute a revolutionary and perhaps hazardous social change with numerous latent consequences should women ever enter politics in great numbers. Even a but partly female-dominated polity may go beyond the parameters of 'healthy' possibility, given the basic conservatism of species. I am concerned less here with isolated women who achieve high office than with a major shift in the sexual composition of dominating bodies. Of course, the whole nature of political action could change were it defined as partly or largely female; certainly there would be major changes in relations between female-dominated states. But like disarmament, it is unlikely that any important nation would develop a female-biased or feminized political system unless other competing nations developed them also.

It appears to be widely believed that men are stronger and tougher, both physically and in terms of social action. To forgo the exclusive or predominant use of men in international relations would involve considerable trust in the intentions and internal controls of other nations. Neither recent nor ancient political history stimulates the conclusion that this form of disengagement from effortful and hard international competition is imminent, or even possible in the foreseeable future. This may mean that female political activity

1. According to ex-U.S. Senator Mrs Maurine Neuberger (personal communication), the involvement of the U.S. in the Vietnam war has been a major discouragement to women who wish for political office. A process of enlarging the confidence and scope of women political activists has been halted and reversed by the dilemmas of the war and by an apparent feeling among women that there is nothing they can do about the war and that they do not understand it. In the mail which Senators receive from female constituents the war is rarely mentioned; it is a major interest of male correspondents.

would concentrate on domestic and local concerns. The complex contribution to political change of which females are potentially the agents may have to be made in a relatively limited sphere. My hunch is that any such changes will be circumscribed and of minor import. While the subject of female political participation may be more carefully and compassionately discussed than ever before, actual socio-political changes will be influenced more extensively and directly by other factors, such as technology, age-composition of the population, the spread of armaments in the world, etc., than by the efforts of females and their striving for political emancipation.

There is an additional relevant factor which links formally to the notion of male bonding. This is that the very scale of modern political societies and the growth of relatively impersonal forms of human communication have made it difficult for politicians to know personally even a small proportion of the people impinging on their political activity. With whom can a politician bond? With how many other politicians? Perhaps politicians are above average in their readiness and ability to deal with large numbers of people; we can say that they are specialists in dealing with the problems arising from moving from species-typical groups of thirty to fifty persons to those vast assemblies which now engage us. But however specialized they are, even their developed skills cannot cope with the range and number of people involved in most political actions.

If we recall that the evolution of the species may have been related to the dominant hierarchies of bonded males, and if we are genetically broadly committed to this pattern still, it can be appreciated how difficult and biologically bewildering it must be for persons entrusted with massive responsibilities who cannot assimilate the sorts of inter-personal stimuli 'required by evolution' for making decisions about social order and defence. In common with other writers, Tinbergen has noted that human ability to manipulate symbols, moral structures, and weapons has far outrun our ability to control our behaviour by interpersonal influence; we can more easily drop a bomb on a village than kill with our hands the inhabitants we wish to destroy.[1] We can also create computer simulations of hostile encounters and seek to make policy decisions on the basis of one-page memos carefully prepared by skilled advisers. But is this suffi-

1. Niko Tinbergen, 'On War and Peace in Animals and Man', *Science*, **160** (28 June 1968), p. 1415.

cient input for politicians? Are love letter. enough for lovers? Are
we so enamoured with our skill with words, symbols, and swift
methods of communication that we do not recall that human communication depends on a host of factors of which words are only one?
Of course, we are committed to words and increasingly to numbers.
But it is likely that our extraordinary symbolic skills have led us into
a social-organizational dilemma: that because of our communication
we can centralize our authority structures, but that the very act of
centralization deprives both government and people of an immediate
and intimate reciprocity which is the necessary basis for patterns of
government reflecting the evolved social and biological needs and
skills we have. Thus in the interests of efficiency our nations and
cities grow – and grow more frightening, cumbersome, violent,
and meaningless as entities to the creatures inhabiting them.

Of course, these are cliché comments about modern politics. I
dare make them only to stress the importance of bearing in mind that
politics is a control and decision-making process which has ancient
roots in an evolution marked by the development of male bonding,
and by the growth of notions of corporate loyalty in terms of the
spinal cord of male bonds which structures any community. Sometimes, in dire situations, this spinal cord holds firm, as in the
response of the Czechoslovakian leadership and people to the Russian
occupation of 1968. But, for example, what about England in Suez
and Rhodesia, the U.S. in Vietnam? It is one thing to say these
actions are moral or immoral; it is another to say they are taken by
men who must operate in a situation of considerable isolation from
both the recipients of their action and the immediate responses of
the population in whose name they formally act.

Morality is not my concern here, but the broadly biological
problem of government and survival is. Max Weber predicted that
with industrialization and the growth of bureaucracies, problems
of politics become problems of administration.[1] But the factor of
size may now turn the administrative bias in social affairs into a
political problem of enormous and uncomprehended magnitude.
This may be so because the business of making decisions depends so
acutely on knowing with whom and for whom decisions are being
taken – a knowledge our skills for other learning and symbolization
may make remote and inaccessible.

1. Reinhard Bendix, *Max Weber: An Intellectual Portrait*, Heinemann, London, 1960, p.
433.

2

Another broad but influential matter – in the more intimate area – to which attention could be profitably turned, is the effect of male–female differences and the male bonding hypothesis on architecture and town-planning. The layout of houses in new towns and suburban developments may preclude the growth of male bonds in new communities and so curtail the range of social experience available to men in their communities of residence. Succinctly stated, men 'need' some haunts and/or occasions which exclude females. Given the decreasing hours of work, and as potential time at home increases, should not men's huts or their equivalent be constructed? Obviously English pubs serve this function already. On the other hand, all-male pubs tend to be restricted to old-established working-class communities. In new developments, planning is based on relatively middle-class norms; foreign to these is the notion that males and females should even temporarily engage in sexually segregated drinking or discussion. Sports facilities may satisfy part of the requirements I am projecting here; but there remains no place which is defined as specifically and exclusively male, and which is not only exclusively male but also anti-female. No necessary hostility between males and females is implied here, but rather an expression in architecture and planning of a kind of social structuring which may be both satisfying and 'constructively' energizing for men. From a planning point of view, it may be equally desirable to provide similar facilities for females. Architects and planners could have the responsibility to recognize formally in their schemes the value of permitting men to enjoy forthright male interaction in sanctioned situations. This would not replace voluntary organizations, hobby and sports groups, political activity, and the host of other activities in which men alone, and men and women together, engage. But proceeding from the observation that simple, pointless, unstructured conversation is a widely desired human activity, and that if friendship patterns, discussion groups at mixed parties, the existence of all-male dining and drinking clubs, etc., are an indication of a human propensity, then the provision of physical facilities for this male activity may be a responsibility of sophisticated planners of physical space.[1]

This may seem to some a retrograde step – in a sense it would be. But some facilities for men, particularly in suburban areas, could

1. Desmond Morris (personal communication) regards conversation as the human equivalent of grooming behaviour among other primates. The pub is an admirable

provide a useful counterbalance for men to the heavy emotional and temporal demands of nuclear family life. It has been claimed often enough that suburban life is child-centred. In part, the reason must be that the institutional life of suburban communities reflects the strongly family-centred concepts of housing. Schools and churches – both family and/or child-centred – are typically the first public buildings to be constructed in new communities and a pattern is established which does not ultimately create a *formally* all-male environment for recreation. Even existing urban clubs are economically afflicted by the movement of their former clientele to suburbs where heterosexual country clubs usurp time men formerly spent in all-male establishments.[1] In other parts of the world, many communities frequently provide places for men either to live or pass time in. In some classes of Euro-American society such facilities exist. But the trend of planning and prejudice or belief is in the direction of curtailing opportunities to establish male-only environments outside of work. Community views about familial activity, females' rights, and the assumed impropriety of all-male groups may deny men a relatively harmless and modest form of pleasure.

Though wives may fear their husbands' congregation in all-male groups because it is assumed they will collectively seek out other women, in fact they do not do this and prefer to drink, talk, or gamble.[2] It is true that many females will regard their husbands' decision to spend time with men rather than their families as a threat to their own appeal and strength as women and wives. The weight of cultural expectations supports this. However, this does not mean the expectations are 'desirable' or even biologically healthy. It is conceivable that – in the same way that children who are too rigorously supervised or women who are too dominated by men may be less likely to be lively and creative – so, also, men dominated by their wives and families may lose a certain constructive maleness of

place in which to talk-groom easily; prices are variable enough to permit most members of the community to spend time in pubs if they wish; the division of the pub into saloon and public bar, far from suggesting only the rigidity of English social class differences (though it obviously does that), also acknowledges the importance of the pub for the community so that it becomes a matter of government policy to provide a place where public-bar beer prices are government-controlled and presumably affordable by the great majority of people.

1. Faced with such economic difficulties, the Oxford and Cambridge Club in London decided to open its membership to graduates of all English universities. However, women, even Oxbridge women, do not meet Oxbridge men on the premises, and there are separate facilities for men and women. In this case, like blood and water, sex seems to be thicker than status.

2. I am grateful to Elizabeth Bott of the Tavistock Institute for this suggestion.

consequence to many of their activities. This seems to be particularly true among North American academic males, a high proportion of whom live in college towns in which work and domestic relationships are closely mixed. It may be also relevant, as Kinsey found, that American academic families have the lowest rate of sexual intercourse of the occupational groups identified in his studies.

3

Numerous other implications of the male-bonding hypothesis must await discussion after further work. I conclude with some comments about the efficacy of managing aggression through the male bond.

First of all it must be stressed that discussion of the male bond in itself is inadequate. We must also recognize that the concept of male validation which Margaret Mead describes is an essential concomitant of the male bonding phenomenon. I have already sought to explain the virtually complete connexion between validation and bonding except in those pathological cases where validation may depend on asocial concepts developed by poorly socialized or otherwise abnormal individuals to cope with their treacherous worlds. The attempts at validation of these pathological individuals may result in physical or appreciable psychological harm to others. This I called violence.

But here I am concerned with aggression. There is a paradox. I have suggested that male associations and the exclusion of females are intimately linked with aggression, which, in turn, may be linked with unhappy social consequences. I have also proposed that failure to engage in male bonding may hinder the search for comprehensive and satisfactory male individual experience. The paradox is in fact a true one, and yet another expression of the dilemma any peacemaker faces who wishes to restrain the encounter of active hostile groups and yet not diminish the internal energy and productivity of the separate groups.

One of the possible resolutions of the paradox lies in the frame of reference within which the bonding–aggression occurs. Konrad Lorenz has already indicated possible ways in which the pattern of bonding may be employed to encourage scientific, artistic, philanthropic, and similarly 'positive' enterprises. But for various reasons – chiefly military, historical, and the need for defence – notions of valid maleness are widely associated with the hard military virtues, with various activities such as hunting, speeding, fighting, and the extraction of substantial sums of money from either natural resources or people. The hard and 'realistic' virtues created the dislocation of the Industrial Revolution in England, scarred the ground, polluted the air, and violently disrupted social life. Those who argued that this was wrong or intemperate were the idealists; they were soft. That later the realists would plant grass on the coal-mine tips, would replan slums and control air pollution, is a question of context; a change in the nature of social awareness has made welfare work in its varied forms tough, real, and partly manly. But none the less the control of goods, power, land, people remains more reputedly masculine than scholarship, art, or chemistry; the advertisements instruct us 'Be a Man – Join the Army' not 'Be a Man – Become a Fabric Designer'.

There are two things to be said about this. Weapons, fast machines, complex and heavy structures, certain social activities such as war, decision-making about major social events, the maintenance of order – these may in fact elicit or stimulate 'maleness' from men more directly and powerfully than designing jewellery, playing the harpsichord, or composing poetry. Maleness may be more forcefully released by certain hard and heavy phenomena in the same way that maternal feelings are better stimulated by a baby than by an aircraft, an elephant, or even an adult. Driving a racing car or leading a platoon are different from writing a good paragraph or having a pleasing idea or forming a friendship; there is a sense of moment, of manly drama. At a high speed any driving error can be dangerous or fatal; there are other drivers to watch and anticipate; there is the condition of tl = road, its curvature, and the line of vision; there is the car to understand and govern. It is this sense of moment, of the *inevitability* of decision, which may be manly, or at least a manliness of a different kind from what happens when a decision must be made about a patient, a lawyer's client, an inadequate student, or the subplot of a play. Perhaps it is this which underlies the war game and the great interest in armament which virtually all nations show. Perhaps for their leaders it is part of the masculine aesthetic. Involvement with guns confers validation and decision-making about armaments elicits a sense of the rigour, providence, and virile realism of the decision-makers.

So the first point is that certain matters and things may be more successfully exciting stimuli for men than others. The second is that within whatever 'natural' limits may exist, cultures define what is more or less masculine. Traditionally the masculine has been the hard and the militant. But traditions change; in the new atomic conditions of life, war is not an ultimate test of power and skill but of self-destructive madness. This may conspire with other forces such as coeducation, increasing sexual freedom, the affluence of the young, the greater catholicism of more-travelled populations, and the very media of communication to promote changes in conceptions of maleness.[1] The new conceptions will encourage the draft-card burner who argues that pacifism is more manly than using powerful weapons to fight Vietnamese peasants; it could allow the man who has his hair waved to disclose this fact in the company of men. Just as more women drive cars, wear trouser suits, and independently enter the labour force, so more men can wear colourful clothes formerly the garb of homosexuals and deviants; they can be flavoured with perfume and cosmetics; in a word they can be dandies but men.

It is undeniable that changes in personal decor have occured – they always do – and in some ways these changes may minimize sexual decorative differences. But also it may be premature to see in this the reflection of large-scale and major shifts in sexual roles and sexual balance of power and access to power. For one thing, the changes are in themselves ambiguous – does the trouser suit balance off the mini-skirt and does the fact that some men (a tiny proportion) have permanent waves balance off the enhanced masculine sexuality implied by tight clothes which betray more crisply the outline of the male body? Or is this simply the difference between good 'hairdressing' and bad 'haircuts'? And how substantial is the group in any community for whom these fashions and changes are of long-standing and decisive significance? And how much does it reflect more coherent age-grading (based on the media) rather than basic change? And is it not the case that the increasing similarity of male and female decor – in some circles – appears to confuse outsiders rather than those boasting the decor (who are accused of promiscuous heterosexual conduct at the same time as they are accused of eliminating various sex differences)?

These are questions which can in part be settled by research. But the answers to them must also be informed by a historical sense, and

1. For a typically provocative suggestion that sex roles are merging, that the 'manly man' becomes a figure of fun and the all-round man becomes the culture hero, see Marshall McLuhan and George Leonard, 'The Future of Sex', *Look* (25 July 1967). A principal reason for this change is the change in the mass-media and the decline of print and print-centred modes of apprehension and the rise of tactile, contextual electronic modes. To be sustained, the argument requires much more justifying data and cross-cultural analysis.

I include in the term 'historical' prehistory and evolutionary history. This is not merely to intone '*plus ça change . . .*', but to suggest that sexual differentiation of role involves a highly charged human core phenomenon, the importance of which is its adaptability to different economic, ecological, and climatic circumstances. That it should change its form and decor should not surprise us. The content remains the same, and it is risky to surmise on the vulgar basis of what is chic and sexy at any moment that basic communal notions of maleness have changed.

Of course, they may have already changed, and it is the task of human biologists to perceive and analyse these changes. But I have argued throughout this book that the changes are slow and possibly invisible to contemporaries of the changes. Though the prestige of militarists may decline in some war-weary or unbelieving communities, some other role or set of roles will be given equivalent status and encouragement because the practitioners of the jobs in question help the community in its contest with other communities for the world's good and privileges. These practitioners will also be seen as tough, manly, and quiet masters of the momentous event.[1] That they will often be successful at the expense of other communities – most conspicuously by taking trade from companies in other countries – is a reiteration of the aggressive pattern discussed earlier. That they may dispossess members of their own community – like the adept explorers for natural gas who have destroyed the livelihood and work morale of many coal miners – is another case of the same process. There will be many, at the same time, who develop drugs, perfect inventions, rescue lives, organize flood relief, who will be rewarded by the community. It is these wholly 'constructive' heroes who may represent a guide for new ways for men to validate themselves, for women to love and breed with validated males, and for boys to learn how to become men and what men do. History is discouraging about the prospects. But this is as much a spur to greater and more careful effort as an invitation to cynicism or despair.

Can women help? The Indian government decreed that Untouchables should have a proportion of seats in legislatures and special

---

1. Harold Wilson has stated (1967) that, in future, militarists and diplomats will receive fewer relatively automatic Honours. More will go to businessmen, particularly those prominent in exporting and some other public services. This may have some long-term effect, though it would be interesting to see what happens were Britain to become involved in military and forceful diplomatic adventures once more.

privileges to redress a historical deprivation. Perhaps women can be guaranteed a proportion of places, not only in legislatures but also in the critical decision-making bodies dealing with finance, defence, and war. This could be effective only if the men involved in these female-populated groups were not permitted to treat the formal group as a largely irrelevant forum for decisions taken by smaller all-male groups possessing the conviction of higher patriotism and realism than any mixed group could boast. This would ensure some democratic representativeness; more important, it would insert a new element into the decision-making which has yielded us a phenomenally well-armed world – a world where since the Second World War, whose ghastliness seemed final at the time, there have been scores of painful and costly military encounters. This new female element could turn out to be much the same thing again, so that there would be no change. But if the theory presented here is correct, modifying the dynamics and repercussions of the male bond may be a crucial feature of altered attitudes to power, to the value of destroying other communities' people and property, and to the concept that manliness is strength rather than flexibility and authority rather than attentiveness to others.

(In the first draft of this sentence, I made what is almost a parody of a 'Freudian slip' and wrote '. . . rather than attentiveness to authors'. But then, authors want to be as effective as anybody else; if the pen is indeed mightier than the sword, the pen bestows a mightiness of which any particular group of scribblers at any particular time seem ungratefully unaware. Perhaps in the long run of posterity the Galileos and Liddell Harts, Marxes and Carveth Reads are able to make their point. But is the lonely poet with a groin full of unused lust consummated because ladies love his work when he is old or dead? That reality is too serious a matter to be left to the realists is well known. But the political and quasi-political structures which intervene between private wish and social action are complex and usually require time to know and befriend. Writers may simply be impatient creatures who cannot spend the time forming the world to their model, so they bestow the model on that imperfect world.)

At the same time, should women join in male enterprises, particularly enterprises which now have the sense of masculine moment, it may necessitate some recognition of the desirability of either permitting or prohibiting sexual relations between participants, or at least recognizing the fact that sexual attraction exists between them and may cause difficulty to the group. This may be less problematic for the older the individuals involved. But the complex series of taboos, titillations, laws, and hedonistic influences surrounding male–female relationships in industrial societies (and most others too) will have to be adjusted to take account of the introduction of the sexual tension into affairs already tense as a result of their importance to communities and their consequences for individual careers.

Equality will cause the problems. Doctors and nurses, executives and secretaries, producers and actresses, can and do manage because there is a status and dominance difference between them. It is relatively 'normal' for men to seek sexual access to females who are their subordinates. Sexual access is not even in itself necessary; Robin Fox has made the point that polygamy is not necessarily about sex but about dominance.[1] It is an overvaluation of merely sexual intercourse which defines polygamy in terms of sex rather than social access and dominance. But where status dominance does not exist it is possible that some effort at stabilizing the internal sexual power system by coitus or flirtation may result from placing men and women as equals in charged situations concerned with power in the first place. In my own sphere, I have been struck at how predictably academics considering employing a younger female will comment upon her attractiveness *qua* female. It is possible to regard this as an anticipation of possible conflict between woman-as-colleague and woman-as-sexual-object. Nor are women unaware of the importance of attractiveness in securing desirable employment in largely male organizations. Currently there appear to be no solid prospects for significant change in this matter, and it seems but sensible to continue to regard it as a hazard in the search for ways of introducing female influence in the councils of power.

It may be unwise, therefore, to be optimistic or even sanguine about the possibility that females will soon stimulate much change in the social sub-systems and systems at the root of war as well as of happier actions. Women stay around and support murderers, thieves, usurers, frauds, and even failures. It is unlikely they will spurn warriors and it is likely there will always be enough – indeed a surplus – of women happy and willing to play the general's or the corporal's lady, to raise their children, and move from base to base living as income and expectations permit. It is their husband's job to kill or declare war or defend territory or condemn a traitor or imprison

1. Robin Fox, op. cit., 1968.

a pacifist; the men must do their job if only because it is too late in life to find another. Usually the job is justified because humans are immensely imaginative, and if indeed women are more realistic than men about the world, they boast the tact to allow men to maintain their own version of the *realpolitik* – it is still this version which prevails where it matters. Nor has Lysistrata's sexual bargaining ever been the answer. Should it come to that, the sexual-reproductive urgency claims more than enough strike-breakers who close the bedroom door behind them; women do not form bonds. Dependent as most women still are on the earnings and genes of men, they break ranks very soon. 'At least let my group survive.'

I have not in this book discussed homoerotic behaviour, and that particular form of male bonding and female bonding loosely called 'the homosexual community'. These large subjects require extensive treatment. But, very briefly, it should be said here that there may be analytic and practical profit in seeing male homosexuality as a specific feature of the more general phenomenon of male bonding. For a variety of obvious and more subtle reasons, male homoeroticism is socially organized differently and occurs more frequently than the female variety. There are a host of other differences which, in part, reflect the biologically based patterns which must accompany such a profound matter as seeking erotic contact, establishing sexual identity, and defining sexual role. The effect of homoerotic relationships in work, political, and other groups is of considerable interest in terms of many of the questions I have raised in this book. From a strictly biological viewpoint, there is no good reason for forbidding or even discouraging homoerotic activity, though in terms of Euro-American family structure and sexual attitudes there may be sociological reasons. As I have tried to indicate, there are important inhibitions in much of Euro-American culture – if not elsewhere too – against expressing affection between men, and one result of this inhibition of tenderness and warmth is an insistence on corporate hardness and forcefulness which has contributed to a variety of 'tough-minded' military, economic, political, and police enterprises and engagements.

Of course, a fear of homoeroticism is not the only reason for this – a number of others have been described here too. But homoerotic activity has been widely and powerfully defined as aberrant (though, as Kinsey has suggested, about half American males have had homosexual activity, while at least a third have had experiences culminating in orgasm).[1] Much guilt and uncertainty must plague many of the participants in these relationships. So must the insecurity about possibly being or becoming 'queer' or 'bent' among other men who may feel drawn to their colleagues and friends in ways I have described but whose repertoire of explanations of their feelings is overwhelmed by their community's assertion that men tender with each other are unmanly and unreliable. It remains a worthy subject of exploration to learn more about the dynamics of tender male interchanges, both for the sake of scientific understanding, and perhaps for providing information on the basis of which greater sympathy and opportunity may confront persons often harassed and disdained by themselves as well as others. That this may accompany a changed ideal of manhood, of corporate structure, of political acumen, and of the role of hard dominance, is not accidental but intrinsic to the whole argument of this book.

4

Which must now come to its conclusion. Being a hunting species, humans must have hope. There must even be a programme for hope springing eternally in our innards. This means that we cannot leave what is not well enough alone. It is obvious that many aspects of our private and communal lives are not well enough. In this book I have described and analysed a variety of situations and actions that cause foul injury to the occasionally elevated notion of ourselves which as a symbolizing species we ambitiously contrive. What can be done? Socrates' frightening demand 'know thyself' still stands as the beginning and the end of a reasonable course of personal study. Perhaps the same rule can and should apply to the species: 'know ourselves'. And here a paradox stares us in the eyes. In order to change how we act, we have to know what we are. Only by knowing what has changed a precious little can we set about changing things a little more. Things fell down before the Law of Gravity. But now – from our point of view – they fall down better, even bombs, because we understand them and can control a few conditions. Once before, when life was very trying, we were advised to attend our private gardens. But now we all share this one huge garden, our only Eden, a strangely tangled, strangely fruitful, strangely mapless garden. We also share a common responsibility to learn what our common responses to the garden are, and to its inhabitants. Only then dare we disturb the universe.

1. Alfred C. Kinsey, *et al.*, *Sexual Behaviour in the Human Female*, op. cit., pp. 487–9.

Bibliography

This bibliography contains all the items referred to in the text of the book. There is also a selection of more pertinent books and articles involved in the study, but not directly mentioned in this report.

1. BOOKS

JANE ADDAMS
Newer Ideals of Peace, Macmillan, New York, 1907.

ALEXANDER ALLAND, JR
Evolution and Human Behavior, American Museum of Natural History, Garden City, New York, 1967.

BRIDGET ALLCHIN
The Stone-Tipped Arrow, Phoenix House, London, 1966.

MICHAEL ALLEN
Rites de Passage, Melbourne University Press (in press).

STUART ALTMANN (ed.)
Social Communication among Primates, University of Chicago Press, 1965.

STANISLAV ANDRESKI
Elements of Comparative Sociology, Weidenfeld and Nicolson, London, 1964.

ROBERT ARDREY
The Territorial Imperative: A Personal Inquiry into the Animal Origins of Property and Nations, Atheneum Press, New York, 1966.

ROBERT ARDREY
African Genesis: A Personal Investigation into the Animal Origins and Nature of Man, Collins, London, 1961.

PHILIPPE ARIÈS
Centuries of Childhood, Jonathan Cape, London, 1962.

A. S. ATTEKAR
The Position of Women in Hindu Civilization, Motilal Banarsidas, Benares, 1956.

D. S. BAILEY
Homosexuality and the Western Christian Traditions, Longmans, Green, London, 1955.

ALBERT BANDURA and RICHARD H. WALTERS
Adolescent Aggression: A Study of the Influence of Child Training Practices and Family Interrelationships, Ronald Press, New York, 1959.

MICHAEL BANTON (ed.)
Darwinism and the Study of Society, Tavistock Publications, London, 1961.

S. A. BARNETT (ed.)
A Century of Darwin, Heinemann, London, 1958.

FRANK BEACH (ed.)
Sex and Behaviour, John Wiley, New York, 1965.

EARL H. BELL and JOHN SIRJAMAKI
Instructor's Manual to Accompany Social Foundations of Human Behaviour (2nd edition), Harper & Row, New York, 1965.

REINHARD BENDIX
Max Weber: An Intellectual Portrait, Heinemann, London, 1960.

THÉRÈSE BENEDEK
Psychosexual Function in Women, Ronald Press, New York, 1952.

JONATHAN BENNETT
Rationality: An Essay Towards an Analysis, Routledge & Kegan Paul, London, 1964.

L. BERKOWITZ (ed.)
Advances in Experimental Social Psychology, vol. 2, Academic Press, New York, 1965.

VERA BILSHAI
The Status of Women in the Soviet Union, Foreign Languages Publishing House, Moscow, 1959.

UNA BIRCH
Secret Societies and the French Revolution, Bodley Head, London, 1911.

RAY L. BIRDWHISTELL
Introduction to Kinesis: An Annotation Systems for Analysis of Body Motion and Gesture, University of Louisville, n.d.

EUGENE L. BLISS (ed.)
Roots of Behavior, Harper & Bros., New York, 1962.

ABBÉ BREUIL
Cave Drawings: catalogue for an exhibition of drawings by the Abbé Breuil, Arts Council, London, 1954.

J. W. BURROW
Evolution and Society: A Study in Victorian Social Theory, Cambridge University Press, 1966.

F. W. BUTT-THOMPSON
West African Secret Societies, Witherby, London, 1929.

KARL W. BUTZER
Environment and Archaeology: An Introduction to Pleistocene Geography, Methuen, London, 1965.

V. F. CALVERTON (ed.)
The Making of Man, Modern Library, New York, 1931.

ELIAS CANETTI
Crowds and Power, Gollancz, London, 1962.

J. D. CARTHY and F. J. EBLING (eds.)
The Natural History of Aggression, Academic Press (for the Institute of Biology), London, 1964.

WALTER LEGROS CLARK
History of the Primates, British Museum (Natural History), London, 1960.

YEHUDI A. COHEN
The Transition from Childhood to Adolescence, Aldine Books, Chicago, 1964.

NORMAN COHN
Warrant for Genocide, Eyre & Spottiswoode, London, 1967.

AUGUST COMTE
Cours de Philosophie Positive (5e edition), Paris, 1893.

JAMES CRAMER
The World's Police, Cassell, London, 1964.

ARKON DARAUL
Secret Societies Yesterday and Today, Muller, London, 1961.

CHARLES DARWIN
The Descent of Man and Selection in Relation to Sex, John Murray, London, 1871 (1st edition); 1894 (2nd edition).

NORMAN DENNIS, FERNANDO HENRIQUES, and CLIFFORD SLAUGHTER
Coal Is Our Life: An Analysis of a Yorkshire Mining Community, Eyre & Spottiswoode, London, 1956.

ALFRED DE VIGNY
The Military Condition (translated by M. Barnett), Oxford University Press, 1964.

IRVEN DeVORE (ed.)
Primate Behaviour: Field Studies of Monkeys and Apes, Holt, Rinehart & Winston, New York, 1965.

PAUL DeVORE (ed.)
The Origin of Man, Aldine Books, Chicago, 1968.

PAUL L. DeVORE (ed.)
The Origins of Man, transcript of a symposium sponsored by the Wenner-Gren Foundation, Wenner-Gren Foundation, New York, 1965.

THEODOSIUS DOBZHANSKY
Mankind Evolving: The Evolution of the Human Species (paperback edition), Yale University Press, 1962.

NORTON T. DODGE
Women in the Soviet Economy, Johns Hopkins Press, 1966.

MAURICE DUVERGER
The Political Role of Women, UNESCO, Paris, 1955.

S. M. EISENSTADT
From Generation to Generation, Free Press of Glencoe, Glencoe, Ill., 1955.

E. E. EVANS-PRITCHARD
The Position of Women in Primitive Societies, Faber & Faber, London, 1965.

JOHANNES FALKENBURG
Kin and Totem: Group Relations of Australian Aborigines in the Port Keats District, Oslo University Press, 1962.

LESLIE H. FARBER
The Ways of the Will: Essays Towards a Psychology and Psychopathology of Will, Constable, London, 1966.

S. M. FARBER and R. H. WILSON (eds.)
The Potential of Women, McGraw-Hill, New York, 1963.

JAMES C. FARIS
Cat Harbour: A Newfoundland Fishing Settlement, Institute of Social and Economic Research, St John's, Newfoundland, 1966.

ELIZABETH FAULKNER BAKER
Technology and Women's Work, Columbia University Press, 1964.

RONALD FLETCHER
Instinct in Man: In the Light of Recent Work in Comparative Psychology, Allen & Unwin, London, 1957.

C. S. FORD and FRANK BEACH
Patterns of Sexual Behaviour, Harper & Bros., New York, 1951.

GILLIAN FREEMAN
The Undergrowth of Literature, Thomas Nelson, London, 1967.

SIGMUND FREUD
Three Essays on the Theory of Sexuality (translated and edited by James Strachey), Hogarth Press, London, 1962.

BETTY FRIEDAN
The Feminine Mystique, W. W. Norton, New York, 1963.

PETER FRYER
Mrs Grundy: Studies in English Prudery, Dennis Dobson, London, 1963.

ROGER GARAUDY
Femmes du XXe Siècle: Semaine de la Pensée Marxiste, Presses Universitaires de France, 1965.

PAUL H. GEBHARD, J. H. GAGNON, W. B. POMEROY, and C. V. CHRISTENSON
Sex Offenders: An Analysis of Types, Heinemann, London, 1965.

JOHN GILLEN (ed.)
For a Science of Social Man: Convergences in Anthropology, Psychology, and Sociology, Macmillan, New York, 1954.

MORRIS GINSBURG
'Introduction to the Ninth Edition', *The Psychology of Society*, Methuen, London, 1964.

ELI GINZBURG, *et al.*
Breakdown and Recovery (vol. 2 of *The Ineffective Soldier*: 3 vols.), Columbia University Press, 1959.

ELI GINZBERG, *et al.*
Life Styles of Educated Women, Columbia University Press, 1966.

LOUIS GINZBURG
Students, Scholars and Saints, Jewish Publications Society of America, Philadelphia, 1928.

CARL GLICK and HONG SHENK HWA
Swords of Silence: Chinese Secret Societies – Past and Present, McGraw-Hill, New York, 1947.

MAX GLUCKMAN (ed.)
Closed Systems and Open Minds: The Limits of Naïvety in Social Anthropology, Oliver & Boyd, Edinburgh, 1964.

MAX GLUCKMAN (ed.)
Essays on the Ritual of Social Relations, Manchester University Press, 1962.

WILLIAM GOLDING
Lord of the Flies, Faber & Faber, London, 1954.

WALTER GOLDSCHMIDT
Comparative Functionalism: An Essay in Anthropological Theory, University of California Press, 1966.

W. J. GOODE
World Revolution and Family Patterns, Free Press of Glencoe, Ill., 1963.

GEOFFREY GORER
Hot Strip Tease and Other Notes on American Culture, Cresset Press, London, 1937.

ALAN P. GRIMES
The Puritan Ethic and Woman Suffrage, Oxford University Press, 1967.

ROBERT E. GRINDER (ed.)
Studies in Adolescence, Macmillan, New York, 1963.

LLEWELLYN GROSS (ed.)
Symposium in Sociological Theory, Row, Peterson, Evanston, Ill., 1959.

E. T. HALL
The Hidden Dimension, Doubleday, New York, 1966.

G. A. HARRISON, J. S. WEINER, J. M. TANNER, and N. A. BARNICOT
Human Biology, Clarendon Press, Oxford, 1964.

E. G. MURRAY HAUSNECHT
The Joiners: A Sociological Description of Voluntary Association Membership in the United States, Bedminster Press, New York, 1962.

TOM HAYDEN
Riot in Newark, Random House, New York, 1967.

WALTER HEAPE
Sex Antagonism, Constable, London, 1913.

CHARLES W. HECKETHORN
The Secret Societies of All Ages and Countries, George Redway, London, 1897.

H. HEDIGER
Studies of the Psychology and Behaviour of Captive Animals in Zoos and Circuses, Butterworth, London, 1955.

FERNANDO HENRIQUES
Prostitution and Society, vol. 2, MacGibbon & Kee, London, 1963.

MAGNUS HIRSCHFELD
The Sexual History of the World War, Panurge Press, New York, 1934.

MAGNUS HIRSCHFELD
Sexual Anomalies and Perversions, Encyclopedic Press, London, 1938.

E. J. HOBSBAWN
Primitive Rebels: Studies in Archaic Forms of Social Movement in the 19th and 20th Centuries, Manchester University Press, 1959

RICHARD HOFSTADTER
Social Darwinism in American Thought: 1860–1915, University of Pennsylvania Press, 1945.

E. P. HOLLANDER
Leaders, Groups and Influence, Oslo University Press, 1964.

F. C. HOWELL and F. BOURLIÈRE (eds.)
African Ecology and Human Evolution, Methuen, London, 1964.

FRANCIS L. K. HSU
Clan, Caste and Club, D. Van Nostrand, Princeton, N.J., 1963.

KINJI IMANISHI and S. H. ALTMANN (eds.)
Japanese Monkeys, Yerkes Regional Primate Center, Atlanta, Ga., 1965.

H. W. JANSON
Apes and Ape Lore in the Middle Ages and the Renaissance, Warburg
Institute, London, 1952.

JUSTIN KAPLAN (ed.)
*With Malice Toward Women: A Handbook for Women-Haters Drawn from
the Best Minds of All Time*, W. H. Allen, London, 1953.

A. G. KELLER
Societal Evolution: A Study of the Evolutionary Basis of Science and Society,
Yale University Press, 1931.

HANS KELSEN
Society and Nature, University of Chicago Press, 1943.

ALFRED KINSEY, *et al.*
Sexual Behaviour in the Human Female, W. B. Saunders, Philadelphia,
1953.

CLIFFORD KIRKPATRICK
Nazi Germany: Its Women and Family Life, Bobbs-Merrill, New York,
1938.

VIOLA KLEIN
Working Wives, Institute of Personnel Management, London, 1960.

A. L. KROEBER
Anthropology, Harcourt, Brace, New York, 1948.

PETER KROPOTKIN
Mutual Aid: A Factor of Evolution, Heinemann, London, 1902.

THOMAS S. KUHN
The Structure of Scientific Revolutions, University of Chicago Press, 1962.

WALTER Z. LAQUER
Young Germany: A History of the German Youth Movement, Routledge &
Kegan Paul, London, 1962.

HAROLD LASSWELL
Psychopathology and Politics, Viking Press, New York, 1960.

HENRI LE CARON
Twenty-five Years in the Secret Service, Heinemann, London, 1892.

GERSHON LEGMAN
Love and Death: A Study in Censorship, Breaking Point, New York, 1949.

GERSHON LEGMAN, H. C. LEAM, T. WRIGHT, G. WITT, SIR A. TENNANT, and SIR W. DUGDALE
The Guilt of the Templars, Basic Books, New York, 1966.

CLAUDE LÉVI-STRAUSS
The Savage Mind, Weidenfeld and Nicolson, London, 1966.

MARION J. LEVY, JR
The Structure of Society, Princeton University Press, 1951.

ROY LEWIS
The Evolution Man, Penguin Books, Harmondsworth, 1963.

R. LINTON (ed.)
The Science of Man in the World Crisis, Columbia University Press, 1945.

SEYMOUR M. LIPSET
Political Man, Doubleday, New York, 1963.

K. L. LITTLE
The Mende of Sierra Leone, Routledge & Kegan Paul, London, 1951.

KONRAD LORENZ
On Aggression, Methuen, London, 1966.

EMERSON H. LOUCKE
The Ku Klux Klan in Pennsylvania, Telegraphy Press, New York, 1935.

ROBERT LOWIE
Primitive Society, George Routledge, London, 1921.

E. E. MACCOBY, et al. (eds.)
Readings in Social Psychology, Holt, Rinehart & Winston, New York, 1958.

BRYAN MAGEE
One in Twenty: A Study of Homosexuality in Men and Women, Secker & Warburg, London, 1966.

B. MALINOWSKI
A Scientific Theory of Culture and Other Essays, University of North Carolina Press, 1944.

MARGARET MEAD
Male and Female, Penguin Books, Harmondsworth, 1962.

MARGARET MEAD
Continuities in Cultural Evolution, Yale University Press, 1964.

MARGARET MEAD AND FRANCES B. KAPLAN (eds.)
American Women: The Report of the President's Commission on the Status of Women, Charles Scribner's Sons, New York, 1965.

E. MILLER (ed.)
Foundations of Child Psychiatry, Longmans, Green, London, 1965.

C. WRIGHT MILLS
The Power Élite, Oxford University Press, 1956.
JOHN MONEY (ed.)
Sex Research: New Developments, Holt, Rinehart & Winston, New York, 1965.
ASHLEY MONTAGU
The Natural Superiority of Women, Allen & Unwin, London, 1954.
ASHLEY MONTAGU
The Biosocial Nature of Man, Grove Press, New York, 1956.
ASHLEY MONTAGU (ed.)
Culture and the Evolution of Man, Oxford University Press, 1962.
W. P. MORGAN
Triad Societies in Hong Kong, Government Press, Hong Kong, 1960.
RICHARD HOGGART
The Uses of Literacy, Penguin Books, Harmondsworth, 1957.
DESMOND MORRIS
The Naked Ape, Jonathan Cape, London, 1967.
DESMOND MORRIS (ed.)
Primate Ethology, Weidenfeld & Nicolson, London, 1967.
FARLEY MOWAT
Never Cry Wolf, Secker & Warburg, London, 1964.
GEORGE P. MURDOCK
Social Structure, Macmillan, New York, 1949.
GARDNER MURPHY
Personality: A Biosocial Approach to Origins and Structure, Harper & Bros., New York, 1947.
BURY PALLISER
Historic Devices, Badges and War-Cries, Sampson Low & Marston, London, 1870.
TALCOTT PARSONS
The Social System, Tavistock Publications, London, 1952.
T. PARSONS, E. SHILS, K. D. NAEGELE, and J. PITT (eds.)
Theories of Society, Free Press of Glencoe, Glencoe, Ill., 1962.
TALCOTT PARSONS and ROBERT F. BALES
Family, Socialization and Interaction Process, Routledge & Kegan Paul, London, 1956.
NICHOLAS PASTORE
The Nature–Nurture Controversy, King's Crown Press, New York, 1949.
DENISE PAULME (ed.)
Women of Tropical Africa, University of California Press, 1964.

KARL PEARSON
Side Lights on the Evolution of Man, Eugenics Laboratory Lecture Series, No. XIV, Cambridge University Press, 1921.

ROBERT N. PEHRSON
The Social Organization of Marri Baluch (compiled and analysed from his notes by Frederick Barth), Viking Fund Publication in Anthropology, vol. 43, Wenner-Gren Foundation, New York, 1966.

N. W. POLSBY
Community Power and Political Theory, Yale University Press, 1963.

HENRI PIRENNE
Early Democracies in the Low Countries, Harper Torchbooks, New York, 1963.

KARL POPPER
The Poverty of Historicism, Routledge & Kegan Paul, London, 1961.

JOHN PORTER
The Vertical Mosaic, University of Toronto Press, 1965.

ADOLF PORTMAN
Animals as Social Beings, Hutchinson, London, 1961.

CARVETH READ
The Origin of Man, Cambridge University Press, 1925.

ANN ROE and GEORGE GAYLORD SIMPSON (eds.)
Behaviour and Evolution, Yale University Press, 1958.

FRITZ ROETHLISBERGER, *et al.*
Management and the Worker, Harvard University Press, 1939.

G. ROHEIM
Psychoanalysis and Anthropology; Culture, Personality and the Unconscious, International Universities Press, New York, 1950.

ISMOND ROSEN (ed.)
The Pathology and Treatment of Sexual Deviation, Oxford University Press, 1964.

H. D. RUITENBECK (ed.)
The Problem of Homosexuality in Modern Society, E. P. Dutton, New York, 1963.

JOHN RUSKIN
Letters and Advice to Young Girls and Young Ladies, John Wiley, New York, 1879.

BERTRAND RUSSELL
Anti-Suffragist Anxieties (pamphlet), People's Suffrage Federation, London, n.d.

BERTRAND RUSSELL
Marriage and Morals, Allen & Unwin, London, 1929.

MARSHALL D. SAHLINS and ELMAN R. SERVICE (eds.)
Evolution and Culture, University of Michigan Press, 1960.

STANLEY SCHACTER
The Psychology of Affiliation: Experimental Studies of Sources of Gregariousness, Tavistock Publications, London, 1961.

ADAM SCHAFF
A Philosophy of Man, Lawrence & Wishart, London, 1963.

I. SCHAPERA
Government and Politics in Tribal Societies, Watts, London, 1965.

C. H. SCHILLER (trans. and ed.)
Instinctive Behaviour: The Development of a Modern Concept, Methuen, London, 1957

MICHAEL SCHOFIELD
The Sexual Behaviour of Young People, Longmans, Green, London, 1965.

ALVIN L. SCHORR
Slums and Social Insecurity, Thomas Nelson, London, 1965.

ROBERT R. SEARS, *et al.*
Patterns of Child Rearing, Row, Peterson, Evanston, Ill., 1957.

HEREWARD SENIOR
Orangeism in Ireland and Britain, 1795–1836, Routledge & Kegan Paul, London, 1966.

ELMAN R. SERVICE
The Hunters, Prentice-Hall, Englewood Cliffs, N.J., 1966.

JORDON N. SHER (ed.)
Theories of the Mind, Free Press of Glencoe, Glencoe, Ill., 1962.

A. and G. SIEVEKING
The Caves of France and Northern Spain, Studio Vista, London, 1962.

ANDREW SINCLAIR
The Emancipation of the American Woman, Harper & Row, New York, 1966.

E. J. SLIJPER
Whales, Hutchinson, London, 1962.

WILLIAM EDWARD SMITH
Christianity and Secret Societies, Meador Publishing, Boston, 1936.

W. J. SOLLAS
Ancient Hunters and Their Modern Representatives, Macmillan, London, 1924.

G. SOMMERHOFF
Analytical Biology, Oxford University Press, 1950

PITIRIM SOROKIN
Contemporary Sociological Theories, Harper & Bros., New York, 1927.

C. H. SOUTHWICK (ed.)
Primate Social Behaviour, D. Van Nostrand, Princeton, N.J., 1963.

NICHOLAS J. SPYKMAN
The Social Theory of Georg Simmel, Atherton Press, New York, 1966
(reissue of 1925 publication).

WILLIAM N. STEPHENS
The Oedipus Complex: Cross-Cultural Evidence, Free Press of Glencoe,
Glencoe, Ill., 1962.

ANTHONY STORR
Human Aggression, Allen Lane, The Penguin Press, London, 1968.

SAMUEL STOUFFER, *et al.*
The American Soldier, vol. 1, Princeton University Press, 1949.

J. M. TANNER (ed.)
Human Growth, Pergamon Press, Oxford, 1960.

SOL TAX (ed.)
The Evolution of Man, University of Chicago Press, 1960.

SOL TAX (ed.)
Horizons of Anthropology, Aldine Books, Chicago, 1964.

E. L. THORNDIKE
Human Nature and the Social Order, Macmillan, New York, 1940.

VERA TOMICH
Education in Yugoslavia and the New Reform, U.S. Department of Health,
Education and Welfare, Washington, D.C., 1963.

J. C. TROTTER
Boxing, George Routledge, London, 1901.

WILFRED TROTTER
Instincts of the Herd in Peace and War, Ernest Benn, London, 1916.

GRAHAM WALLAS
The Great Society: A Psychological Analysis, Macmillan, London, 1914.

GRAHAM WALLAS
Human Nature in Politics, Constable, London, 1908.

S. L. WASHBURN (ed.)
The Social Life of Early Man, Aldine Books, Chicago, 1961.

MAX WEBER
The Theory of Social and Economic Organization, Free Press of Glencoe,
Glencoe, Ill., 1947.

HUTTON WEBSTER
Primitive Secret Societies, Macmillan, New York, 1932.

LESLIE T. WILKINS
Social Deviance, Prentice-Hall, Englewood Cliffs, N.J., 1965.

RUPERT WILKINSON
The Prefects: British Leadership and the Public School Tradition, Oxford University Press, 1964.

PETER WILLMOTT
Adolescent Boys of East London, Routledge & Kegan Paul, London, 1966.

KURT H. WOLFF (trans. and ed.)
The Sociology of Georg Simmel, Collier-Macmillan, London, 1964 (Free Press paperback edition).

MERVYN L. WYNNE
Triad and Tabut: A Survey of the Origin and Diffusion of Chinese and Mohammedan Secret Societies in the Malay Peninsula, A.D. 1800–1935, Government Printing Office, Singapore, 1941.

V. C. WYNNE-EDWARDS
Animal Dispersion in Relation to Social Behaviour, Hafner, New York, 1962.

FRANK YOUNG
Initiation Ceremonies: A Cross-Cultural Study of Status Dramatization, Bobbs-Merrill, New York, 1965.

W. C. YOUNG (ed.)
Sex and Internal Secretions, vol. 2 (3rd edition), Baillière, Tindall & Cox, London, 1961.

SOLLY ZUCKERMAN
The Social Life of Monkeys and Apes, Kegan Paul, London, 1932

2. ARTICLES IN JOURNALS, PUBLISHED AND UNPUBLISHED PAPERS, AND INDIVIDUAL LECTURES

DAVID F. ABERLE, URIE BRONFENBRENNER, ECKHARD H. HESS, DANIEL R. MILLER, DAVID M. SCHNEIDER, and JAMES N. SPUHLER
'The Incest Taboo and the Mating Patterns of Animals', *American Anthropologist*, **65**, 2 (April 1963).

CORINNA ADAM
'Gretel's Old Look', *New Statesman* (21 February 1964).

CORINNA ADAM
'Duels and Jobs for the Boys', *New Statesman* (18 June 1965).

J. ANTHONY AMBROSE
'The Study of Human Social Organization: A Review of Current

Concepts and Approaches', *Symposia of the Zoological Society*, No. 14, London.

IRIS ANDRESKI
'The Baby as Dictator', *New Society* (15 December 1966).

YU. P. AVERKIEVA
On the Earliest Forms of Inheritance, a paper presented to the Sixth World Congress of Sociology, Evian, September 1966: Nauka Publishing House, Moscow, 1966.

HERBERT BARRY, III, MARGARET K. BACON, and IRVIN L. CHILD
'A Cross-Cultural Survey of Some Sex Differences in Socialization', *Journal of Abnormal and Sexual Psychology*, 55, 3 (November 1957).

F. BARTH
'Anthropological Modes and Social Reality' (The Second Royal Society Nuffield Lecture), *Proceedings of the Royal Society*, 165, 998 (July 1966).

MARSTON BATES
'On Being Man', *The American Scholar*, 36, 1 (Winter 1966–7).

FRANK BEACH
'The Snark was a Boojum', *American Psychologist*, 5 (1950), pp. 113–27.

ROBIN BEST
'Against High Density', *New Society* (24 November 1966).

LEWIS R. BINFORD and SALLY R. BINFORD
'A Preliminary Analysis of Functional Variability in the Mousterian of Levallois Facies', *American Anthropologist*, 68, 2 (April 1966).

E. WILBER BOCK
'The Female Clergy: A Case of Professional Marginality', *American Journal of Sociology*, 72, 5 (March 1967).

KENNETH E. BOCK
'The Comparative Method of Anthropology', *Comparative Studies in Society and History*, 8, 3 (April 1966).

WILLIAM F. BRAINERD
'Masonic Lecture', John March, New London, 1825; *Encyclopaedia Britannica* (11th edition), vol. 23, Cambridge, 1911.

PETER BROOK
'Filming a Masterpiece', *Observer Weekend Review* (26 July 1964).

NONA B. BROWN
'Inquiry into the Feminine Mind', *New York Times Magazine* (12 April 1964).

WAYNESBURG COLLEGE LIBRARY
WAYNESBURG PA.

232 MEN IN GROUPS

JEAN BUXTON
'Animal Identity and Human Peril: Some Mandari Images', *Man*, 3, 1 (March 1968).

ROBERT L. CARNEIRO and STEPHEN F. TOBIAS
'The Application of Scale Analysis to the Study of Cultural Evolution', *Transactions of the New York Academy of Sciences* (Series II), vol. 26, No. 2 (December 1963).

ROBERT CARRICK
'Ecological Significance of Territory in the Australian Magpie', unpublished paper, 1965.

M. R. A. CHANCE
'Attention Structure as the Basis of Primate Rank Orders', *Man*, 2, 4 (November 1967).

M. R. A. CHANCE and ALAN MEAD
'Social Behaviour and Primate Evolution', *Symposia*, vol. 7, Society for Experimental Biology, London, 1953.

MICKEY CHIANG
'Use of Tools by Wild Macaque Monkeys in Singapore', *Nature*, 214 (17 June 1967).

J. DESMOND CLARK
'Acheulian Occupation Sites in the Middle East and Africa: A Study in Cultural Variability', *American Anthropologist*, 68, 2, Part 2 (April 1966).

WERNER COHN
'Social Stratification and the Charismatic', *Midwestern Sociologist*, 21, 1 (December 1958).

WERNER COHN
'Social Status and the Ambivalence Hypothesis: Some Critical Notes and a Suggestion', *American Sociological Review*, 25, 4 (August 1960).

LEWIS A. COSER
'Political Functions of Eunuchism', *American Sociological Review*, 29, 6 (December 1964).

EARL W. COUNT
'Comment on Steps toward a Unified Anthropology', *Current Anthropology*, 8, 1–2 (February–April 1967).

EARL W. COUNT
'The Biological Basis of Human Sociality', *American Anthropologist*, 60, 6 (December 1958).

URSULA M. COWGILL
'The Season of Birth in Man', *Man*, 1, 2 (June 1960).

JOHN HURRELL CROOK
'Cooperation in Primates', *Eugenics Review*, 58, 2 (June 1966).

JOHN HURRELL CROOK
'Evolutionary Change in Primate Societies', *Science Journal* (June 1967).

J. H. CROOK and J. S. GARTLAN
'Evolution of Primate Societies', *Nature*, 210 (18 June 1966).

R. H. S. CROSSMAN
'War Crime', *New Statesman* (3 May 1963).

F. FRASER DARLING
'Social Life in Ungulates', in *Structure et Physiologie des Sociétiés Animales*, Colloques Internationaux du Centre Nationale de la Recherche Scientifique, Paris, 1952.

RAYMOND DART
'The Minimal Bone-Breccia Content of Makapansgat and the Australopithicine Predatory Habit', *American Anthropologist*, 60, 5 (October 1958).

JAMES A. DAVIS
'The Campus as a Frog Pond: An Application of the Theory of Relative Deprivation to Career Decisions of College Men', *American Journal of Sociology*, 72, 1 (July 1966).

P. CHOMBART DE LAUWE
'Introduction', *Images of Women in Society: International Social Science Journal*, 14, 1, UNESCO, Paris.

ROBERT E. EDGERTON
'Pokot Intersexuality: An East African Example of Resolutions of Sexual Incongruity', *American Anthropologist*, 66, 6 (December 1964).

IRENAUS EIBL-EIBESFELDT
'The Fighting Behaviour of Animals', *Scientific American* (December 1961).

JOHN F. EISENBERG and ROBERT E. KEUHN
'The Behaviour of *Ateles Geoffroyi* and Related Species', *Smithsonian Miscellaneous Collections*, 151, 8 (1966).

JOHN F. EISENBERG
'The Social Organization of Mammals', *Handbuch der Zoologie*, 10, 7 (May 1964).

NORBERT ELIAS and ERIC DUNNING
'Dynamics of Group Sports with Special Reference to Football', *British Journal of Sociology*, 17, 4 (December 1966).

J. MERRITT EMLEN
'Natural Selection and Human Behaviour', *Journal of Theoretical Biology*, 12 (1966).

ERIK ERIKSON
'Sex Differences in the Play Configurations of Pre-Adolescents', *American Journal of Orthopsychiatry*, 21, 4 (October 1951).

ROBERT ERWIN
'Civilization as a Phase of World History', *American Historical Review*, 71, 4 (July 1966).

WILLIAM M. EVAN
'Dimensions of Participation in Voluntary Associations', *Social Forces*, 36, 2 (December 1957).

COLIN FLETCHER
'Beat and Gangs on Merseyside', *New Society* (February 1964).

CLELLAN S. FORD
'A Comparative Study of Human Reproduction', in *Yale University Publications in Anthropology*, vol. 3, Yale University Press, 1945.

R. F. FORTUNE
'Omaha Secret Societies', in *Columbia University Contributions to Anthropology*, vol. 14, Columbia University Press, 1932.

ROBIN FOX
'The Evolution of Human Sexual Behaviour', *New York Times Magazine* (24 March 1968).

ROBIN FOX
'In the Beginning: Aspects of Hominid Behavioural Evolution' (London School of Economics and Political Science, Malinowski Memorial Lecture, 1967), *Man*, 2, 3 (September 1967).

ROBIN FOX
'Incest, Inhibition and Hominid Evolution', paper presented to Wenner-Gren Symposium, Burg Wartenstein (August 1968).

J. G. FRAZER
'Observations in Central Australian Totemism', *Journal of the Royal Anthropological Institute* (n.s.), 1, 3–4 (February–May 1899).

DEREK FREEMAN
'Social Anthropology and the Scientific Study of Human Behaviour', *Man*, 1, 3 (September 1966), pp. 330–42.

HOWARD E. FREEMAN, EDWIN NOVAK, and LEO G. REEDER
'Correlates of Membership in Voluntary Associations', *American Sociological Review*, 22, 5 (October 1957).

EDGAR Z. FRIEDENBERG
'A Violent Country', *New York Review of Books* (20 October 1966).

HAROLD GARFINKLE
'Conditions of Successful Degradation Ceremonies', *American Journal of Sociology*, 61, 5 (March 1956).

CLIFFORD GEERTZ
'The Impact and Concept of Culture on the Concept of Man', *Bulletin of the Atomic Scientists* (April 1966).

VALERIUS GEIST
'Working with the Mountain Sheep', *Animals* (July 1967).

MARTHA GELLHORN
'A Tale of Two Wars', *Guardian* (14 April 1967).

ERNEST GELLNER
'Nature and Society in Social Anthropology', *Philosophy of Science*, 30, 3 (July 1963).

M. T. GHISELIN
'On Semantic Pitfalls of Biological Adaptation', *Philosophy of Science*, 33, 1–2 (March–June 1966).

HELEN GIDEON
'A Baby is Born in the Punjab', *American Anthropologist*, 64, 6 (December 1962).

NOEL P. GIST
'Secret Societies: A Cultural Study of Fraternalism in the United States', *University of Missouri Studies*, 15, 4 (1 October 1940).

RONALD GOLDMAN
'Cultural Influences on the Sex Ratio in the Incidence of Stuttering', *American Anthropologist*, 69, 1 (February 1967).

E. H. GOMBRICH
'Ritualized Gesture and Expression in Art', *Royal Society Philosophical Transactions*, Series B, Biological Sciences No. 772, 25 (December 1966).

MICHAEL GRAHAM
'Crowds and the Like in Vertebrates', *Human Relations*, 17 , 4 (1964).

E. F. GREENMAN
'The Extraorganic', *American Anthropologist*, 50, 2 (April–June 1948).

EDWARD GROSS
'Plus Ça Change . . . The Sexual Structure of Occupations Over Time', presented to the American Sociological Association Meeting, San Francisco, 1967.

OSWALD HALL
'Gender and the Division of Labour', in *Implications of Traditional Divisions Between Men's Work and Women's Work in Our Society*, Department of Labour of Canada, Ottawa, 1964.

A. IRVING HALLOWELL
'Personality Structure and the Evolution of Man', *American Anthropologist*, 52, 2 (April–June 1950).

DAVID A. HAMBURG
'Evolution of Emotional Responses: Evidence from Recent Research on Nonhuman Primates', *Science and Psychoanalysis*, 12 (1968).

H. F. HARLOW and M. H. HARLOW
'Affection in Primates', *Discovery*, 27, 1 (January 1966).

RICHARD S. HARTIGAN
'Augustine on War and Killing', *Journal of History of Ideas*, 27, 2 (April–June 1966).

KATHY HASSARD
'Spirit of Feminism Political Lack Today', *Vancouver Sun* (2 October 1963).

HARRY B. HAWTHORN
'A Test of Simmel on the Secret Society: The Doukhobors of British Columbia', *American Journal of Sociology*, 62, 1 (July 1956).

BRUCE A. HERTIG
'Acclimatization of Women during Work in Hot Environments', *Federation Proceedings*, 22, 3 (May–June 1963).

JAMES N. HILL
'A Prehistoric Community in Eastern Arizona', *Southwestern Journal of Anthropology*, 22, 1 (Spring 1966).

ROBERT A. HINDE
'The Nature of Aggression', *New Society*, 9, 231 (2 March 1967).

RALPH L. HOLLOWAY, JR
'Tools and Teeth: Some Speculations Regarding Canine Reduction', *American Anthropologist*, 69, 1 (February 1967).

ROGER HOLMES
'Freud and Social Class', *British Journal of Sociology*, 16, 1 (March 1965).

ROGER HOLMES
'The University Seminar and the Primal Horde', unpublished paper, London School of Economics and Political Science, London, 1966.

JOHN J. HONIGMANN
'Cultural Dynamics of Sex', *Psychiatry*, 10, 1 (February 1947).

THELMA HUNT
'Australian Women', *Australian Quarterly*, 35, 1 (March 1963), pp. 79–84.

G. I. C. INGRAM
'Displacement Activity in Human Behaviour', *American Anthropologist*, 62, 6 (December 1960).

NICHOLAS JOHNSON
'What do Children Learn from War Comics', *New Society* (7 July 1966).

SIDNEY JOURARD
'Privacy: The Psychological Need', *New Society* (25 May 1967).

MIRRA KAMOROVSKY
'The Voluntary Associations of Urban Dwellers', *American Sociological Review*, 11, 6 (December 1964).

FRANK KERMODE
'The Meaning of It All', *Books and Bookmen*, 5 (October 1959).

A. KORTLANDT and M. KOOIJ
'Protohominid Behaviour in Primates', *Symposia of the Zoological Society of London*, No. 10 (1963).

A. KORTLANDT
'Comment on the Essential Morphological Basis for Human Culture', *Current Anthropology*, 6 (1965).

LANDAU, JACOB M.
'Prolegomena to a Study of Secret Societies in Modern Egypt', *Middle Eastern Studies*, 1, 2 (January 1965).

MARK LANE
'The Eternal Feminine', printed for private circulation, 1922.

CHRISTOPHER LASCH
'The Trouble with Black Power', *New York Review of Books*, 10, 4 (29 February 1968).

EARL LATHAM
'The Group Basis of Politics: Notes for a Theory', *American Political Science Review*, 46 (June 1952).

W. S. LAUGHLIN
'The Importance of Hunting in Human Evolution', paper presented to the Man the Hunter Conference, University of Chicago, April 1966.

EDMUND LEACH
'Don't Say Boo to a Goose', *New York Review of Books* (15 December 1966).

RICHARD B. LEE
'What "Hunters" Do for a Living: Or, How to Make Out on Scarce Resources', paper presented to the Man the Hunter Conference, University of Chicago, April 1966.

ROBERT E. LEVINE
'Sex Roles and Economic Change in Africa', *Ethnology*, **5**, 2 (April 1966).

SEYMOUR LEVINE
'Sex Differences in the Brain', *Scientific American*, **214**, 4 (April 1966).

CLAUDE LÉVI-STRAUSS
'The Scope of Anthropology', *Current Anthropology*, **7**, 2 (April 1966).

NORMAN LEWIS
'The Honored Society', *New Yorker* (8 February 1964).

OSCAR LEWIS
'Husbands and Wives in a Mexican Village: A Study of Role Conflict', *American Anthropologist*, **51**, 3 (July–September 1949).

KENNETH LITTLE
'The Role of Voluntary Associations in West African Urbanization', *American Anthropologist*, **59**, 4 (August 1957).

KENNETH L. LITTLE
'The Role of the Secret Society in Cultural Specialization', *American Anthropologist*, **51**, 1 (January–March 1949).

FRANK B. LIVINGSTONE
'Reconstructing Man's Pliocene Pongid Ancestors', *American Anthropologist*, **64**, 2 (April 1962).

PETER LOMAS
'Childbirth Ritual', *New Society* (31 December 1964).

KONRAD LORENZ
'The Evolution of Behaviour', *Scientific American* (December 1958).

G. A. LUNDBERG
'The Natural Science Tradition in Sociology', *American Journal of Sociology*, **61**, 3 (November 1955).

STANFORD LYMAN
'Chinese Secret Societies in the Occident: Notes and Suggestions for Research in the Sociology of Secrecy', *Canadian Review of Sociology and Anthropology*, **1**, 2 (1965).

GLEN MCBRIDE
'The Conflict of Crowding', *Discovery*, **27**, 4 (April 1966).

W. C. MCCLELLAND
'Women's Weeklies', *New Society* (31 December 1964).

JAMES V. MCCONNELL
'A Tape Recorder Theory of Memory', *Worm Runner's Digest*, **7**, 2 (September 1965).

ALASTAIR MCKINNON
'God, Humanity and Sexual Polarity', *Hibbert Journal* (July 1954).

MARSHALL MCLUHAN and GEORGE LEONARD
'The Future of Sex', *Look* (25 July 1967).

JOHN S. MCNEIL and MARTIN B. GIFFEN
'Military Retirement: The Retirement Syndrome', *American Journal of Psychology*, **123**, 7 (January 1967).

DAVID G. MANDELBAUM
'The Plains Cree', *Anthropological Papers*, **37**, 2 American Museum of Natural History, New York, 1940.

MARGARET MEAD
'The Mountain Arapesh', *Anthropological Papers*, **36**, 3, American Museum of Natural History, New York, 1938.

RICHARD MEANS
'Why Worry About Nature?', *Saturday Review* (2 December 1967).

RICHARD MEANS
'Sociology, Biology and the Analysis of Social Problems', *Social Problems*, **15**, 2 (Fall 1967).

P. B. MEDAWAR
'Onwards from Spencer', *Encounter* (September 1963).

WALTER R. MILES
'Chimpanzee Behaviour: Removal of Foreign Body from Companion's Eye', paper presented to the 100th Annual Meeting of the National Academy of Sciences in Washington, D.C., May 1963.

C. WRIGHT MILLS
'The Structure of Power in American Society', *British Journal of Sociology*, **60**, 1 (March 1958).

GERALDINE R. MINTZ
'Some Observations on the Function of Women Sociologists at Sociology Conventions', *American Sociologist*, **2**, 3 (August 1967).

URSULA MITTWOCH
'Sex Differentiation in Mammals', *Nature*, **214** (May 1967).

BARBARA MOON
'For the Sake of Argument', *Maclean's Magazine* (5 October 1963).

LEWIS MUMFORD
'Speculations on Prehistory', *American Scholar*, **36**, 1 (Winter 1966–7).

GEORGE P. MURDOCK
'Comparative Data on the Division of Labour by Sex', *Social Forces*, 15, 4 (1937).

ROBERT F. MURPHY
'Social Structure and Sex Antagonism', *Southwestern Journal of Anthropology*, 15, 1 (Spring 1959).

ROBERT F. MURPHY
Review of Denise Paulme (ed.), *Femmes D'Afrique Noire*, in *American Anthropologist*, 64, 5 (October 1962).

JOHN NAPIER
'The Antiquity of Human Walking', *Scientific American*, 216, 4 (April 1967).

PAT NASH
Homeless Men at Home, unpublished paper, Columbia University, New York, 1965.

CARL NIEMEYER
'The Coral Island Revisited', *College English*, 22 (January 1961).

EDWARD NORBECK, DONALD E. WALKER, and MIMI COHEN
'The Interpretation of Data: Puberty Rites', *American Anthropologist*, 64, 3 (June 1962).

KENNETH P. OAKLEY
'The Problem of Man's Antiquity: An Historical Survey', *Bulletin of the British Museum (Natural History) Geology*, 9, 5 (1964).

GORDON ORIANS
'Natural Selection and Ecological Theory', *American Naturalist*, 96, 890.

ANTHONY M. ORUM
'A Reappraisal of the Social and Political Participation of Negroes', *American Journal of Sociology*, 72, 1 (July 1966).

GEORGE ORWELL
'Boys' Weeklies', *Inside the Whale*, Secker & Warburg, 1940.

TALCOTT PARSONS
'Evolutionary Universals in Society', *American Sociological Review*, 29, 3 (June 1964).

T. T. PATERSON
'Ritual in Industrial Societies, A Discussion of Ritualizations in Animals and Man', *Royal Society Philosophical Transactions*, Series B, Biological Sciences No. 772, 25 (December 1966).

MELVIN L. PERLMAN
'The Changing Status and Role of Women in Toro (Western Uganda)', *Cahiers d'Études Africaines*, **6**, 4 (1966).

JOHN PFEIFFER
'When Homo Erectus Tamed Fire, He Tamed Himself', *New York Times Magazine* (11 December 1966).

JEAN PIAGET
'Biology and Cognition', *Diogenes*, No. 54 (Summer 1966).

JEAN PIAGET
'Le Probleme des Mechanismes Commune dans les Sciences de l'Homme', *Transactions of the Sixth World Congress of Sociology*, vol. 1, International Sociological Association, Geneva, 1966.

DAVID R. PILBEAM
'Man's Earliest Ancestors', *Science Journal*, **3**, 2 (February 1967).

MIHAILO POPOVICH
'What the American Sociologists Think About their Science and its Problems', *American Sociologist*, **2** (May 1966).

ALVIN F. POUSSAINT
'The Stresses of White Female Workers in the Civil Rights Movement in the South', *American Journal of Psychiatry*, **123**, 4 (October 1966).

JOHN DOUGLAS PRINGLE
'The British Commune: Thoughts on the Public School', *Encounter*, **16**, 2 (February 1961).

FROELICH G. RAINEY
'The Whale Hunters of Tigara', *Anthropological Papers*, **42**, 2, American Museum of Natural History, New York, 1911.

VERNON REYNOLDS
'Kinship and the Family in Monkeys, Apes and Man', *Man*, **3**, 2 (June 1968).

VERNON REYNOLDS
'Open Groups in Hominid Evolution', *Man*, **1**, 4 (December 1966).

AILEEN D. ROSS
'Control and Leadership in Women's Groups; An Analysis of Philanthropic Money-Raising Activity', *Social Forces*, **37**, 2 (December 1958).

JOHN C. SCOTT, JR
'Membership and Participation in Voluntary Associations', *American Sociological Review*, **22**, 3 (June 1957)

JOHN FINLAY SCOTT
'The Role of the College Sorority in Endogamy', *American Sociological Review*, **30**, 4 (August 1965).

JEAN SHARP
'Widows Are Often Successful Running for Political Office', *Montreal Star* (22 December 1964).

EDWARD A. SHILS and MORRIS JANOWITZ
'Cohesion and Disintegration in the Wehrmacht in World War II', *Public Opinion Quarterly*, **12** (1948).

E. L. SIMONS
'Fossil Evidence Relating to the Early Evolution of Primate Behaviour', *Annals of the New York Academy of Sciences*, **102**, Article 2 (December 1962).

E. L. SIMONS
'In Search of the Missing Link', *Discovery*, **1**, 2 (Spring 1966).

E. L. SIMONS
'Some Fallacies in the Study of Hominid Phylogeny', *Science*, **141**, 3584 (6 September 1963).

E. L. SIMONS
'New Fossil Apes for Egypt and the Initial Differentiation of the Huminoides', *Nature*, **205** (1965).

RITA JAMES SIMON, SHIRLEY MERRITT CLARK, and KATHLEEN GALWAY
'The Woman Ph.D.: A Recent Profile', *Social Problems*, **15**, 2 (Fall 1967).

GEORGE GAYLORD SIMPSON
'The Biological Nature of Man', *Science*, **132**, 3721 (22 April 1966).

PHILIP E. SLATER
'On Social Regression', *American Sociological Review*, **28**, 3 (June 1963).

DAVID HORTON SMITH
'A Psychological Model of Individual Participation in Formal Voluntary Associations', *American Journal of Sociology*, **72**, 3 (November 1966).

ROBERT SOMMER
'Studies in Personal Space', *Sociometry*, **22** (1959).

DAVID STEA
'Territoriality, The Interior Aspect: Space, Territory and Human Movements', *Landscape* (Autumn 1965).

JULIAN H. STEWARD
'Hunting as a Factor in the Evolution of Social Structures', presented to the Man the Hunter Conference, University of Chicago, April 1966.

ANTHONY STORR
'The Psychology of Aggression', *New Society* (11 October 1962).

H. SUTHERLAND and IAIN STEWART
'A Critical Analysis of Premenstrual Syndrome', *Lancet*, **7397** (5 June 1965).

YONINA TALMON
'Sex Role Differentiation in an Equalitarian Society', in T. E. Lasswell, J. H. Burne, and S. H. Aronson (eds.), *Life in Society*, Scott, Foreman, Chicago, 1965.

J. M. TANNER
'Galtonian Eugenics and the Study of Growth: The Relation of Body Size, Intelligence Tests Score, and Social Circumstances in Children and Adults', *Eugenics Review*, No. 38, 3 (September 1966).

SUSAN D. TAYLOR, M. WILTON, R. OSNOS
'The Wives of Drug Addicts', *American Journal of Psychiatry*, **123**, 5 (November 1966).

W. I. THOMAS
'The Gaming Interest', *American Journal of Sociology* (1906).

KYRIL TIDMARSH
'Right to do the Hardest Work', *The Times* (16 February 1967).

LIONEL TIGER
'Diplomats, Monkeys and the New Biology', *International Journal* (Winter 1967).

LIONEL TIGER
'A Program for the Study of the Biological Aspects of Human Male Association Patterns', unpublished paper presented to the meeting of the Association for the Study of Animal Behaviour, Oxford, July 1965.

LIONEL TIGER and ROBIN FOX
'The Zoological Perspective in Social Science', *Man*, 1 (n.s.), 1 (March 1966).

NIKO TINBERGEN
'On Aims and Methods of Ethology', *Zeitschrift fur Tierpsychologie*, **20**, 4 (1963).

NIKO TINBERGEN
'The Search for Roots of Human Behaviour', unpublished paper, University of Oxford, 1965.

NIKO TINBERGEN
'On War and Peace in Animals and Man', *Science*, **160** (28 June 1968).

P. U. TOBIAS
'New Discoveries in Tanganyika: Their Bearing on Hominid Evolution', *Current Anthropology*, 6, 4 (October 1965).

BRUCE G. TRIGGER
'Engels on the Part Played by Labour in the Transition from Ape to Man: An Anticipation of Contemporary Anthropological Theory', *Canadian Review of Sociology and Anthropology*, 4, 3.

JEREMY TUNSTALL
'Trawling: A Murderous Trade', *New Society* (8 February 1968).

F. G. VALLEE
'Kabloona and Eskimo in the Central Keewatin', Development of Northern Affairs, Ottawa, 1962

MARGARET VARLEY and DAVID SYMMES
'The Hierarchy of Dominace in a Group of Macaques', *Behaviour*, 27, 1–2 (1966).

G. H. R. VON KOENIGSWALD
'Early Man: Facts and Fantasy' (Huxley Memorial Lecture, 1964), *Journal of the Royal Anthropological Institute*, 194, 2 (1964).

IRVING WARDLE
'Evolutionary Stage', *New Society* (May 1967).

S. L. WASHBURN, PHYLLIS C. JAY, and JANE B. LANCASTER
'Field Studies of Old World Monkeys and Apes', *Science*, 15, 370 (1966).

HITOSHI WATANABE
'The Ainu: A Study of Ecology and the System to Social Solidarity Between Man and Nature in Relation to Group Structure', *Journal of the Faculty of Science, University of Tokyo*, Section 5, 11, 6 (30 July 1964).

CAMILLA H. WEDGEWOOD
'The Nature and Functions of Secret Societies', *Oceania* (July 1930).

J. P. WELCH, *et al.*
'Psychopathy, Mental Deficiency, Aggressiveness and the XYY Syndrome', *Nature*, 214 (29 April 1967).

CHARLES E. WOODHOUSE and H. J. TOBIAS
'Primordial Ties and Political Process in Pre-Revolutionary Russia: The Case of the Jewish Bund', *Comparative Studies in Society and History*, 8, 3 (April 1966).

DENNIS WRONG
'The Over-Socialized Conception of Man in Modern Sociology', *American Sociological Review*, 26, 2 (April 1961).

F. W. YOUNG
'The Function of Male Initiation Ceremonies', *American Journal of Sociology*, **68**, 4 (January 1962).
F. W. YOUNG and ALBERT A. BACDAYAN
'Menstrual Taboos and Social Rigidity', *Ethnology*, **4**, 2 (April 1965).
BASIL G. ZIMMER and AMOS H. HAWLEY
'The Significance of Membership in Associations', *American Journal of Sociology*, **65**, 2 (September 1959).
SOLLY ZUCKERMAN
'Myths and Methods in Anatomy', *Journal of the Royal College of Surgeons, Edinburgh*, 11 (1966), pp. 87–114.

3. REPORTS

Children and Their Primary Schools, Department of Education and Science, H.M.S.O., London, 1967.
Labour in Britain — Survey of Women's Employment, Survey of British and Commonwealth Affairs, 2, No. 11 (24 May 1968).
Women in the Labour Force in Nine Countries of Europe, Women's Bureau, Department of Labour, Government of Canada, Ottawa, 1962.
Women and Top Jobs: An Interim Report, P.E.P., London, 1967.
Women at Work in Canada, Government of Canada, Department of Labour of Canada, Ottawa, 1958.

4. NEWSPAPER ITEMS

'Doing Away with Grades in Toronto', *The Times Educational Supplement* (13 January 1967).
'Stock Exchange May Admit Women', *The Times* (18 January 1967).
'Canadians return to Vimy Ridge', *The Times* (10 April 1967).
'Women wanted in Norway's Politics', *The Times* (23 February 1967).
'Slow March of the Matriarchy', *Guardian* (leader) (3 November 1966).
'U.S. Sets Out to Destroy North Vietnam Air Force', *New York International Herald Tribune and Washington Post* (4 January 1967).
'Equal-wage Bill is Voted in House', *New York Times* (Western edition) (24 May 1963).
' "No" to Vote for Women in Zurich', *Guardian* (21 November 1966).

Index

About the Author

Lionel Tiger was born in Montreal in 1937. He studied at McGill University, taking his M.A. there and his Ph.D. at the London School of Economics. At present he is Associate Professor of Anthropology at Livingston College, Rutgers University, and was Assistant Professor of Sociology at the University of British Columbia from 1963-68. His studies in the relationship of animal and human behavior and male bonding and grouping go back over several years, and he has published many papers on these and related topics.

WAYNESBURG COLLEGE LIBRARY
WAYNESBURG, PA.